OVERTURE OPERA GUIDES

in association with

The publisher John Calder began the Opera Guides series under the editorship of the late Nicholas John in association with English National Opera in 1980. It ran until 1994 and eventually included forty-eight titles, covering fifty-eight operas. The books in the series were intended to be companions to the works that make up the core of the operatic repertory. They contained articles, illustrations, musical examples and a complete libretto and singing translation of each opera in the series, as well as bibliographies and discographies.

The aim of the present relaunched series is to make available again the guides already published in a redesigned format with new illustrations, many revised and newly commissioned articles, updated reference sections and a literal translation of the libretto that will enable the reader to get closer to the intentions and meaning of the original. New guides of operas not already covered will be published alongside the redesigned ones from the old series.

Gary Kahn
Series Editor

Sponsors of the Overture Opera Guides

for the 2012/13 Season at ENO

Eric Adler
Frank and Lorna Dunphy
Richard Everall
Ian and Catherine Ferguson
Ali Khan
Andrew Medlicott
Ralph Wells

Daniel de Marsillac and Richard Everall
are gratefully acknowledged
for their assistance in the 2020 reprint of this volume

Carmen

Georges Bizet

Overture Opera Guides
Series Editor
Gary Kahn

Editorial Consultant
Philip Reed

OVERTURE

OVERTURE OPERA GUIDES
in association with

Overture Publishing
an imprint of

ALMA BOOKS LTD
3 Castle Yard
Richmond
Surrey TW10 6TF
United Kingdom

Articles by Richard Langham Smith, Lesley A. Wright, George Hall and Gary Kahn first published in this volume © the authors, 2013

This *Carmen* Opera Guide first published by Overture Publishing, an imprint of Alma Books Ltd, 2013. This revised edition first published in 2020.

© Alma Books Ltd, 2013, 2020
All rights reserved

Translation of libretto © Richard Langham Smith

Printed in United Kingdom by CPI Group (UK) Ltd, Croydon CR0 4YY

ISBN: 978-1-84749-855-7

All the pictures in this volume are reprinted with permission or presumed to be in the public domain. Every effort has been made to ascertain and acknowledge their copyright status, but should there have been any unwitting oversight on our part, we would be happy to rectify the error in subsequent printings.

All rights reserved. No part of this publication may be reproduced, stored in or introduced into a retrieval system, or transmitted, in any form or by any means (electronic, mechanical, photocopying, recording or otherwise), without the prior written permission of the publisher. This book is sold subject to the condition that it shall not be resold, lent, hired out or otherwise circulated without the express prior consent of the publisher.

Contents

List of Illustrations	8
Carmen: From Mérimée to Bizet Richard Langham Smith	9
Carmen and the Opéra-Comique Lesley A. Wright	35
A Selective Performance History George Hall	56
Carmen's Early Lovers Gary Kahn	81
Sources and Editions Richard Langham Smith	84
Thematic Guide	87
Carmen, Libretto	93
Note on the Libretto	95
Act One	101
Act Two	185
Act Three	263
Act Four	313
Recitatives	337
Select Discography	365
Carmen on DVD: a Selection	370
Select Bibliography	373
Bizet Websites	375
Note on the Contributors	376
Acknowledgements	376

List of Illustrations

1. Georges Bizet in 1875
2. Prosper Mérimée
3. Henri Meilhac and Ludovic Halévy
4. The second Salle Favart
5. Poster of the first production
6. The tobacco factory in Seville
7. *Cigarreras* with their children at the tobacco factory in Seville
8. Engraving from *L'Illustration*, 1875
9. Célestine Galli-Marié
10. Emma Calvé
11. Minnie Hauk
12. Maria Gay
13. Italo Campanini (Metropolitan Opera Archives)
14. Enrico Caruso (Metropolitan Opera Archives)
15. Suzanne Adams (Metropolitan Opera Archives)
16. Ezio Pinza (Metropolitan Opera Archives)
17. Jon Vickers and Grace Bumbry (Carolyn Mason Jones/San Francisco Opera Company)
18. Regina Resnik and Nicolai Gedda (Louis Malaçon/Metropolitan Opera Archives)
19. Mirella Freni (Louis Malaçon/Metropolitan Opera Archives)
20. Denyce Graves (Catherine Ashmore)
21. Harry Belafonte and Dorothy Dandridge in *Carmen Jones*
22. Carl Johan Falkman and Hélène Delavault in *La Tragédie de Carmen* (Marc and Brigitte Enguerand)
23. Lucian Pintilie's production at Welsh National Opera (Clive Barda)
24. Steven Pimlott's production at Earl's Court, London (Clive Barda/ArenaPAL)
25. Lina Wertmüller's production at the Bayerische Staatsoper (Winfried Rababus)
26. Franco Zeffirelli's production at the Metropolitan Opera (Winnie Klotz/Metropolitan Opera Archives)
27. Shirley Verrett and Plácido Domingo (Reg Wilson)
28. Plácido Domingo and Julia Migenes-Johnson (Second Sight)
29. Barry McCauley and Maria Ewing (Guy Gravett)
30. Agnes Baltsa and José Carreras (Clive Barda)
31. John Treleaven and Sally Burgess (Clive Barda/ArenaPAL)
32. Antoni Garfield-Henry and Ruby Philogene (Stephen Vaughan)
33. Anna Caterina Antonacci (Catherine Ashmore)
34. Genia Kühmeier, Nikolai Schukoff and Sylvie Brunet (Marie-Noelle Robert)
35. Elīna Garanča and Roberto Alagna (Ken Howard)
36. Calixto Bieito's production at the Gran Teatre del Liceu, Barcelona (Antoni Bofill)

1. Georges Bizet in 1875, the year of the premiere of *Carmen*, photographed by Étienne Carjat.

2. Prosper Mérimée, the author of the novella on which the opera is based, in an engraving by Jean-Denis Nargeot (left).

3. Henri Meilhac and Ludovic Halévy, the librettists of *Carmen* (right).

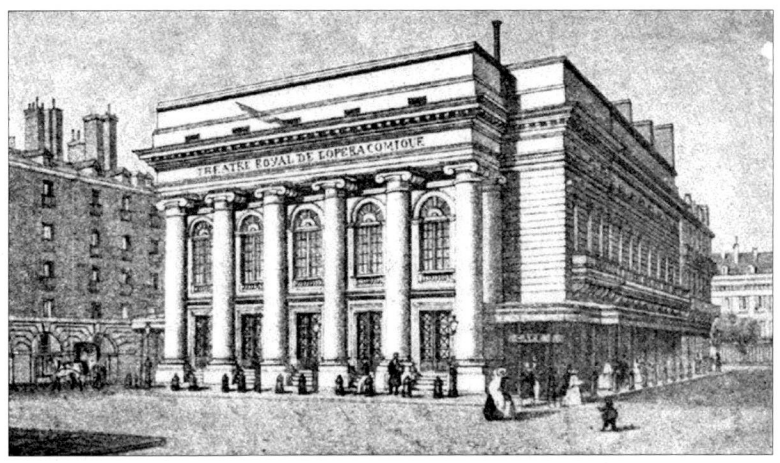

4. The second Salle Favart, where the Opéra-Comique performed from 1840 until 1887 and where *Carmen* had its premiere in 1875 (above).

5. Poster by Prudent Leray showing the end of Act Four and printed for the publisher Choudens at the time of the first performances (left).

Engravings by Gustave Doré from *Voyage en Espagne* by Jean-Charles Davillier, published in 1874: 6. The tobacco factory in Seville (above). 7. *Cigarreras* with their children at the tobacco factory in Seville (below).

8. Engraving of the first production, from the Paris periodical *L'Illustration*, 1875.

Four early Carmens: 9. Célestine Galli-Marié, the first Carmen (top left). 10. Emma Calvé, who sang Carmen many times, including the thousandth performance at the Opéra-Comique in 1904 (top right). 11. Minnie Hauk, who appeared in the role over five hundred times (bottom left). 12. Maria Gay, the first Spanish singer to establish herself in the role (bottom right).

Four other early performers: 13. Italo Campanini, the first Don José at the Metropolitan Opera, 1884 (top left). 14. Enrico Caruso as Don José in 1906 (top right). 15. Suzanne Adams as Micaëla in 1901 (bottom left). 16. Ezio Pinza as Escamillo in 1928 (bottom right).

17. Jon Vickers as Don José and Grace Bumbry as Carmen at the San Francisco Opera in 1966 (top left). 18. Regina Resnik as Carmen and Nicolai Gedda as Don José at the Metropolitan Opera in 1967 (top right).
19. Mirella Freni as Micaëla at the Metropolitan Opera in 1972 (bottom left).
20. Denyce Graves as Carmen at the Royal Opera House in 1984 (bottom right).

21. Harry Belafonte and Dorothy Dandridge in Otto Preminger's 1954 film of *Carmen Jones*, based on Oscar Hammerstein II's Broadway adaptation (left).

22. Carl Johan Falkman and Hélène Delavault in *La Tragédie de Carmen*, directed by Peter Brook and designed by Chloé Obolensky, at the Théâtre des Bouffes du Nord in Paris in 1981. The production was subsequently filmed with each of the three original casts (above).

23. Act Four of Lucian Pintilie's production, designed by Radu and Miruna Boruzescu, at Welsh National Opera in 1983 (above).
24. Act One of Steven Pimlott's arena production, designed by Stefanos Lazaridis, at Earls Court, London, in 1989 (below).

25. Act One of Lina Wertmüller's production, designed by Enrico Job, at the Bayerische Staatsoper in 1992. A representation of the Seville tobacco factory in the background (above).
26. Act Three of the production directed and designed by Franco Zeffirelli at the Metropolitan Opera in 1996 (below).

Carmen and Don José at the end of the final scene of Act Four: 27. Shirley Verrett and Plácido Domingo in the production directed by Michael Geliot and designed by Jenny Beavan and David Fielding at the Royal Opera House in 1973 (above). 28. Plácido Domingo and Julia Migenes-Johnson in the film directed by Francesco Rosi in 1984 (right).

29. Barry McCauley and Maria Ewing in the production directed by Peter Hall and designed by John Bury at the Glyndebourne Festival in 1985 (above).
30. Agnes Baltsa and José Carreras in the production directed by Michael Geliot and designed by Jenny Beavan and David Fielding, restaged at the Royal Opera House in 1983 (below).

31. John Treleaven as Don José and Sally Burgess as Carmen in the production directed by David Pountney and designed by Maria Bjørnson at ENO in 1986 (above). 32. Antoni Garfield-Henry as Don José and Ruby Philogene as Carmen in the production directed by Phyllida Lloyd and designed by Tim Hatley at Opera North in 1998 (below).

33. Anna Caterina Antonacci as Carmen in Francesca Zambello's production, designed by Tanya McCallin, at the Royal Opera House in 2006 (above).
34. Genia Kühmeier as Micaëla, Nikolai Schukoff as Don José and Sylvie Brunet as Carmen in the production directed by Martin Kušej and designed by Jens Kilian at the Théâtre du Châtelet in 2007. This was the first production to use the new Peters Edition of the score prepared by Richard Langham Smith (below).

35. Elīna Garanča as Carmen and Roberto Alagna as
Don José in the production directed by Richard Eyre and designed by
Rob Howell at the Metropolitan Opera in 2009 (above).
36. Act Three of Calixto Bieito's much travelled production, designed by
Alfons Flores, at the Gran Teatre del Liceu, Barcelona, in 2010 (below).

Carmen: From Mérimée to Bizet

Richard Langham Smith

Although *Carmen* is often seen as the starting point for a chain of French pieces on Spanish themes, it was in its time merely a stepping stone in the rush of French enthusiasm for Spanish culture which arose in the mid nineteenth century in the wake of Napoleon's defeat in the Peninsular War. Chabrier's *España*, Debussy's *Ibéria* and Ravel's *Boléro* and *L'Heure espagnole* may have drawn inspiration from *Carmen* but Bizet's opera was only a high point in the fashion – if not mania – for things Spanish (and in particular Andalusian) which snowballed from the 1830s onwards.

After the Napoleonic defeat many Spanish citizens who had supported his cause – the 'afrancesados', considered collaborators – were forced to flee north, particularly to the cultural magnet of Paris. Among them were intellectuals, artists, musicians and dancers who captivated the French with their arts but also hoped to perfect them there.[1] Hosted enthusiastically in French salons, they fostered a taste for learning the guitar and for flamenco costume and dancing. Spanish spectacle flourished on the Parisian stage: celebrated flamenco dancers delighted French audiences and a prosperous industry in the publication of dual-language Spanish songs grew up. Some publishers simply provided French texts for pre-existent Spanish music, others commissioned newly composed

---

1 For further detail on this, see Montserrat Bergadà, 'Musiciens espagnols à Paris entre 1820 et 1868', in Louis Jambou (ed.), *La Musique entre France et Espagne: Interactions stylistiques, 1870–1939* (Paris: Presses de l'Université de Paris-Sorbonne, 2003), pp. 17–38.

pieces by Spanish composers who had established themselves in France.²

In literature, travelogues from visitors to the country across the mountains were much in fashion. Prosper Mérimée's novella *Carmen*, on which Bizet's opera is based, was to some extent one of these but had been preceded by such writers as Théophile Gautier in several genres. Among visual artists, Goya had visited Paris and enjoyed particular popularity – Delacroix in particular was at one time greatly influenced by him – and among French painters bitten by the Spanish bug were Chassériau (who painted the celebrated dancer Petra Camara), Manet (who painted Lola de Valence) and Degas who used a Spanish guitarist as a model. The taste was fostered not only by Hispanic exhibits at the various *Expositions universelles* but also by King Louis Philippe's founding of a *Galerie espagnole* in the Louvre in 1835.

Particular individuals were central in encouraging a French interest in Spain. The last Empress of France, Eugénie (née de Montijo, 1826–1920), was by birth Andalusian. She married Bonaparte's nephew, Napoleon III (1808–73), and fostered a taste for Spanish arts. Mérimée, incidentally, had been an intimate of hers since her childhood. Among Spanish musicians working in Paris were the dancer, guitarist and composer Fernando Sor (1778–1839) and later on Sebastián Yradier (1809–65) who had been a singing teacher to Eugénie. As will be seen, Bizet modelled his celebrated Habanera on a song by Yradier.

Also important were the García family who settled in France. The father, Manuel García (1775–1832) was an actor, opera singer and composer and a committed francophile. His son, also Manuel, was author of a celebrated singing treatise, considered a key text on *bel canto* even today. The two daughters were also highly influential: Maria (1808–36), a celebrated singer known under the name of her husband, Malibran, fell off her horse and died in Manchester at an early age. Her sister Pauline (1821–1910) sang and composed in the Spanish style. Their pictures often adorned the bilingual sheet music

---

2   For details of this wave of Spanish fever, see Gerhard Steingress, ...*y 'Carmen' se fue a París* (Córdoba: Almuzara, 2006).

which flooded the market in the early and mid nineteenth century. Pauline and her husband, Louis Viardot, provided a direct link with Bizet since both their out-of-town retreat on the Seine at Bougival, where Bizet worked on *Carmen* in 1874, and their Paris residence, were close to his, and he became a family friend. Viardot was himself a learned Hispanist with a particular interest in Spanish gypsies, on whom he wrote an extensive article in the *Dictionnaire Larousse*.[3]

The operatic stage had been by no means impervious to Spanish fever, and although no one had incorporated as much Spanish-style music as Bizet would do in *Carmen*, there were notable exceptions. For example in Massenet's *Don César de Bazan* of 1872, the Overture, supported by *tambours de basque*, has a motif with decidedly Spanish syncopations followed by a choral *Boléro* and a *Ballade aragonaise*. Several of the original cast of *Carmen*, incidentally, had sung in this opera. Before this, Auber, in *Le Domino noir* (1837) and *Les Diamants de la couronne* (1841), had used elements of music from the Iberian Peninsula. Adolphe Adam was another composer who employed Spanish settings, notably in *Giralda* (the name of the grand tower in Seville) and *Le Toréador*.[4] Both the Spanish context in general, and Bizet's friendship with the Viardots, not to mention his early friendship with Sarasate, were without doubt catalysts for his attraction to Mérimée's masterly novella about an alluring Spanish gypsy.

It was a rival to Bizet's two librettists, Louis Gallet, who first remembered how Mérimée's *Carmen* was recognized as a potential opera subject well before Halévy and Meilhac took it up. He recalled a conversation after sitting on a jury:

> 'Would you like me to recommend a subject?' proposed one of the judges: 'I'll give it to you, for I'm only a critic myself. It's *Carmen*, for there you have an opera in the same genre as *Fra Diavolo* with a part for an Englishman, think about it!'

---

3 *Grand Larousse Universel*, article 'Bohémien, -ienne' (no precise date but probably 1860s), p. 868.
4 See Hervé Lacombe, 'L'Espagne à l'Opéra-Comique avant *Carmen*', in François Lesure (ed.), *Échanges musicaux franco-espagnols* (Paris: Klincksieck, 2000), pp. 161–94.

Just think, we could have done this *Carmen* without ever having foreseen the other. And despite our own preoccupations, in deference to our advisor, there could have been a role for an Englishman, just as in *Fra Diavolo*.[5]

Leaving aside Gallet's comments about an Englishman – which will be returned to – why was Mérimée's *Carmen* so attractive and so successful in its transformation into a libretto? It is usually categorized as a '*nouvelle*', as opposed to a '*conte*', which is more of a 'tale', a chronological narrative telling a story. Mérimée's *Carmen* is quite different, more a compressed novel, not continuous and with a double narrative, with events at first observed by an erudite historian interested in the culture and history of other places, in this case remains of antiquity in Andalusia. Comparisons with Mérimée himself are inevitable for he was essentially a traveller, an inspector of public buildings all over France, responsible for the allocation of substantial funds for their restoration. In the novella the observer shows off his erudition with frequent references to gypsy, Basque and local culture, even in the form of footnotes extending into Greek.

He enthusiastically meets a notorious bandit, Don José, who is about to be garrotted for murdering Carmen. José, as the second narrator, recounts the events of his life from the perspective of a condemned man, centred on his meeting with Carmen and his affair with her. The novella thus dwells on Carmen from two perspectives: the narrator's, who seems intrigued by her and carries little cigars to lubricate engagement with women; and José's, whose interest in her begins not with her personality but with her legs. Even in prison he looks out between the bars recalling the delicious holes in her stockings!

For transformation into the opera libretto this double narrative was unworkable, so the novella is turned back into a story, and the erudite observer is eradicated, although the libretto retains details not only from the whole novella, but also from Mérimée's other reminiscences

---

5   Louis Gallet, *Notes d'un librettiste: Musique contemporaine* (Paris: Calmann-Lévy, 1891), pp. 265–67.

of Spain which included essays on a bullfight and an execution and an interview with a bandit.[6]

The novella was in another sense a travelogue, first published in a celebrated periodical (*La Revue des deux mondes*) which informed readers about life abroad. Its essence is that it observes details as well as embroidering them, just as Mérimée's compatriot in the field of the visual arts, Gustave Doré, did a little later on in his series of over two hundred engravings of Spanish life first published in another *revue* with a similar agenda, *Le Tour du monde*.[7] *Carmen* was the result of Mérimée's second visit to Spain in the 1840s, a significant date falling just after the formation of the Guardia Civil, an armed force whose principal mission was to rid Spain of bandits. Andalusia was allocated a particularly strong force and one crucial theme in the opera is the conflict between the soldiers and the bandits, encapsulated in Don José's change from one side to the other.

The libretto softens many aspects of the novella while developing others. Mérimée's Carmen has a horrible, murderous, one-eyed husband called García who is removed from the libretto. On the other hand, the libretto invents an operatic foil, Micaëla, the angel of the fireside. Where Carmen is a dark-skinned Andalusian, a sexually adventurous gypsy dressed in red, Micaëla is a blonde-haired Catholic virgin dressed in blue. Micaëla's devotion to José and her friendship with his mother are thus inventions of the librettists though she is developed from hints of a northern girl in the novella. Similarly, Escamillo is developed from mention of a picador who has a fling with Carmen into a fully-fledged torero, a macho foil to the lily-livered José who makes it clear in the opera – though not in Mérimée's original – that he is also a virgin:

car jamais, jamais femme, jamais femme avant toi[8]

---

6   Prosper Mérimée, *Nouvelles* (contains *Lettres d'Espagne*, essays previously published separately in *Revue de Paris* in the 1830s) (Paris: Michel Lévy, 1852).
7   Jean Charles Davillier, *Voyage en Espagne*, illustrated by Gustave Doré (Paris: Hachette, 1874). See also Gustave Doré, *Doré's Spain: All 236 Illustrations from Spain* (Mineola: Dover Editions, 2004).
8   'For never, never a woman, never a woman before you'.

he sings to Carmen in the crucial scene where he has to choose between love and duty. As if we hadn't guessed he was inexperienced, and as if his chastity will impress her! Quite the reverse.

Bizet's librettists also strengthen the novella's other main aspect: its sense of place, enhanced on stage (of course) by costume and scenery over which tremendous care was taken. First comes the *plaza* where all classes and occupations meet. A main conflict in the opera is projected: that of imposed masculine order against gypsy, female unruliness. The final version of the set strengthens this, pitting the guardhouse against the factory on opposite sides of the stage – the factory had originally been backstage, with a cumbersome fountain in the centre.

In Act Two the topos is the *venta*, or inn, sordid in the novella but a flamenco dance hall in the opera. In Act Three the wilderness of the sierra, or mountains, is portrayed: the hideout of the bandits who make excursions to the coast and to Gibraltar to rob their victims and even murder them, particularly if they are English. This terrain was finely captured by Doré. Finally we get to a double representation of the bullring (which we hear but don't see) and to the events outside.

Carmen has many claims to originality, not least because of its incorporation of so much Spanish-style music and its fusion of this with other styles: the tear-jerking *opéra-comique* arias and duets (such as José's duet with Micaëla [12][9] and his Flower Song [23]); the gypsy elements on a strange, oriental-sounding scale (Carmen's recurrent motif first heard at the end of the Prélude [4], again in the card scene predicting her death [27], and finally at her murder [36]); elements of Spanish dance such as the Séguedille [16], the Chanson bohème [18] and the final Entr'acte [32]; and continuous musical dialogue which takes over in the final act, but is also extended in the scene where Carmen taunts José as he is torn between love and duty after her dance for him [22]. There is also a touch of religiosity about Micaëla's music: her first duet with José is introduced by an imitation of organ music as she tells him how she has been to church with his

---

9   Numbers in square brackets refer to the Thematic Guide on pp. 87–92 [Ed.].

mother, and the hymnic line of her subsequent aria, accompanied by legato strings and harp, is reminiscent of a style of religious music used in fashionable Parisian churches, sometimes known as the '*style saint-sulpicien*' [13]. There's also a fugal style used for Carmen's condemnation in the finale of this act; its ordered entries perhaps express the control imposed on her violent behaviour [17].

More important overall, however, is the opera's realism, often using diegetic effects where the music is part of the action, for example the Chanson bohème [18], and the offstage music emanating from the bullring in the final act. Carmen's several dance songs are also more a part of the action than the average operatic aria since they involve dancing in front of an onstage audience.

The Prélude [1–4], essentially a paso doble, plunges us straight into the music of the bullring, and it returns when the bullfight occurs. Paso dobles, or *pas redoublés* as they were known in France, were the stock-in-trade of the military bands that played (and still play) during *corridas* – in English they are quaintly known as the 'military two-step'. They were originally used for training soldiers to march at double pace, and there were many examples to be found in the music of composers such as Rossini, Cherubini and Offenbach, to name a few. What Bizet does is to introduce a Spanish inflection by the use of a flamenco scale (with a flat supertonic, i.e. the second note of the scale) which listeners immediately recognize as Spanish: it is sometimes referred to as the 'Spanish tetrachord'. The following music examples show various ways in which this Spanish hallmark is applied:

Example 1: A repeated motif based on the tetrachord C sharp, D, E, F sharp, centred on C sharp, is appended to the second idea in the Prélude, recurring later at various repetitions.

Example 2: Carmen's so-called 'Séguedille' uses the tetrachord in several forms to give the movement an entirely authentic Spanish feel. Here the tetrachord descends, centred on B it starts on the flat sixth, another characteristic of flamenco music, G, F sharp, E, D, C, B.

Example 3: The entire ritornello to the Chanson bohème which opens Act Two is based on a four-note motif descending from E to B via a flattened C.

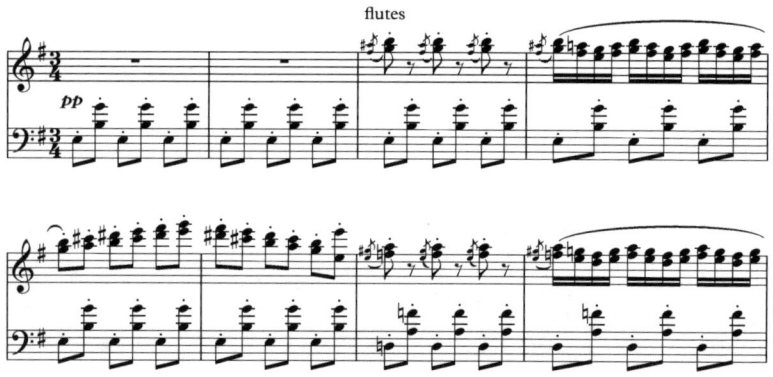

Example 4: Bizet immediately impregnates the final act with the flavour of a Spanish fiesta with the stereotypical opening to the final Entr'acte, using not only the flattened supertonic, but the clash of major and minor versions of the third degree of the scale. Hemiolas characterize the dance on which it is based, the *polo*, and it is not immediately clear whether we are in duple or triple time.

Bizet also introduces into the Prélude an element specific to the *Pasodoble taurino* by using the 'Toreador theme' which will later appear as Escamillo's [3]. Essentially sectional, and using fanfare motives, the paso dobles used at bullfights would include a lyrical melody as the final section before a recapitulation: this tune – the hallmark of the piece – would be identified with a victorious bullfighter. So in a sense, the Prélude is the paso doble 'El Escamillo'. Published paso dobles were rare at this time and it is possible that Bizet knew of this convention through the sizeable Spanish community in Paris who, among other patriotic activities, held bullfights in Montmartre. After all, the composer had lived on the borders of Montmartre from 1869 when it was rather more separate from Paris than it is today.

The relentless vamping of the Prélude's accompaniment – to which men could march and horses could trot – is disturbed with great effect as the postlude changes suddenly to the 'Requiem' key of D minor, announced in a style somewhat conventional for foretastes of death or destruction: tremolando strings. Against this, a motif based on a scale with two augmented seconds is heard, possibly owing a little to the composer who was above all the world authority on gypsies, Franz Liszt.[10] This is sounded on bassoons and clarinets; rasping low notes on the horns punctuate [4].

After the scene in the *plaza* [5], a crowd scene ubiquitous in *opéras-comiques* of the period, comes a fascinating variant: a '*Scène et Pantomime*' found in the first vocal score but subsequently eradicated in all other early editions [7]. This is an extraordinary movement in several ways: first, because it has Moralès addressing the audience; second, because it uses mime; and thirdly because it is very funny, not a characteristic much found elsewhere in the opera. Only from the two surviving production books held at the Bibliothèque Historique de la Ville de Paris do we learn what this scene is about. Clearly marked in the *Livret de mise-en-scène* as the '*Scène de l'Anglais*' it explains Gallet's comment about the potential for a spoof at the expense of the English.

The idea of an elderly 'milord' cuckolded by a sexy young Spaniard had already been exploited in Auber's *Fra Diavolo*, an Opéra-

---

10 The scale is used at the opening of Liszt's B minor Piano Sonata. Liszt also wrote a lengthy essay on gypsies.

Comique favourite. Here it's turned into a mime, with the Englishman accompanied by an attractive young lady from the *corps de ballet*. The scene was included in the printed libretto, the first vocal score and the orchestral parts. One critic, Jules Guillemot, writing in *Le Soleil*, advised his readers

> to look out particularly for a meaningful pantomime between an old husband, a young wife and a lover, commented upon by the *brigadier* Moralès who whispers the words spoken by the miming characters behind him, which we do not hear: it's an original and witty idea and the production brought this out well.[11]

This scene was apparently written because the baritone Edmond Duvernoy, who took the role of Moralès, thought he hadn't got enough to sing, and Bizet and his librettists took the chance further to exploit the English presence in the novella. Only a brief aside was otherwise retained in the libretto when Le Remendado comes back from Gibraltar reporting that the place is full of English people and raising a laugh by reminding us that the English are 'a bit cold, but distinguished' (see libretto, p. 209). The lines are finely delivered in the 1911 recording (see Select Discography, p. 365).

This seems not to have been the only change caused by singers throwing their toys out of the pram. Célestine Galli-Marié was also dissatisfied, in her case with the crucial aria following her dramatic entry whose manner is distilled in the accompanying stage direction: 'Carmen enters. Her entrance and costume should be exactly as described by Mérimée' (see libretto, p. 131).

Since we are pointed back to the novella for Carmen's characterization, it is perhaps worth a glimpse at the two first encounters with her which so brilliantly encapsulate her conflicting aspects: first in the words of the erudite narrator, and then in those of Don José:

---

11 Jules Guillemot, 'Revue dramatique', *Le Soleil* (9th March 1875). Despite this critic's admiration for the scene, it was unpopular with the directorate. A common view, as reported by Bizet's early biographer Charles Pigot, was that it sidetracked the plot and made Act One overlong.

One evening, after it had grown quite dusk, I was leaning over the parapet of the quay, smoking, when a woman came up the steps leading from the river, and sat down near me. In her hair she wore a great bunch of jasmine – a flower which, at night, exhales a most intoxicating perfume. She was dressed simply, almost poorly, in black, as most work-girls are dressed in the evening. Women of the richer class only wear black in the daytime, at night they dress *a la francesa*. When she drew near me, the woman let the mantilla which had covered her head drop on her shoulders… I perceived her to be young, short in stature, well proportioned, and with very large eyes. I threw my cigar away at once. She appreciated this mark of courtesy, essentially French, and hastened to tell me she was very fond of the smell of tobacco, and that she even smoked herself, when she could get very mild *papelitos*. I fortunately happened to have some such in my case, and at once offered them to her. She condescended to take one, and lighted it on a burning string which a child brought us, receiving a copper for its pains. We mingled our smoke, and talked so long, the fair lady and I, that we ended by being almost alone on the quay.[12]

There follows some banter in which the narrator, emphasizing her otherness, skirts round the question of whether she is a Jewess. She replies:

'Oh come! You must see I'm a gypsy! Wouldn't you like me to tell you *la baji*? [your fortune] Did you never hear tell of Carmencita? That's who I am!'[13]

Where the narrator is intrigued, José is smitten. His narrative begins by gloating over her physical assets. Beginning with her legs, he then moves his gaze to her assets under her chemise:

---

12 Prosper Mérimée, *Carmen*, trans. Lady Mary Loyd, reprinted in *'Carmen': a Romance by Prosper Mérimée with a Study of the Opera of the Same Name by Winton Dean* (London: The Folio Society, 1949), pp. 17–18. Adapted by the present author for the mistranslation of '*cassie*' as acacia.
13 Ibid., p. 19.

She was wearing a very short skirt, below which her white silk stockings – with more than one hole in them – and her dainty red morocco shoes, fastened with flame-coloured ribbons, were clearly seen. She had thrown her mantilla back, to show her shoulders, and a great bunch of cassia that was thrust into her chemise. She had another cassia blossom in the corner of her mouth, and she walked along, swinging her hips, like a filly from a Cordova stud farm. In my country anyone who had seen a woman dressed in that fashion would have crossed himself.[14]

It is clearly from this description that the librettists' stage direction is drawn. She continues introducing a new theme, strengthened in the libretto, which not only emphasizes José's obedience as a good soldier, but also mocks him for being effeminate. In this respect the librettists develop the image into a diametric contrast with Escamillo, the macho bullfighter who has myriad women ready to loosen their underclothes for him.

'*Compadre*,' said she, in the Andalusian fashion, 'won't you give me your chain for the keys of my strongbox?'
'It's for my priming pin,' said I.
'Your priming pin!' she cried, with a laugh. 'Oho! I suppose the gentleman makes lace, as he wants pins!'
Everyone began to laugh, and I felt myself getting red in the face, and couldn't hit on anything in answer.
'Come, my love!' she began again, 'make me seven ells of black lace for my mantilla, my pet pin-maker!'
'And taking the cassia blossom out of her mouth she flipped it at me with her thumb so that it hit me just between the eyes. I tell you, sir, I felt as if a bullet had struck me. I didn't know which way to look. I sat stock-still, like a wooden board.[15]

José has already introduced himself as a mummy's boy, bursting into song in the middle of Micaëla's dialogue, the minute she mentions

---

14 Ibid., pp. 28–29.
15 Ibid., pp. 29–30.

his mother [14]. His weakness is stressed in many ways, one of which is that he has no real aria of his own, nor a motif like Carmen. From the thinly veiled implication of the dialogue, it might be deduced that he has to resort to masturbation, unlike Escamillo: after all, he spends an awful lot of time fiddling about with his priming-pin.

As an incorrigible habitué of the brothel when he was on excursions, and even a commentator on how many times a night – and how loudly – La Malibran enjoyed orgasm with her lover, the violinist Charles de Bériot, it is hardly surprising that Mérimée, highly sexed and with a taste for obscenity, should introduce sexual metaphors into his novella.[16] Nor that Bizet should endorse them, for he too had freely indulged in loose women in his youth. His best biographer, Hervé Lacombe, after having given us a page of confessions from various inns and brothels, concludes that Bizet categorized his women as either 'saints or whores', a polarization not exactly irrelevant to the plot of *Carmen*.[17]

Before the final version with the Habanera, Bizet had already composed an aria to follow Carmen's entry and very lovely it is. In its way. It uses material from the 6/8 section sung by the *jeunes gens*, in the rhythm, it has been suggested, of a tarantella. It was already a dance song whose central section, for an extended setting of the word *l'amour*, is deliciously lyrical: a sugar-plum number so typically in the manner of the Opéra-Comique.[18] If the supposition is that Galli-Marié thought it not strong enough, since she made Bizet alter it no fewer than thirteen times, then she was right: Bizet's first version, lovely though it is, was not characteristic of a gypsy. The composer's solution was the Habanera [11]. He remodelled the words to fit a dance song in this form, which he had found in an anthology of Spanish songs with French translations, and the page of his manuscript adapting these exists to this day.[19]

---

16 For a résumé of Mérimée's letters recounting his sexual exploits, see Mario Bois, *La Trilogie de Séville* (Paris: Marval, 1999), pp. 132–33.
17 Hervé Lacombe, *Georges Bizet* (Paris: Fayard, 2000), p. 254 et seq.
18 The original version has been recorded as an extra in the 2003 EMI recording conducted by Michel Plasson (see Select Discography, p. 369).
19 From Paul Bernard and Dieudonné Tagliafico (eds.), *Chansons espagnoles del maestro Yradier* (Paris: Heugel, 1865).

The Habanera, apart from its stronger characterization of Carmen, is also dramatically more convincing since it is in part a chorus, particularly where Carmen's confidantes (or one might say partners-in-crime) – Frasquita and Mercédès – as well as the crowd around, join in with Carmen's interjections about free love which are the essence of the aria: 'Love! Love!', says the original text, 'is the spice of life, whether it lasts a day, a week or a month' (no one suggests it lasts for ever):

> Chance and whim,
> That's how loves begin!
> And there it is for life,
> Or for six months, or a week perhaps.
> One chance morning on a road
> You meet love: there it is!
> It comes, and just when you least expect it, it goes away.
>
> It takes you, carries you away
> And it does what it wants with you!
> It's a delight, a dream
> And it lasts as long as it can![20]

What the text loses by dropping these lines, it surely gains in dramatic impetus through its hybrid form as part dance, part aria, part chorus.

Before moving to some commentary on Act Two it is worth turning from text to context, in particular to the tobacco factory in Seville, built to accommodate the changing fashion for imbibing tobacco, from snuff to all kinds of cigars and cigarettes. The enormous factory and its regime were famous internationally: it is now used by the University of Seville and is free to visit. Several issues connected with it are explored in both novella and libretto. The imposing building

---

[20] For the full text, see the liner notes to the Plasson recording. The French reads: *Hasard et fantaisie, / Ainsi commencent les amours ! / En voilà pour la vie, / Ou pour six mois, ou pour huit jours ! / Un matin sur la route, / On trouve l'amour, il est là ! / Il vient, sans qu'on s'en doute, il s'en va ! // Il vous prend, vous enlève, / Il fait de vous tout ce qu'il veut ! / C'est un délice, un rêve, / Et ça dure ce que ça peut !*

was illustrated in several of Doré's engravings, one of them depicting – as does the opera – the moment when the bell rings and the factory workers come out (see plate 6). The factory was well known for its unique employment of women, in particular the gypsy underclass who resided across the Guadalquivir River in Triana, now connected by a bridge. In the earlier days of the factory the gypsy *cigarreras* came over by boat, as is attested in early photographs.

Its regime was celebrated for the chance it gave to women – often already with children – to earn money legitimately rather than be forced into prostitution: Doré captures this aspect too (see plate 7). On the other hand some saw it as exploitative since women could be paid less than men for similar work. The scene depicting the dispute is also an embroidery of reality: the girls were paid by the piece – the number of cigars they produced – and the speed at which they could fashion these was determined by the quality of the tobacco leaves given to them. Records from the factory show that a number of girls were dismissed for insubordination and aggression and this issue forms a major part of the interest of Act One of the opera.[21] The presence of children in and around the factory is also developed into a number by the librettists as they imitate the soldiers in their 'urchins' chorus' [8]. But their attitude here raises a question: do they imitate the soldiers because they want to be soldiers when they grow up, or is there an element of parody here? This question is reflected later when Carmen mocks José by imitating their bugle calls [22].

The origins of Carmen's insolent interrogation are also interesting, especially an indication in the first vocal score that she should sing her 'tra-la-las' under her breath rather than in your face [15]! Her melody is a known (if not well-known) folk song, in this case from Ciudad Real. By singing it *sotto voce* she emphasizes not only her refusal to answer Zuniga's questions, but her vow to remain silent. All too often modern Carmens blurt it out. The idea is once again taken from another of Mérimée's works, in this case a translation

---

21 Information provided to the present author by Jose M. Rodríguez Gordillo, curator of the archives of the tobacco factory, currently in the new factory (still in operation) on the opposite side of the river. Gordillo has published widely on the history of tobacco in Seville.

of a poem by Pushkin where a country girl, tired of her lover, quietly hums a folk song, refusing to speak to him.[22]

Her so-called 'Séguedille' which ends the act is puzzling, not least because it bears about as much relation to a real seguidilla as a minuet does to a sarabande [16]. Seguidillas (or sevillanas) are like boleros: six quavers in a bar, with the second quaver divided into two or three, often emphasized by castanets. The three-quaver dance, though not a real seguidilla, is nonetheless very Spanish, not least because Bizet impregnates it with the Spanish tetrachord already mentioned. It's modelled on a *tirana* or a *vals* (waltz) and this rhythm is emphasized by the anacrusis to the second beat. Even more puzzling is the fact that its text mentions that Carmen will go to Lillas Pastia's tavern and dance the seguidilla with José. Why say this if she's already doing one? Perplexing.

The number does, however, retain one essential quality of the real seguidilla, outlined in a detailed article by Fernando Sor, a dancer as well as guitarist and composer.[23] At the end of a typical seguidilla there was no reprise: the piece ended suddenly as does this number. At this point the dancers froze. If the audience liked the pose in which they ended the dance they would shout ¡*Bien parado!*: 'Well stopped!'. The sudden ending of this number – seguidilla or not – on a high note seems to reflect this perfectly.

Act Two transforms Mérimée's sordid *venta* (inn) into a very different place from the original which José advised the narrator against, and in which, ignoring the wise advice, he was savagely bitten by bedbugs. In the first staging it was set on three levels with plenty of room for a nicely choreographed gypsy dance replete with 'Carmen elbows', guitars, mantillas and amply pleated skirts. The delightful representation of it from the widely distributed magazine *L'Illustration* captures it well (see plate 8).

The Chanson bohème which opens the act fulfils Carmen's promise to dance the seguidilla, although José is still in prison [18]. Unlike

---

22 Prosper Mérimée, 'Les Bohémiens' ('Tsygany'), translation of Pushkin in *Nouvelles*, op. cit.
23 Fernando Sor, 'Le boléro', in Adolphe Ledhuy and Henri Bertini (eds.), *Encyclopédie pittoresque de la musique* (Paris: H. Delloye, 1835), pp. 88–97.

its preceding number, it is clearly in the bolero rhythm of the *seguidillas manchegas*, appropriated by the Andalusians as the sevillana. Although it is not prescribed, some early performances introduced castanets into this movement, with extra clicking added (in duplets, triplets or even quadruplets) to the second quaver of each bar: a nice touch. Essential is the sense of increasing frenzy: a characteristic of elaborate gypsy dances highlighted, among other accounts, by Louis Viardot, the singer Pauline Viardot's erudite husband, in his dictionary article:

> The women get up, young or old, and begin to dance, or rather to slide onto the dance floor, with their arms and shoulders, their thighs and even their entire bodies overtaken with bizarre tremblings, uncoordinated movements which throw them little by little, like the *bayadères* and *almées* of the East, into a sort of trance or inebriation.[24]

The quotation crystallizes perfectly the essence of Bizet's number: a trance is induced by increasing volume and tempo, reflected in the text, driven by the beating of the onstage tambourine, often found in illustrations of gypsy dances of the time.

No doubt the librettists' researches on gypsies would have included reading the most important work before those of George Borrow:[25] that of Heinrich Grellmann, first published in German and subsequently translated into both French and English.[26] In the French version, Grellmann notes particularly the use of a pair of flutes in gypsy dances, while Fernando Sor, in his article on the seguidilla, remarks that the music for such dances is usually in the major key, with the one exception of the use of the 'guitar key' of E minor: the exact key of this movement. This gypsy tableau, giving such fertile opportunity for stagers, directors and choreographers, has been

---

24 See p. 11, footnote 3.
25 George Borrow (1803–81). Writer of travelogues, especially concerning gypsies.
26 Heinrich Grellmann, *Histoire des Bohémiens ou Tableau des mœurs, usages et coutumes de ce peuple nomade, suivie de recherches historiques sur leur origine* (Paris: J. Chaumerot, 1810).

interpreted richly, sometimes with real flamenco dancers imported from Spain. In any case, the stage directions are particularly copious in the various staging manuals as well as the libretto; note particularly the indication of mimed guitars onstage.

The next scenes are concerned with the arrival of Escamillo, the torero, with a use of the *coulisses* (wings) preparing us for the more extended use of them to depict the bullfight at the end of the opera. Bizet was wrong to have dismissed praise for his Toreador Song as '*cochonnerie*' (muck). But composers – dare one suggest – are rarely the best critics of their own successes. The song surely characterizes the three elements of a toreador just perfectly:

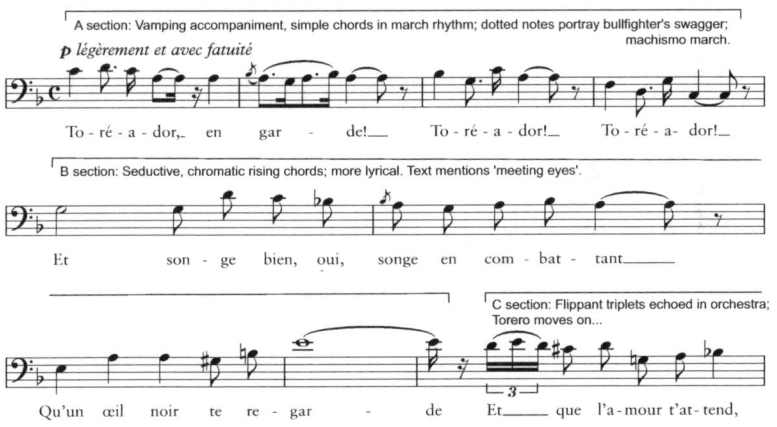

After the assembled company has toasted '*le grand art de la tauromachie*' ('the great art of bullfighting'), the key drops to F minor – later a 'death key' after Carmen has dealt herself the black tarot cards and the flattest key in the opera. The rhythm returns to that of the *pasodoble taurino* of the Prélude but the new melody, characterized with macho syncopations, is adorned with all the finery of the toreros' costumes, made for the original 1875 Paris production, incidentally, by the same haberdashers responsible for embroidering ecclesiastical robes [19]. A nice touch added in the 1875 production book is that Carmen smokes a cigarette while watching Escamillo. Were we hearing the opera for the first time, we would only now realize the significance of the bullfighter's melody embedded in the Prélude to the opera. Note the reference to the 'black look': the look of death given by the bull, the bullfighter or a woman.

The inn has by now acquired a function rather different from that in the novella: as a meeting place for all the factions of the drama. These include: the soldiers; their prey the smugglers who are on the borders of banditry; the gypsy women; the bullfighter and his entourage, as well as locals. In terms of its function, the following quintet prepares us for the criminal escapade into the mountains which comprises Act Three [20]. For the delight of the audience, Bizet invents some pungent, chromatic harmonies which – judging by the approximate rendering of the 1911 Opéra-Comique recording – presented problems for the singers of the day who, although they may have captured the spirit of a bunch of unruly brigands, were unable to cope with the intricacy of Bizet's fleet ensemble writing.

Woven into the spoken dialogue are the first hints that José does not have enough mettle for life as a bandit. Le Dancaïre points out that although Carmen had slipped him a file in a loaf of bread while he was in prison, he didn't have the guts to use it: too afraid of punishment. The ensuing scene, prescribed as a melodrama with speech superimposed over José's monodic song, 'Halte-là', was recorded in a different way in the 1911 recording, with the speech interpolated between the two verses of the song [21].

Several points are worth mentioning regarding the following duo between Carmen and José. The idea comes from the novella, where Carmen follows gypsy tradition by dancing a *romalis*: a dance song preceding coition [22]. Mérimée has introduced his readers to the gypsy terms *rom* and *roma* – the gypsy man and woman – to prepare for their understanding of this scene. It is only in the later Choudens orchestral score published in 1877 (see p. 95) that it is suggested that the castanets can be played by either the orchestra 'or the artist responsible for the role of Carmen'.

Some jiggery-pokery may be necessary for interpreters depending on whether Carmen accompanies herself with broken crockery – as in Mérimée's depiction of this scene – or finds her castanets in the nick of time. For Carmens who use the castanets a little alteration to dialogue needs to be made: for Carmens who don't, the text indicating that she finds them needs to be deleted. An alteration made in green ink to the working score used at the Opéra-Comique goes back to the novella and describes the dance as a *romalis*, altering the text of the recitative which begins the scene: '*Je vais en ton honneur danser la Romalis. / Et tu verras, mon fils, / Comment je sais moi-même accompagner ma danse*' are the words used to replace the text in the vocal score.[27]

Most important about the movement [22] is its key role as the number in which José effectively changes sides from the hunter to the hunted: he becomes the prey whose extermination was the *raison d'être* for the founding of the Guardia Civil in which José was originally a corporal, though stripped of this rank for releasing Carmen. This is projected in musical terms by Bizet's masterful use of conflicting musical languages, the first being the only example of highfalutin *grand opéra* recitative in the opera, standing out also because in the original text she addresses José as '*vous*' and calls him '*seigneur*'. This mock formality melts into her gypsy dance, once again characterized by untexted ululation. The contrast of this one satirical doff of the cap at the tradition of *grand opéra* is of course lost when the recitative version of the opera is used.

---

27 Variants of this sort are given in full in my 'Performance Urtext' of the score published by Peters Edition (London: 2013).

What is so particularly skilful about this crucial scene is the way in which Bizet extends it into a conflict of genres between the gypsy song and the accompanying military band, and the way the librettists weave this comically into the text as Carmen makes light of the situation in her line *'il est mélancolique de danser sans orchestre'* ('it's a bit sad to have no orchestra to dance to'), impervious to the severity of José's acute 'love and duty' turmoil. The approach of the band, growing in volume as it passes the inn, is also a masterstroke: projecting José's increasing distress as well as adding yet another realistic element. As it fades into the distance, the sense of José's having lost his moment of choice is driven home. In her fury, because José does not adhere to the gypsy code where love dominates over duty, Carmen indulges in another of the many echoes and foreshadowings which unify the opera: like the urchins earlier on, she mocks the ubiquitous bugle calls of the soldiers: 'ta-ra-ta-ra'. If the urchins were merely playing soldiers rather than mocking them, we are now in no doubt of Carmen's contempt for the forces of authority: even José's famous Flower Song is to no avail in calming her rage [23].

Once again the seeds of the next act are sown in the following duet which underlines the value gypsies place on the freedom of the open road [24]. At the same time, José's burning of his bridges is further advanced as he insults Zuniga. *'La liberté,'* shriek the chorus as the act ends. Is the lovely flute solo of the following Entr'acte a paean of praise to *'La liberté'*? The feature film of the opera directed by Francesco Rosi and released in 1984 portrays it with a bird flying over open landscape: a convincing interpretation [25].

Act Three begins with a long trudge [26]. Its danger and its nighttime setting are emphasized by its relentless rhythm, its length and its dark orchestration. In the novella the danger of armed conflict is far stronger. On one occasion, García, Carmen's hideous one-eyed husband, shoots Le Remendado in the face with a blunderbuss rather than have him captured: 'He'd be a clever fellow who could recognize him now,' he gloats, 'looking at his face, cut to pieces by a dozen pieces of shot'.[28] In the opera this episode is omitted but the danger is still there as the chorus keep reminding themselves 'not to take a false step'.

---

28 Prosper Mérimée, *Carmen*, op. cit., p. 52.

Another echo occurs in the card scene [27]. Carmen has previously faced José with the prospect of romantically whisking her away on horseback: a dream which was never to be. Now, as Mercédès and Frasquita enjoy good fortune with the tarot cards, they talk of similar adventures. The description of the card game, realistically portrayed in the music by opportunities for choreographed cutting and shuffling – '*Mêlons! Coupons!*' – clearly indicates the use of tarot cards. First cards are dealt from the *Arcanos Mayores* which establish the type of fortune being played for: life and death; health and illness; love; fortune in the sense of money, and so on. Then the familiar cards of the four suits are used. It is in the life-death sphere that Carmen deals her hand of black cards as the music descends to the D minor 'death' key which had first introduced her fateful motive at the end of the Prélude. She shares the key of F minor, in her first real aria [28] (as opposed to dance song), with that first sung by Escamillo: the professional dealer in life and death. It is also the first time she reflects inwardly. Life, however, must go on and her reflections on the fortune the cards have revealed are contrasted with the light-hearted musings of her two gypsy companions [27].

The duping of the customs men is once again a softening of the murderous banditry depicted in the novella, often ending with the murder of the '*écrevisses*', the British soldiers known as 'crayfish' because of their red uniforms and lobster-like plumes [29]. It is interesting that the spoken dialogue preceding Micaëla's aria with the four horns was replaced even at the Opéra-Comique by Guiraud's recitative, perhaps because it strengthens the trajectory of the opera towards an uninterrupted musical flow. This fine aria, skilfully voiced for the two pairs of horns in different keys, reintroduces the Christian faith of Micaëla to contrast with the developed picture we now have of Carmen's priorities to which Micaëla's reaffirmation of family duties and of forgiveness act as a foil [30].

The first edition of the vocal score has a far longer version of the following duel scene between José and Escamillo, particularly in the duel itself [31]. It would seem that although this was elaborate in the first staging, the scene was considered overlong and the 'sparrings' somewhat ridiculous. And how rare to have a pair of opera singers who can sustain a stage fight! The cut version appeared in the second vocal score and all subsequent scores except certain modern urtexts which have rightly restored the original music, perhaps more successful and balanced.

The final Entr'acte [32] is modelled on a *polo* by Manuel García senior, *Cuerpo bueno, alma divina,* thoroughly Spanish in both its syncopations and its borrowing of a characteristically flamenco use of key where the dominant seems to be the tonic: it's essentially in D minor but begins and ends on A. The librettists are exact in their depiction of the following cuadrilla: the procession leading to the bullring has been carefully researched and the opening paso doble of the Prélude is now heard in its proper context [1].

First come the two *alguazils* or *alguacilillos* (mounted bailiffs) who traditionally wore seventeenth-century costumes. Then come the picadors and finally the red-shirted *monosabios* and *mulilleros*, assistants who aid the matadors with the mounting of horses, help the fallen and generally look after the ring. These latter are not indicated in the libretto whose climax is the arrival of the *Espada*, a word indicating both the sword and the matador, in this case Escamillo who is accompanied by a triumphant rendering of his Toreador Song, carefully introduced in A major. In between fanfares are heard: perhaps modelled on the smaller band of musicians who signalled the various stages of the fight to the torero, and particularly the moment when the president of the ring estimated that it was time for the killing: '*la hora de la verdad*', the moment of truth. The whole effect is of a brilliant stage spectacle, with fanfares, the chorus inside the ring and the tune of the paso doble ringing out on the *cornets à pistons* (valved cornets which were used in French orchestras at the time of *Carmen*).

Although the music for the last scene is continuous, and completely free of spoken sections, it is characterized by unexpected key changes and alternation between the music inside and outside the arena. There is also a quick succession of changes of genre where the final drama outside the ring is masterfully superimposed over the bloodthirsty killings inside: heard but not seen in a virtuosic use of the age-old Opéra-Comique tradition of the *coulisses*, the wings of the stage. Also crucial is the quick succession of reminiscences – of the themes from the Prélude, and of Escamillo's triumphant Toreador Song now intensified by being transposed up a tone to G major. In fact wrenching up the keys to increase the frenzy – both inside and outside – is a technique central to the effect of the opera's terrible denouement. Bizet's extraordinary further screwing up of the key to F sharp major as José reflects on what he has done never fails to chill the spine, even though the final, crucial appearance of the torero, indicated in the score and illustrated on the original poster, is all too often ignored in modern-day productions.

What is it that we have witnessed, we may ask ourselves as we exit the theatre? Certainly an opera whose interpretations have changed over the years. It used to be simpler perhaps: the gypsy whore had got her just reward. What else would you expect from those sun-tanned southerners whose sexuality was seen as in proportion to the colour of their skin?

How many of us come out singing Micaëla's lovely aria, certainly the easiest melody of the opera, which soars upwards and sharpwards, winging over the harp and shimmering strings? So different from Carmen's sexy, but angular motive, always plunging downwards, as did her Habanera entry.

More modern interpretations of the opera's story have turned the idea of Carmen as an over-sexed *femme fatale* on its head. She is, after all, only behaving as men always have: moving from one sexual partner to another, taking her pleasure with whoever she wants. Susan McClary's groundbreaking – and in its time controversial – book introduced these ideas claiming *Carmen* as only one of many French theatrical fantasies involving race, class and gender.[29] Seen in the context of Spanish history, Carmen came from an underclass which the soldiers are employed to repress in a province ruled by relatively few landowners who kept the masses in medieval-style serfdom.

---

29 Susan McClary, *Georges Bizet: 'Carmen'* (Cambridge: Cambridge University Press, 1992), especially Chapter 3, 'Images of race, class and gender in nineteenth-century French culture'.

Her social climbing through her affair with a lieutenant, and then a bullfighter, while dancing for the aristocracy, is merely her means of transcending her repression.

Many opera-goers may still come out of a performance of *Carmen* with much the same view as its earliest audiences, and with Micaëla's lovely tune ringing in their ears – what a masterstroke on Bizet's part to recapitulate a little snatch of it towards the end of the opera! It prompts them to ask that so-obvious question: 'What if José had married Micaëla?' He'd certainly have saved himself a lot of bother, but we wouldn't have had an opera.

Carmen and the Opéra-Comique

Lesley A. Wright

In 1869 Georges Bizet was exultant as he wrote to his friend and student Edmond Galabert: 'Change of leadership! The new management of the Opéra-Comique has asked me in writing for a work! We are looking for a big piece in three or four acts. It is Du Locle, Perrin's nephew [...] Leuven will stay on as a formality[1] [...] Death to *La Dame blanche*!'[2] Understanding that this would also be a step toward entry into the prestigious venue of *grand opéra*, the Paris Opéra itself, Bizet had ambitious plans. Here was the opportunity not only to advance his career but also to transform the genre so beloved by the French public and so closely identified with the institution of the Opéra-Comique – this intention, years before he proposed to his librettists using a story based on Mérimée's widely read novella, *Carmen*.

1   Before he became co-director of the Opéra-Comique, Camille Du Locle (1832–1903) learnt about the theatre as an assistant to Émile Perrin at the Paris Opéra, 1862–70. He also wrote libretti for Jules Duprato and Ernest Reyer, finished the libretto of Verdi's *Don Carlos* (1867) and adapted Auguste Mariette's scenario for *Aida* (1871). Émile Perrin (1814–85) was an expert administrator who directed the Opéra-Comique (1848–57, 1862, 1876), the Théâtre-Lyrique (1854–55), the Paris Opéra (1862–71) and the Comédie-Française (1872–85). Adolphe de Leuven (1800–84), who had directed the Opéra-Comique since 1862, with Eugène Ritt, would stay on as co-director with Du Locle until 1874.
2   Georges Bizet, letter of February 1869, Edmond Galabert (ed.), *Lettres à un ami (1865–72)*, (Paris: Calmann-Lévy, 1909), p. 176. Written to a libretto based on the works of Sir Walter Scott, *La Dame blanche* (1825) by François-Adrien Boieldieu (1775–1834) was hugely popular in nineteenth-century France. Like other young French composers, Bizet resented the fact that access to lyric stages was blocked or reduced by repertory that his generation regarded as outdated.

Bizet understood the politics of cultural life in Paris and the power of theatre directors in aiding young composers' careers and shaping the repertory. A month after his letter to Galabert, he was already grumbling that Camille Du Locle had not yet provided him with a libretto, but he must have hoped that the new director's reputation as a cultivated, modern literary man would lead to changes that supported his own vision of progress. His target, Boieldieu's *La Dame blanche* (1825), was a charming work emblematic of the traditional Opéra-Comique repertory. With brave and benevolent Georges Brown as a gentleman hero returning to his ancestral lands, a brilliant lyric tenor part, tunefulness that rivalled Rossini's, Scottish local colour and a touch of the supernatural, it satisfied the public on every count and showed remarkable staying power, reaching its thousandth performance at the Opéra-Comique during 1862. Several other *opéras-comiques* achieved the '*reprise millénaire*' at this house during the last three decades of the nineteenth century: all were tuneful and ended with the prospect of happy nuptials or a plot resolution that otherwise reinforced family values.[3] Though only a few others would ever achieve such iconic status on the stage that gave them birth, one of them would be Bizet's *Carmen*. After its much discussed premiere on 3rd March 1875, it returned to the Opéra-Comique's stage in 1883 and had its thousandth performance there on 23rd December 1904.

In 1869 the Opéra-Comique drew almost half of its repertory from works written before 1845. Limited access frustrated ambitious younger composers. The state required this house to give Prix de Rome winners their official stage debuts with one-act curtain raisers, but these rarely stayed long in the repertory. By contrast, the Paris Opéra was normally reserved for those with major reputations or unusually good connections. Its director Perrin had rejected Bizet's *Ivan IV* in 1865, but by the late 1860s was cultivating him for the future. In the meantime the young composer had at least had the good fortune to see his

---

3   The list of *millénaires* includes: *Le Pré aux clercs* (Ferdinand Hérold, 1832), *Le Chalet* (Adolphe Adam, 1834), *Le Domino noir* (Daniel François Esprit Auber, 1837), *Les Noces de Jeannette* (Victor Massé, 1853) and *Mignon* (Ambroise Thomas, 1866). *Le Domino noir*, set in Spain during the Bourbon Restoration, includes an often excerpted bolero that circulated as 'La gitana' ('The Gypsy').

operas performed. Supported by his teacher Fromental Halévy, a successful composer in the previous generation, Bizet won a competition sponsored by Jacques Offenbach to bring attention to his new theatre, the Bouffes-Parisiens, where Offenbach would also present a string of his own wildly popular operettas beginning with *Orphée aux enfers* (1858). Both Bizet and his co-winner Charles Lecocq received eleven performances in 1857 of their light one-act operas on the libretto of *Le Docteur Miracle*, written by Léon Battu and Ludovic Halévy. In the next decade Léon Carvalho twice welcomed Bizet to the Théâtre-Lyrique (the highly regarded third lyric theatre in Paris for French opera). Both operas had exotic settings: Ceylon for *Les Pêcheurs de perles* (1863) and Scotland (à la Sir Walter Scott) for *La Jolie Fille de Perth* (1867). Carvalho also helped Gounod's operatic career by launching several of his operas, among them *Faust* (1859), *Mireille* (1864) and *Roméo et Juliette* (1867). The Théâtre-Lyrique's varied repertory included not only *opéras-comiques* but also operas with recitatives and operas in translation. Much to the chagrin of Bizet's generation, it disappeared with the onset of the Franco-Prussian War, after an existence of scarcely more than two decades. Though there were several attempts to establish a similar venue in the later nineteenth century, none succeeded for long. As a result, the Opéra-Comique became still more important for the *jeune école* ('young school') in the 1870s and was even more closely watched by both critics and tastemakers.

Opéra-Comique and opéra-comique

Opéra-Comique and *opéra-comique* must be understood as both institution and genre. As an institution, this was one of the four *grands théâtres* authorized by imperial decrees in 1806 and 1807, along with the Opéra, the Comédie-Française and the Odéon. Its activities were controlled via its state subsidy (linked to a contract between the state and the theatre director(s) which specified the mission in great detail) and state censorship. The government decreed that the repertory of the Opéra-Comique would consist of French works only – spoken comedies or dramas mixed with sung *couplets*, *ariettes* and ensembles. Plots were not always comic, but frequently sentimental and sometimes dramatic. Even death was not unheard of, for in Auber's *Manon Lescaut* (1856) the heroine expires onstage in exotic Louisiana.

The government's contract for the theatre in 1874 stipulated that the director present French works of the genre specified in 1807. To stage other repertory, even for special occasions or benefit performances, the director had to seek and obtain authorization from the Minister of the Interior. Numerous other Parisian theatres, including the Bouffes-Parisiens and the Théâtre-Lyrique, also staged works in French with varying amounts of music and spoken dialogue, but only in the 1870s, after the demise of the Théâtre-Lyrique, did the Opéra-Comique apply for permission to present operas with recitatives or in translation. Maintaining restrictions on the repertory in the 1870s reinforced the widely held view that the Opéra-Comique served as a bulwark against foreign cultural invasion. This was a matter of particular urgency immediately after political defeat in the war with Prussia and was stressed by the theatre's directors in a funding request to the National Assembly in 1871: 'If state support is withdrawn from the Opéra-Comique, its production will inevitably be halted. Stages in the provinces and abroad will not be slow to suffer the effects from this state of affairs, and Italian and German music will dominate everywhere to the detriment of French music.'[4]

Like the Comédie Française, the Opéra-Comique gave daily productions throughout the year (until a summer closure became an annual event in the late 1870s) and often played more than one work in an evening. Despite close oversight of its budget and stipulations about the type of repertory and number of new acts required each year, state politics had less influence here than at the Paris Opéra, and 'did not play a comparable role in the chase after prestige and extravagant grandeur'.[5] This '*genre moyen*', neither as frothy as operetta nor as serious as *grand opéra*, was popular among a broad swath of Paris-

---

4 Hervé Lacombe, 'L'Opéra-Comique au XIXe siècle: Un genre défini par sa législation', in Lorenzo Frassà (ed.), *The Opéra-Comique in the Eighteenth and Nineteenth Centuries* (Turnhout, Belgium: Brepols, 2011), p. 198.

5 Arnold Jacobshagen, 'A National Genre in an International Context', in Frassà (ed.), op. cit., p. 177.

ians, and, with its lowest-price tickets in the peanut gallery costing less than seats for popular spoken theatre, it was accessible to many.[6] In fact, the Opéra-Comique was a haven for works that embodied values aligned with French self-image and family values. The *soiriste* Frou Frou summed up its character as follows:[7]

> The Opéra-Comique is, without question, the most patriarchal theatre in Paris. Even on the evenings of first performances, it is like being with the family. It is a tranquil space for parents who have daughters to marry off. On the ceiling, the portraits of composers, who have so often brought together Adolphe and Clara and Colin and Colinette through their music, smile beneficently on the young ladies in quest of husbands and on bachelors in quest of wives. There is in the repertory of the theatre something good, sweet and honest which brings to the Opéra-Comique a clientele of young girls from boarding schools, escorted by their mothers. Even the boxes are more spacious than everywhere else and arranged in such a way that they can hold the double family of the fiancés.
>
> (*Le Figaro*, 2nd December 1872)

Opéra-comique was the 'best-loved and most-played type of stage performance of its day, not only in Paris but also – especially – in the French provinces.'[8] (It was even popular abroad.) Updating this genre '*éminemment national*' was a delicate process. Its public was comfortable with, even emotionally connected to, classics like *La Dame blanche*, and a group of journalists supported them. In any new opera, 'Wagnerian' influence (in other words, a more active

---

6   Olivier Bara, *Le Théâtre de l'Opéra-Comique sous la Restauration* (Hildesheim-Zurich-New York: Georg Olms Verlag, 2001), pp. 513–15 and Jacobshagen in Frassà (ed.), op.cit., p. 177.

7   The *soiristes* were less experienced journalists than the major critics and had the job of providing the readers with a 'rapid impression of a new play the day after its opening performance'. They would often list who attended and comment on audience reactions during the evening. See F.W.J. Hemmings, *The Theatre Industry in Nineteenth-Century France* (Cambridge: Cambridge University Press, 1993), p. 76.

8   Jacobshagen in Frassà (ed.), op. cit., p. 177.

orchestra and more complex harmonies) could even be attacked as unpatriotic, especially in the 1870s, whether or not the score had any significant ties to Wagner's innovations. And so we read comments like Henri Heugel's: 'May our young composers think about this. They hold the French lyric school in their hands: Germanized, it is lost! Let us stay French' (*Le Ménestrel*, 15th July 1877).

From 1870 to 1874 Du Locle and de Leuven (1800–84) directed the Opéra-Comique. Bizet's letter of 1869 implies that Du Locle took a leadership role in soliciting new repertory from the time he was first nominated for the post. Then, from 1874 to 1876 he directed the theatre alone. These two men of different generations were incompatible in every way. Director of the Opéra-Comique beginning in 1862, de Leuven had written the libretti for numerous *opéras-comiques* in the old style. Du Locle had been assistant to Perrin at the Opéra from 1862 and looked to the future. He had the odd habit, however, of criticizing to everyone within earshot his own theatre's productions, particularly if they were works that he judged old-fashioned. These chestnuts of the repertory were not only what de Leuven cherished but also what any practical director would programme to keep less adventurous subscribers interested in buying tickets while he patiently sought to open their ears to the beauties of newer scores. As the composer Henri Maréchal put it, Du Locle was 'firing on his own troops' by saying things like: 'Finally! I succeeded in making just eight hundred francs with *La Dame blanche*!'[9]

A well-educated literary man, Du Locle had some ideas that worked well. In 1872 and 1873 he probably suggested bringing Mozart's *Le nozze di Figaro* (sung in French) and Gounod's *Roméo et Juliette* over to the Opéra-Comique from the defunct Théâtre-Lyrique and arranged for the acclaimed and financially successful performances of Verdi's Requiem in the spring of 1874 and 1875. He also brought Massenet's oratorio *Marie-Magdeleine* to the theatre for a Lenten performance in 1874. In truth, he did commission the right young composers in his attempt to build new repertory for his institution. However, except for Bizet, none of them was yet ready to produce an operatic masterpiece.

---

9   Henri Maréchal, *Lettres et souvenirs (1871–74)* (Paris: Hachette, 1920), p. 221.

The Opéra-Comique closed during the Franco-Prussian War and the Commune, like other theatres in Paris, and did not reopen until July 1871 when it presented *Le Domino noir* as a tribute to Auber, who had died that May.[10] Afterwards, Du Locle was forced to scale back his plans to rejuvenate the theatre's repertory. He did arrange for the widely discussed premieres of three one-act *opéras-comiques* in April, May and June 1872: Émile Paladilhe's *Le Passant*, Bizet's *Djamileh* and Camille Saint-Saëns's *La Princesse jaune*. Each pushed at the boundaries of the genre, with music that was perceived as 'Wagnerian' and libretti that emphasized poetry and reverie over dramatic action. Louis Gallet, who wrote the libretti of the two orientalist one-acters in this series, recalled that he could not bring himself to use de Leuven's mockingly proffered solution to remedy audience boredom – have one of the characters drop a pile of plates.[11] Despite all the attention they garnered for the house, each of these operas had less than a dozen performances, and none was revived in the 1872–73 season. Nonetheless, both Paladilhe and Bizet were encouraged to begin full-length *opéras-comiques*, and Paladilhe's *L'Amour africain* had its premiere in May 1875, just two months after *Carmen*'s. At the end of 1872, Massenet's three-act Spanish work, *Don César de Bazan*, fared little better than the one-acters with only thirteen performances.

By bringing Gounod's *Roméo et Juliette* and then *Mireille* to his theatre in 1873 and 1874, Du Locle introduced serious themes, tragic endings and more modern scores in his effort to move the repertory away from the *opéra-comique*'s typically light or sentimental plots with joyful wedding celebrations at the final curtain. Not all supported this broadening of subject matter at the Opéra-Comique. Rumblings in the press grew louder on behalf of the increasingly unhappy public, and box-office receipts diminished as Du Locle's innovative programming met resistance. Achille de Lauzières, later one of the harshest critics of *Carmen*, lamented these changes:

---

10 Although the Franco-Prussian War began in July, the Opéra-Comique carried on until 3rd September 1870. Immediately after the French defeat in March 1871, the popular uprising called the Paris Commune began; it came to a bloody end in May.

11 See Louis Gallet, *Notes d'un librettiste* (Paris: Calmann-Lévy, 1891), pp. 24–25.

Why not stay with well-bred subjects, with piquant stories and with witty dialogue; why not stay with this lively, sparkling, animated music that does not deafen you and that does not break out in a big laugh, but always smiles? Or if it sometimes tugs at a sentimental string, limits itself to moving you without saddening the soul and the gaze of the spectator with lamentable tableaux, lugubrious episodes and bloody catastrophes...

(L'Art musical, 12th June 1873)

Other critics allowed that Du Locle should definitely search for new masters but continued to remind him that the genre's essence depended on grace and simplicity combined with tender or witty melodies.

By the time *Carmen* was in rehearsal, Du Locle needed a resounding success to fill the theatre's coffers. True to form, he engaged in nervous comments about the work, undercutting the artists and making the rehearsals even more strained. The actor Pierre Berton later claimed that these remarks circulated outside the theatre and set the opera up as a target for criticism. He also asserted that Du Locle failed to take a normal, basic precaution in support of his investment and pay off the usual corrupt journalists to write good reviews of the premiere.[12] And so, despite Du Locle's penchant for adventurous programming, it turned out that he lacked the business skills to run the Opéra-Comique, even with the aid of a state subsidy. He also seemed unwilling to believe wholly in what he presented. In March 1876 he turned the house over to his mentor and relative Émile Perrin, but the theatre, without funds to operate, had to close for the summer. When it reopened in August, Léon Carvalho was its new director.

The Genesis of Carmen

Shortly after the unsuccessful première of *Djamileh* (1872), Bizet reported to his friend Galabert that the Opéra-Comique had given him a commission for a three-act work that would be written by

---

12 Pierre Berton, 'Georges Bizet', *Souvenirs de la vie de théâtre* (Paris: P. Lafitte, 1913), pp. 209–73.

Henri Meilhac (1831–97) and Ludovic Halévy (1834–1908). This team produced the books for numerous light operas, including Offenbach's *La Belle Hélène*, *La Grande-Duchesse de Gérolstein* and *La Vie parisienne*. No wonder Bizet predicted that his opera would be gay and stylish, but he himself suggested Mérimée's *Carmen* as the subject. The novella was well known and had gone through dozens of printings since its first publication in 1845. It had already served, in a much altered version, for an *opéra-comique* in 1862 with libretto by Jules Barbier and music by amateur composer Jules Beer, the immensely wealthy nephew of Giacomo Meyerbeer. (Here the gypsy heroine decides to devote herself to God during the final ensemble, while the country folk celebrate the impending nuptials of her former lover and his loyal village sweetheart.) Victor Massé had corresponded with Victorien Sardou in 1864 about setting the novella, too. He planned to have his heroine die at the end and to have Célestine Galli-Marié (later Bizet's Carmen) play the title character.

Aware of the plot's conclusion and the title character's immorality, Bizet's librettists decided to speak to Du Locle about this idea for their project, and he warned them that the subject would frighten his co-director. Halévy's father (the historian and dramatist Léon) and uncle (the composer Fromental Halévy) had known de Leuven for decades, and so he was tapped to go to speak to the older man. Three decades later, when *Carmen* achieved its thousandth performance at the Opéra-Comique, he recalled that meeting. De Leuven interrupted him immediately, very upset, as soon as he broached the subject: '*Carmen*!... Mérimée's *Carmen*! Isn't she assassinated by her lover?... And this milieu of thieves, gypsies and cigar makers!... At the Opéra-Comique!... the theatre for families!... the theatre for marriage interviews!... We have, every evening, five or six boxes rented out for these interviews... You'll put our public to flight... it's impossible!'[13] Halévy promised that Carmen would be much sweetened and attenuated, that there would be an innocent, chaste girl among the characters, that the gypsies would be comic ones and that the inevitable death would be slipped in at the very end after a lively act. De Leuven finally agreed,

---

13 Ludovic Halévy, 'La Millième Représentation de *Carmen*', *Le Théâtre* No. 145 (January 1905), pp. 5–14.

reluctantly, but asked that the librettists try to avoid the death scene: 'Don't make her die! Please, my dear child.' (Halévy was about forty.) He speculated that de Leuven's horror at the prospect of *Carmen* on his stage led to his resignation in 1874. Of course, the director was then seventy-four, and, more importantly, his business savvy may have encouraged him to get out before financial disaster struck. Du Locle's leadership would result in his bankruptcy just two years later.

Bizet began to write the score of *Carmen* in 1873, initially anticipating rehearsals in autumn of that year. He also worked on *Don Rodrigue*, a *grand opéra* based on Guillén de Castro's story of *El Cid*. Bizet liked its 'real Spanish colouring' and its potential for scenes featuring Jean-Baptiste Faure, the star bass-baritone at the Opéra. He dropped this project to focus again on *Carmen* later in the same year. In summer 1873 a rumour circulated that the dynamic Zulma Bouffar, star of Offenbach's operettas, would be playing Bizet's Carmen. Its accuracy is dubious, but we do know that Marie Roze (a star at Mapleson's opera company in London and from 1877 wife of his son, Henry) actually turned the role down in early September after an interview with the composer: she thought the part too shocking to suit her and, more importantly, that she would not be suited to it either. At that point negotiations began with Célestine Galli-Marié to undertake the lead role; she finally accepted in December 1873 and at that point expected performances to begin in October 1874. After Bizet orchestrated the score during two months in the summer of 1874, rehearsals finally began that autumn.

Documents show that Bizet was directly involved in making the verse more vivid at specific important moments, like the Habanera and the Card Trio. However, many details of *Carmen*'s genesis will never be known because Ludovic Halévy, first cousin of Bizet's wife Geneviève, lived in the same apartment building as the Bizets. Meilhac is also supposed to have come there on Wednesday evenings to play whist. Other documents, now missing, were probably destroyed (see George Hall's article, p. 57). As the librettists prepared the book, they focused on only one section of Mérimée's novella and changed many things, not the least of which was omitting Carmen's criminal husband, García the One-Eyed, and Don José's murder of him. They added a sweet soprano from the Basque country, Micaëla, and Carmen's friends Frasquita and Mercédès. They created comic smugglers in the bantering pair, Le Dancaïre and Le Remendado. The self-enamoured toreador Escamillo was fabricated from Lucas, a minor character in the novella. Although the librettists accommodated certain *opéra-comique* stereotypes, they retained many of Carmen's gypsy traits, showed Don José's collapse from honourable soldier to murderer, and even borrowed some of Mérimée's phrases verbatim (see Richard Langham Smith's article for a detailed examination of the *Carmen* libretto). And, of course, Meilhac and Halévy set up the opportunity for *couplets*, duets, choruses and large finales. As in other progressive *opéras-comiques* of that decade, dialogue is relatively limited, especially later in the work, and the role of the choruses more prominent.

Bizet wrote some music that was deliberately accessible in order to acknowledge the tradition of the theatre and the tastes of its patrons. He incorporated more numbers with catchy melodies and overtly exotic Spanish sounds. The score teems with colour and felicitous orchestration. As a member of the *jeune école*, Bizet could not resist making his orchestra a commentator and a partner with the voices in creating the musical fabric. His harmonies sometimes slip into distant regions, as in the cadential area of the Flower Song, and the music for the arguments between José and Carmen achieves an intensity that few have ever surpassed. As Peter Rabinowitz has pointed out, the narrative audience perceives Carmen's death as 'not so much a murder as a suicide – she taunts José into killing her, preferring a freely chosen death to a life of wifely submission'. He also mentions that 'in a certain literary tradition – which reached its peak in such writers as Hemingway and Camus – choosing your death is the ultimate act of (masculine) freedom'.[14] Here is a real threat to social order: this outsider, a gypsy, refuses to become subservient to a man or to bourgeois society's laws and customs. The darkening mood of *Carmen*'s last two acts leads to an ending as tragic as in *grand opéra*, though transposed to a seamier part of society. Nonetheless, Bizet seems to have felt that this tragic

---

14 Peter Rabinowitz, 'Singing for Myself: *Carmen* and the Rhetoric of Musical Resistance', in Elaine Barkin and Lydia Hamessley (eds.), *Audible Traces: Gender, Identity and Music* (Zurich: Carciofoli Verlagshaus, 1999), p. 143.

opéra-comique would succeed: 'People make me out to be obscure, complicated, tedious, more hampered by technical skill than lit by inspiration. Well, this time I have written a work that is all clarity and vivacity, full of colour and melody.'[15]

After rehearsals began in the theatre in October 1874, Bizet was there frequently, but his librettists came only occasionally prior to February. In January 1875, Bizet wrote to Ambroise Thomas of the hectic schedule that an opera in full rehearsal creates for its composer: '*Carmen* no longer leaves me an instant of rest. I'm accompanying myself, I'm reducing the score myself.'[16] A magnificent pianist and experienced transcriber, Bizet usually prepared the piano-vocal versions of his operas himself instead of turning to another. His autograph manuscript and the parts used by the Opéra-Comique orchestra show that he also made numerous revisions to the score. According to his friend Ernest Guiraud, Bizet wrote thirteen versions of Carmen's entrance piece before coming up with the Habanera we know today, which was possibly a last-ditch attempt to please Galli-Marié, and various documents point to at least three.[17] Rehearsal problems were not confined to the diva's entrance song. The orchestra members, used to the simple accompaniments of *La Dame blanche* and other scores from the earlier nineteenth century, claimed their parts were unplayable. And Halévy recalled that after two months of rehearsals, the chorus threatened to go on strike over the 'unperformable' cigar girls' entrance chorus and bloody scuffle during the arrest of Carmen. In mid-February 1875, Bizet pleaded with Du Locle to add ten female choristers so that these pieces in the first act could be performed and offered to rehearse them himself. Though he got the extra singers, it appears that later cuts were still necessary. Shortly before the premiere, Du Locle (nervous about the ending) called in Perrin to judge whether

---

15 Quoted in Winton Dean, *Bizet* (London: Dent, 1965, rev. 1975), pp. 108–9.
16 Georges Bizet, letter to Ambroise Thomas, *c*.20th January 1875, in Lesley A. Wright (ed.), *Letters in the Nydahl Collection* (Stockholm: Royal Swedish Academy of Music, 1988), p. 41.
17 On this, see Hervé Lacombe, 'La Version primitive de l'air d'entrée de Carmen: Réflexion sur la dramaturgie et "l'autorialité" d'un opéra', in Jean-Christophe Branger and Vincent Giroud (eds.), *Aspects de l'opéra français de Meyerbeer à Honegger* (Lyon: Symétrie, 2009), pp. 29–45.

it had to be changed. Perrin hated the piece and predicted a failure if the work stayed in its current form. Still, with the support of his star performers, Bizet succeeded in beating back changes.

Insecure about a solo directorship he had held for barely a year and well aware of his puny cash flow, Du Locle apparently did take precautions, for, as Halévy mentions, several newspapers had announcements on the morning of the premiere that warned the public of the opera's scandal value.[18] The theatrical gossip column of *Le Gaulois* (a place where announcements were often paid for by the line) declared on 3rd March that Meilhac himself checked to make sure that no journalists came to the dress rehearsal, the reason being that '*Carmen* presents characters that are so shocking and situations that are so risky that, overall, the piece might easily be taken badly' – and, of course, such reports by journalists could unduly influence the opening night. The original poster used to advertise *Carmen* on the kiosks that dotted the streets of Paris shows Don José in front of the bullring as Escamillo and the spectators exit, with a knife below one hand and the body of Carmen on his other arm (a clear warning to theatregoers that despite the theatre's tradition of happy endings, Carmen would not survive this time).

The audience for the premiere on 3rd March 1875 was filled with major figures from the literary and artistic world (see George Hall's article, p. 57), not to mention all the major critics. Many years later Jacques-Émile Blanche, son of the famous society doctor who had treated members of the Halévy family at his retreat in Passy, reported what he heard at the premiere as he sat next to Bizet's long-time mentor Charles Gounod. For this fourteen-year-old, it was the first lesson in hypocrisy, for Gounod praised the new opera to Bizet's face, and then exclaimed after Micaëla's *air* in Act Three: 'That melody is mine! Georges has robbed me; take the Spanish tunes and mine out of the score and there remains nothing to Bizet's credit but the sauce that masks the fish.'[19] Not just Gounod, but the audience as a whole cooled through the evening. Bizet was crushed. Afterwards, according

---

18 Halévy, op. cit., p. 8.
19 See Mina Curtiss, *Bizet and His World* (New York: Alfred A. Knopf, 1958), p. 391.

to Halévy, they returned to their apartment building on the slopes below the Place Blanche: 'on foot, silent. Meilhac accompanied us. The lack of success for an *opéra-comique* libretto was not a serious matter for him and me [...] we were only thinking of Bizet.'[20] A decade after the premiere Bizet's first biographer, Charles Pigot, claimed that the composer took the arm of his dear friend Ernest Guiraud, and they wandered together across Paris until dawn as Bizet poured out his bitter disappointment. Whatever transpired the night after the premiere, the disillusionment must have been profound, for Bizet was now thirty-six, and it was time for him to have his first big success.

The reviews began to appear the next day, but many more were published on Monday, 8th March, the day many of the authoritative critics (*les lundistes*) let their opinions be known in a weekly column; most other assessments appeared within the next two weeks. Bizet had already learnt to dismiss bad reviews, but two of these Monday reviews he found particularly upsetting. Achille de Lauzières (*La Patrie*) contemptuously dismissed Bizet's title character as nothing more than a savage and a prostitute. He went on to accuse Bizet of plagiarism in the Toreador Song and of tasteless scoring. A more authoritative musician and writer, Oscar Comettant (*Le Siècle*), also fulminated against the immorality of the subject: 'A plague on these females vomited from hell and what an odd *opéra-comique* [...]! To preserve good social order and security among the impressionable dragoons and toreadors who surround this demoiselle, she should be gagged, a stop put to her wild hip movements; she should be fastened into a straitjacket after being cooled off by a jug of water poured over her head'; furthermore, he added that the 'uterine' frenzies of Carmen were impossible to convey through ingenious orchestration and harsh dissonances. Rossinian melody was what was needed. Bizet 'thinks too much and doesn't feel enough; even his best inspirations lack sincerity [...] He has to *unlearn* many things to become a dramatic composer.' A few weeks later Bizet, with fury in his eyes, confronted Comettant in the lobby of the Conservatoire and upbraided him loudly. The incident rattled the critic enough that he recounted it (from his point of view) when he reviewed *Carmen* again in 1883.

---

20 Halévy, op. cit., p. 8.

While only a few critics attacked *Carmen* this viciously, not many others wholly supported it. Most writers ended up being tepid, dishing out praise and criticism in more or less equal portions, and basically giving their readers no particular encouragement to head off to the box office. Some acknowledged Bizet's 'progress' since *Djamileh*, for he had made this score more overtly melodious. Most found specific moments or numbers to praise, but, with the exception of Micaëla's prayer, chose pieces that fell largely in the first two acts. More perceptive than most about the score itself, the composer Victorin de Joncières (*La Liberté*, 8th March 1875) specifically differentiated between Bizet's music, which he thought showed enormous talent if perhaps too much search for originality, and the dubious libretto – 'not that the piece was not done with skill, but because the regular clientele of the Opéra-Comique is not yet inured to the daring effect of a scene so risqué as that in the act inside the tavern'. Although he liked the first act best, he singled out pieces throughout the score: the Habanera was a 'jewel', the Séguedille charming, tender and passionate, and Micaëla's message from José's mother full of feeling and melody; in the second act the Chanson bohème and the duet between Carmen and Don José were excellent (but the Toreador Song vulgar, even though the audience encored it); in the third act, he praised the colourful smugglers' chorus and the Card Trio, especially Carmen's dark prediction, and the theatrically effective Act Three finale (but not a word about Micaëla's *air*). Finally, Joncières was virtually alone in praising the emotional power of the *grand duo* that closes the opera.

Many found fault with the *scabreux* (shocking) situations in the libretto. Some felt that Bizet had erred in choosing a subject that belonged elsewhere, perhaps at a boulevard theatre like the Théâtre Ambigu. They complained that the characters and situations introduced the mores of the street, of the underclass or, more specifically, of Belleville (a working-class quarter that had also been a major centre of the Commune uprising) to a theatre and genre identified with sweet, proper sentiments and situations. Jules Guillemot (*Le Soleil*, 9th March) even likened *Carmen's* plot to a newspaper report: 'Yesterday the residents of Rue Oberkampf were deeply upset by a murder scene: Mr. J…, sergeant of the 102nd Infantry, met the young woman C… and after a heated exchange of

words, he plunged a knife into her heart: death was instantaneous [...].'
The portrait of Carmen was not the only problem – Guillemot felt the public would not be able to feel sympathy for a hero like Don José, an honourable soldier ruined by his passion ('Real or not, a love that abases a man to that point is not a sight to show publicly').

And then there was Carmen on the stage, vividly sung and convincingly acted by Galli-Marié. Here was a threat quite different from Mérimée's original portrait, which had been safely distanced from reality in an elegant narrative of past events. Galli-Marié performed her role so very well. 'It is difficult to go further without [...] provoking intervention by the police,' reported François Oswald (*Le Gaulois*, 6th March); 'Madame Galli-Marié [...] is common; she has photographed the gestures, the look, the costume of the ladies of the street corner [...]. Let us not fall so low, please, on the pretext of exactitude,' complained Daniel Bernard (*L'Union*, 8th March). How could young girls come to this theatre with their mothers and witness Carmen's sensuality, so present, so vivid and so knowingly portrayed by a mature woman aware of her charms? Émile Cardon (*La Presse*, 9th March) chastised the director:

> M. Du Locle cannot be blamed for his efforts to renew the repertory of the Opéra-Comique and to expand the scope of his theatre, but isn't he overshooting his goal when he presents works like *Carmen*, by M. Georges Bizet? I am afraid so and sincerely regret it. The Opéra-Comique has a public whose taste is not the most cultivated [...]. Their taste can be improved. An artist-director should even try to do so; but if he wants to succeed he should only do this slowly, and M. Du Locle is wrong in wanting to go too fast.

The gifted poet and writer Théodore de Banville, one of the few wholeheartedly to endorse Bizet's assault on the traditional *opéra-comique*, also addressed its creators: 'Take care, M. Du Locle, M. Bizet, M. Meilhac, M. Halévy, for Lady Macbeth was right. Despite all the perfumes of Araby, there will always be the smell of blood, and from now on how can the lieutenant of *La Dame blanche* [...] be brought back?' (*Le National*, 8th March).

Bizet died three months to the day after *Carmen*'s premiere. Though he planned to write the recitatives for the Vienna performance the following autumn, he had decided to return to his work on an oratorio called *Geneviève de Paris* and was in contact with his librettist Louis Gallet. In the meantime, *Carmen* continued its run, with respectable but not impressive box-office receipts. Galli-Marié, who enormously enjoyed her role, lobbied to keep it on the stage until the middle of June. A brief series of performances the next autumn may have been mounted to capitalize on the sympathy generated by Bizet's untimely death, or perhaps Du Locle was motivated by his budget woes, which had escalated with the failure of Paladilhe's *L'Amour africain* in May, to try to wring a bit more value from the expensive production he had mounted for *Carmen*. After thirteen more performances, the Opéra-Comique dropped it from the repertory, and its forty-ninth presentation there would have to wait until 1883.

Carmen: *Life after Death*

In the later 1870s, while Léon Carvalho was repairing damage by the previous administration to the profitability of an institution he would guide for most of the next two decades, *Carmen* was making its way from triumph to triumph around the stages of Europe and the world. Certainly aware of this, members of the press waged a campaign of increasing intensity in the early 1880s to bring *Carmen* back to the Opéra-Comique. Now that his theatre was on a secure footing financially, Carvalho did bow to their pressure, despite his basic disaffection with the opera. He was not alone in wanting to avoid the controversies of 1875 and proposed to the librettists a different star for the title role in the revival. Adèle Isaac, a blonde still in her twenties, was known for her superb high soprano voice, not her acting skills. Halévy, Meilhac and Bizet's widow agreed with Carvalho's decision to cast a tamer interpreter: 'In truth, the piece was not sung in Paris, and it will be this time.'[21]

---

21 Françoise Balard, *Geneviève Straus: Biographie et correspondance avec Ludovic Halévy, 1855–1908* (Paris: CNRS Éditions, 2002), p. 138.

When *Carmen* reached Carvalho's stage on 21st April 1883, rumours swirled about the production in artistic circles and in the press. Writing to Vincent d'Indy, Ernest Chausson was highly critical of the quality of the performance he saw and doubted the director's commitment to the revival:

> Carvalho is doing everything possible to make *Carmen* fail; it shocks the virginal purity of his soul. It is very badly staged, like something that isn't cared about. The choruses in the first act raise the hairs on your head. Nonetheless, I wouldn't be surprised if success grows. The subscribers (!!) find that it is more entertaining than *Jean de Nivelle*, and that horrible Toreador Song makes them believe that they understand advanced music.[22]

While it is unlikely that the director, not only a businessman but also a supporter of Bizet since the time of *Les Pêcheurs de perles*, tried to make *Carmen* fail, Carvalho quite likely held back on pouring money into a lavish production, wanting to test gingerly the reaction of his subscribers and the critics. He was a gifted stage director, too, who would have been able to tone down the acting of his lead singers for this production in a way that Bizet and Galli-Marié would never have permitted in 1875. Forced to adapt the theatre's schedule to the illnesses of various stars, he hurried along the rehearsals of *Carmen* so that the production would open just a week after the world premiere of Delibes's *Lakmé* and two months before the end of the spring season. Some in the cast were not in good voice on opening night. For those who saw this revival as the reparation of an injustice done to Bizet, its deficiencies caused great disappointment. The audience cheered many pieces in the first two acts and then became less enthusiastic. Supporters blamed the performance for being so boring that the hall dozed off; a few detractors reiterated what the opening-night critics in 1875 had maintained (that the first two acts, lighter and closer to the *opéra-comique* tradition, were simply more successful). But the press no longer emphasized 'Wagnerian' connections. With the

---

[22] Ernest Chausson, letter of 26th April 1883, 'Lettres inédites à Vincent d'Indy', *La Revue musicale* (1st December 1925), p. 130.

aura of success already buoying *Carmen*'s reputation, it was more comfortable for the critics to agree that the score was a masterpiece – colourful, realistic and quintessentially French. Auguste Vitu in *Le Figaro* (23rd April 1883) attributed this to 'the limpidity of its musical thought, the clarity of its phrasing, and even [...] its abundance of ideas'. 'Bizet is a melodist,' he maintained, 'who is not afraid to hobnob with Boieldieu, Auber, Gounod, Halévy and even Adolphe Adam under the vaulted ceilings of the Opéra-Comique.'

Isaac sang beautifully, but she was not a true Carmen. Frimousse (Raoul Toché), the *soiriste* of *Le Clairon* (22nd April), called her a 'family Carmen, always serious, always buttoned up'. While Galli-Marié had exuded provocative sensuality as soon as she entered the stage, the chaste Isaac threw her corsage at Don José 'with so much modest grace that you would believe you were watching a young girl at a charity bazaar' (Arnold Mortier, 'Un Monsieur de l'orchestre', *Le Figaro*, also 22nd April). Critics seized on the opportunity to deflect attention from any mistakes they had made in assessing *Carmen* initially by focusing on the problems in Carvalho's production, and there was consensus that the time had come to dispense with quibbles about the morality of the subject and accept *Carmen* as a strong, beautiful and truthful work. Box-office receipts were good that spring. Parents apparently did bring their daughters to see the show; after all, by 1883 the Habanera was already propped up on the piano stand in every salon.

At the suggestion of many, Carvalho hastened to bring Galli-Marié back for the 'true reprise' on 27th October. News of her Carmen portrayals around Europe must have filtered back to Paris, increasing anticipation. In the meantime she had added touches of realism (incorporating dance moves learnt in Barcelona and using the carnation as Carmen's flower, like the *manolas* of Spain). Carvalho put together a stronger cast, redid the staging, had new costumes prepared for the procession in Act Four, and gave the chorus and orchestra ample rehearsal. In other words, he lavished attention on this production knowing that it would reap great profits for his theatre. Galli-Marié was at first engaged for only twenty performances, but her portrayal was unforgettable. This was an artist who 'expends body and soul to give the spectator the most intense illusion of reality' (Alphonse Duvernoy, *La République française*, 31st

April). When she left the theatre for other commitments, other talented Carmens immediately materialized, and the opera became a staple of the Opéra-Comique's repertory.

On 7th December 1898, the new Salle Favart (finally rebuilt after the disastrous fire of 1887) opened in a gala performance, which included Act Two of *Carmen*. This theatre still stands on the Place Boieldieu, and it was here that the Opéra-Comique began its season on 8th December 1898, with its 756th performance of *Carmen*. The production featured Georgette Leblanc in the title role, new sets by Lucien Jusseaume, Marcel Jambon and Alfred Lemeunier and a new staging by Albert Carré, who was in the first year of his long tenure as director of that house (1898–1914). For the thousandth performance of *Carmen* on 23rd December 1904, Carré chose Emma Calvé to sing the title role. Like Galli-Marié, this compelling singer and legendary Carmen had done her homework to add realistic touches (touring Spain, visiting gypsy encampments and watching female workers go in and out of cigarette factories).[23] Galli-Marié, nearing the end of her life, sent Calvé a note of support from her retirement home outside Nice for that evening's performance. Ludovic Halévy and Bizet's widow came to the celebration. But Meilhac had already passed away; so too, had Comettant, Lauzières, Banville, Joncières... and most of the other critics who had reviewed *Carmen* in 1875. The work, dubbed a masterpiece some two decades earlier, was now raised up as an icon, virtually indivisible from Parisian pride and Frenchness itself. '*Ô Paris, ce chef-d'œuvre aimé, vainqueur du temps / C'est la millième fois ce soir que tu l'entends; / Et plus on s'en remplit le cœur, plus on acclame / Ses rythmes de lumière et ses chansons de flamme,*'[24] gushed Jean Richepin in a lengthy poem reprinted the next day on the front page of *Le Figaro*. For the celebratory evening it was recited by an emotional Julia Bartet, who, as a teenager some thirty years earlier, had played Vivette in Bizet's and Alphonse Daudet's *L'Arlésienne*.

---

23 See Steven Huebner, 'La Princesse paysanne du Midi', in Annegret Fauser and Mark Everist (eds.), *Music, Theater, and Cultural Transfer* (Chicago: Chicago University Press, 2009), pp. 361–78.

24 'O Paris, this beloved masterpiece, vanquisher of time, / It is the thousandth performance that you hear this evening; / And the more the heart is filled with it, the more one acclaims / Its rhythms of light and its songs of flame.'

All the press sang the praises of Bizet's music. In *Le Petit Journal*, Léon Kerst found it 'so luminous, so alive, so inspired, so perfectly French'; and in *Le Figaro* on 24th December 1904, Gabriel Fauré paid tribute to a score that was 'all clarity, candour, sensibility and charm'. Some wondered how the music could ever have been misunderstood, even if the libretto had stepped beyond the norms tolerated at the Opéra-Comique in 1875. Perhaps the most luminous homage came from Gustave Charpentier.[25] He began with a quote and a question:

> 'Art aims at conquering death,' wrote Saint-Georges de Bouhélier in his book *The Passions of Love*. What artist will have fulfilled his hope better than Bizet? [...] The man who left us *Carmen* will always be alive.
>
> (*Le Figaro*, 23rd December 1904)

For Charpentier, *Carmen* was a font of contemporary opera and had lit the future, like a Mount Etna 'of love and fiery music'. This eruption had initially inspired charges of vulgarity from those accustomed to earlier *opéras-comiques* ('Pale *Zampa*s shuddered before it'). Bypassing the score's exoticism, Carmen's otherness and her unswerving commitment to personal freedom, he focused instead on naturalism and passion, in a work where man, buffeted by internal storms, becomes a slave to passion and perishes as a result. If Bizet might have been surprised that Charpentier passed lightly over *Carmen*'s overt tunefulness and other conscious accommodations to the *opéra-comique* tradition, he might still have been pleased that its musico-dramatic strengths were viewed as a rupture with the past, not to mention a roadmap toward the future. In the end, however, he might have been even more satisfied to learn that in 1904 *Carmen* had more than three dozen performances at the Opéra-Comique, and *La Dame blanche* only six.

---

25 Appropriately enough, his *Louise*, the first new production of the Opéra-Comique in the twentieth century, would also have one thousand performances at this house – reaching the milestone in 1956, a few months after Charpentier's death.

A Selective Performance History

George Hall

First Night

Unlike the first nights of such famous operas as *Il barbiere di Siviglia*, *Norma* or *Madama Butterfly*, the premiere of *Carmen* was not a fiasco, though it was a failure. Also unlike the other works listed above, there was no immediate volte-face at the second performance – which, in the case of *Butterfly*, was held up for three months because Puccini instantly withdrew the piece and revised it before moving it to another theatre in another city. The aura of failure surrounding *Carmen* – and that despite its continuing its run – was slower to dissipate, and lingered in Paris for several years. The issue of the work's reception was also complicated by the unexpected death of Bizet himself three months after the first night at the early age of thirty-six – an event widely held, both at the time and later, to be partially the result of severe disappointment and depression; a rumour of suicide even briefly did the rounds. Bizet's martyrdom at the hands of his critics has become part of the opera's legend.

Yet *Carmen* surprised its first-night audience by going on to become a classic, and indeed to assume a prime position as one of the most viable candidates for the title of the world's most popular opera, which it continues to hold today. Some of those who had buried it eventually returned to praise it. Others, more closely involved with the composer and his creation, were understandably anxious to present themselves as having been supportively onside during the crucial period leading up to the opera's premiere and on into its sadder aftermath.

Because, also, of ongoing difficulties within Bizet's marriage to Geneviève Bizet (née Halévy) – who suffered from bouts of mental and other illnesses that prevented her from attending either the first night of *Carmen* or her husband's funeral, and who at times lived separately from him – documents that might have provided vital information about the creation and reception of *Carmen*, but which would also have revealed family secrets, have either been destroyed or defaced. Most notoriously, large sections of the journal of Ludovic Halévy – one of *Carmen*'s co-librettists, and also Geneviève Bizet's cousin – have either been cut out and presumably destroyed, or scrawled over to the point of obliterating the text beneath. Family letters, too, are almost entirely missing from 1873 onwards; out of a similar sense of loyalty, Bizet's friend and pupil Edmond Galabert destroyed his correspondence from Bizet covering an identical period. Some of the discrepancies between the accounts of those present on the first night – not only concerning their interpretation of the work's reception, but even specific events and conversations – remain difficult to resolve; a number of them, of course, date from many years afterwards.

Carmen opened at the Opéra-Comique on 3rd March 1875 before an audience that included a host of figures from the Parisian musical and literary worlds, many of them friends and colleagues of Bizet's. Among them were Gounod, Ambroise Thomas, Delibes, Offenbach, Massenet and Ernest Guiraud, younger talents such as Benjamin Godard and Vincent d'Indy, the operetta composer Charles Lecocq, Hortense Schneider and Zulma Bouffar – both stars of Offenbach's operettas – various opera singers and publishers, the conductor Jules Pasdeloup and, representing literature, Alphonse Daudet and Alexandre Dumas *fils*. The cast consisted of Célestine Galli-Marié (Carmen), Paul Lhérie (Don José), Jacques Bouhy (Escamillo) and Marguerite Chapuy (Micaëla);[1] Adolphe Deloffre conducted and the *mise en scène* was by Charles Ponchard. The sets were unusually

---

1 Earlier Galli-Marié, Lhérie and Bouhy had all taken part in the 1872 premiere of another opera with a Spanish setting, Massenet's *Don César de Bazan*, whose numerous Iberian musical references included a 'sevillana' entr'acte later adapted as a coloratura soprano showpiece (see Richard Langham Smith's article, p. 11).

lavish. Georges Clairin, who had visited Spain and knew the country well, designed the costumes; Édouard Detaille, a specialist military artist, the dragoons' uniforms.

The creator of the central role, Galli-Marié (1840–1905) was an extraordinary artist and one of the most notable French singers of the day; her commitment to *Carmen* and to Bizet himself was never in doubt. Born in Paris, the daughter and pupil of the leading tenor Mécène Marié de l'Isle (who had created the role of Tonio in Donizetti's *La Fille du régiment* at the Opéra-Comique in 1840), she commenced her career in 1859. An early marriage to a sculptor called Galli extended her name, which she retained in its longer form following his death in 1861. Admired more as an actress and musician than for her purely vocal abilities, she appeared in the premieres of operas by composers such as Massenet (Lazarille in *Don César de Bazan*) and Offenbach (Vendredi in *Robinson Crusoé* in 1867, the title role in *Fantasio* in 1872), in addition to her two most famous creations: Ambroise Thomas's *Mignon* (1866) and *Carmen*. Her dedication to and aptitude for Bizet's character led her to reprise the role regularly internationally, including in Naples, Barcelona and at Her Majesty's Theatre in London in 1886; her final performance was as Carmen in 1890 on an evening dedicated to raising funds for a monument to Bizet. Interestingly, given the alacrity with which many sopranos have taken up the role of Carmen, Galli-Marié had suggested the tessitura of Marguerite in *Faust* to Bizet as a model; though many would view its rich mezzo depths as an essential part of its dramatic colouring.

Bizet's other main supporter in the company was the tenor Paul Lhérie (originally Lévy, 1844–1937) who had joined the troupe at the Opéra-Comique in 1866 and created the role of Charles II of Spain in *Don César de Bazan* and Benoît in Delibes's *Le Roi l'a dit* (1873) before Don José came along. In 1882 he moved down to the baritone register, appearing as Posa in the revised version of Verdi's *Don Carlos* at La Scala in 1884, and in 1887 singing several major baritone roles at Covent Garden, including Zurga in Bizet's *Les Pêcheurs de perles*. Subsequently he created Rabbi David in Mascagni's *L'amico Fritz* in Rome in 1891 and in 1894 Gudleik in César Franck's *Hulda* at Monte Carlo, after which he retired. No less a judge than Toscanini thought highly of him. 'He had a great talent, more so than [Victor] Maurel. He did not possess Maurel's voice, but he was more refined.'[2]

Escamillo was sung by the Belgian baritone Jacques Bouhy (1848–1929), who had made his debut at the Opéra as Méphistophélès in Gounod's *Faust* in 1871 and went on to create the title role of Ernest Reyer's *Erostrate* in its French premiere that same year. At the Opéra-Comique he created the title role of *Don César de Bazan* as well as appearing in the premieres of works by Victor Massé and Gaston Salvayre. During the 1882 season he appeared at Covent Garden, his roles including Escamillo in the first performances of *Carmen* at the theatre. Bouhy spent the years 1885 to 1889 in New York, where he was asked to establish a municipal conservatory; he then returned to Paris, where he continued to perform at the Opéra and elsewhere.

The creation of the role of Micaëla is the major claim to fame of the soprano Marguerite Chapuy (originally Chopis, 1850–1936). The daughter of two professional ballet dancers (her father was a soloist at the Opéra), she herself sang regularly at the Opéra-Comique from 1872, appearing as Philomèle in the premiere of Delibes's *Le Roi l'a dit* the following year, as well as Susanna in *Le nozze di Figaro* (in French) and the title role of Auber's *Haydée*. According to the London-based impresario James Henry Mapleson, she also won exceptional success at Drury Lane in *Il barbiere di Siviglia* and *La traviata* under his management, but in September 1876 she married Louis André, then a staff officer in the French army and subsequently the French Minister of War, thereupon retiring from the stage.

The numerous other significant premieres led by the conductor Deloffre (1817–76) in Paris around this time included: Gounod's *Faust* (1859), *Philémon et Baucis* (1860), *Mireille* (1864) and *Roméo et Juliette* (1867); Berlioz's *Les Troyens à Carthage* (1863); the revised version of Verdi's *Macbeth* (1865); Bizet's *Les Pêcheurs de perles* (1863), *La Jolie Fille de Perth* (1867) and *Djamileh* (1872); and Massenet's *Don César de Bazan*.

Ludovic Halévy, who was closely involved as co-librettist as well as a friend and relative by marriage of the composer, gave a detailed

---

2 Harvey Sachs, *Toscanini* (London: Weidenfeld & Nicolson, 1978), p. 60.

account of the premiere at the time of the thousandth performance at the Opéra-Comique in 1904:

> The entrance of Carmen was well received and applauded, as was the duet between Micaëla and Don José. As the first act ended there were many curtain calls. Backstage, Bizet was surrounded, congratulated!
> The second act, less enthusiasm. It opened brilliantly. The entrance of Escamillo was most effective. But then the audience cooled... [becoming] surprised, unhappy, ill-at-ease. Backstage, fewer admirers, congratulations restrained. No enthusiasm at all for the third act except for Micaëla's aria. The audience was frigid during the fourth act. Only a few devotees of Bizet came backstage. *Carmen* was not a success. Meilhac and I walked home with Bizet. Our hearts were heavy.[3]

In an earlier account, which survives in his journal (dated 16th March 1875), though with some words crossed out, Halévy attempted to interpret the audience reaction up to that point:

> The later performances have been excellent. The audience included members of the company all of whom had lived with this music for three or four months and consequently had time to penetrate its singularities. We were very confident on the evening of the first performance. But alas! What occurred in the public performance was what we ourselves had experienced in those first days. We needed a bit more time to reach the point of loving and admiring this score. At first we had been [illegible] more astonished than ravished. That was the impression evident amongst the public on the first night... the impact of the performance was uncertain, indecisive [...] Not bad, but not good either.[4]

Strange though it may appear to modern audiences, *Carmen* had presented its first listeners – who were used to a simpler, less sophis-

---

[3] See Ludovic Halévy, 'La Millième Réprésentation de Carmen', *Le Théâtre* No. 145 (January 1905), pp. 5–14.
[4] See Rémy Stricker, *Georges Bizet* (Paris: Éditions Gallimard, 1999), pp. 315–16.

ticated musical language at the Opéra-Comique – with challenging musical novelty, as one or two of the more perceptive reviewers noted (see Lesley Wright's article, pp. 48–50, for a full discussion of the initial reviews).

Bizet's death early on the morning of 3rd June 1875 came three months after the premiere of *Carmen*. The story has been often told how during the performance on the preceding evening Galli-Marié was struck by some sort of mysterious premonition and fainted following the Card Scene. After the announcement of Bizet's death she was too upset to carry on performing *Carmen*, which was replaced by Boieldieu's *La Dame blanche* – a work Bizet cordially loathed.

Despite the blow to Bizet's self-esteem occasioned by the cold public reaction to the first night, and the personal and professional hurt he suffered at the hands of some reviewers, it is important to view this setback in the context of Bizet's career. Neither of his two previous full-length works – *Les Pêcheurs de perles* at the Théâtre-Lyrique in 1863, and *La Jolie Fille de Perth* at the same venue four years later, each of which achieved just eighteen performances – won the success he so keenly desired. *Djamileh* (1872), his previous commission from the Opéra-Comique, was a small masterpiece but made even fewer waves with its eleven performances. *Carmen* was his great opportunity, and at the time of his death he must have believed that it, too, would vanish from the repertory. Yet two other operas premiered at the Opéra-Comique in the same year did far worse and were quickly dropped. The theatre's director Camille Du Locle, whether spurred on by Galli-Marié's determination or inspired by some partial belief in the work itself, retained it in the repertory until the end of the season and beyond. With thirty-five performances in its first season, and thirteen more in its second, *Carmen* enjoyed a more substantial initial run than any of Bizet's earlier operas.

Carmen *Abroad*

Soon the opera's fortunes would change, though on foreign soil. *Carmen* made its international debut in Vienna, sung in German at the Hofoper on 23rd October 1875. It is uncertain whether Ernest Guiraud's recitatives, commissioned by the publisher Choudens in order to facilitate performances in foreign theatres, were used on this occasion; some spoken dialogue was certainly retained and a ballet inserted into the final act. But thereafter Guiraud's recitatives were widely performed and, together with his ballet utilizing extracts from *L'Arlésienne* and the *Danse bohémienne* from *La Jolie Fille de Perth*, became standard additions to Bizet's score in the world's major houses; had he lived, he would certainly himself have composed recitatives for the use of foreign theatres where spoken dialogue was not employed.

The opera won a considerable success in Vienna. In the *Neue Freie Presse*, the influential critic Eduard Hanslick poured scorn on the notion prevalent in the French press that Bizet's idiom was Wagnerian, instead placing it 'halfway between the sentimentality of Gounod and the *esprit* of Ambroise Thomas'. Overall, however, his praise was surprisingly lukewarm. 'In Georges Bizet's score, we cannot salute either the work of a creative genius or that of an accomplished musician; but it is still necessary to recognize in it an interesting production of spirit and talent.'[5]

Next, on 3rd February 1876, *Carmen* made a significant impact in Brussels. In 1904 François-Auguste Gevaert, by then the head of the Brussels Conservatoire, recalled how on the first night 'a warm and spontaneous welcome [was] given by my compatriots to this work of our dear and lamented Bizet. Our public is not, by nature, very demonstrative, but it has a singularly acute musical sense, and [...] *it knows how to listen without talking*. Since that memorable premiere, *Carmen* has enjoyed continuous favour here, disappearing from the La Monnaie programme only to reappear almost immediately.'[6]

Productions followed in Antwerp (1st April 1876), Budapest (28th October 1876), St Petersburg (28th February 1878), Stockholm (22nd March 1878), London (at Her Majesty's Theatre, 22nd June 1878), Dublin (9th September 1878) and New York (at the Academy of Music, 23rd October 1878). Few of these performances were in

---

5 Eduard Hanslick, *Musikalische Stationen: Der Modernen Oper*, II Theil (Berlin: Allgemeiner Verein für Deutsche Literatur, 1885), p. 146.
6 Halévy, op. cit., p. 12.

French. Some were in the vernacular, others in Italian; ironically, what acquired and would long maintain the status of the standard Italian translation was the work of Achille de Lauzières, whose scathing review of the piece had been singled out by Bizet as one of the most offensive. Though *Carmen* was played at Covent Garden in French in 1890, the Italian translation would continue to be used there on a regular basis for many more years.

It had also been employed for the opera's first appearance in London at Her Majesty's Theatre in 1878, when Minnie Hauk sang the title role and Italo Campanini appeared as Don José. Having seen the success of the work in Brussels, the impresario Mapleson decided to include *Carmen* in his London season, and clearly made a good job of it. As the critic of the *Morning Post* wrote on 24th June 1878:

> Rarely has an opera been so well or so perfectly mounted, or rehearsed with such care as to secure an almost faultless representation on the first night: rarely has such brilliant and dashing music been presented to an admiring audience from an unexpected source: and still more rarely has it been the good fortune of opera patrons to be delighted with the exhibition of such piquant and fascinating histrionic talent as shown by Mdlle Minnie Hauk in the part of Carmen.

Hauk was a leading American soprano (later mezzo-soprano) who made a speciality of Carmen during her international career; she sang the role some 500 times, in four languages. Campanini, meanwhile, would also go on to present the first Don José in New York and also the first at the Metropolitan in its opening season of 1883–84. Initially, though, neither he nor the baritone singing Escamillo, Giuseppe Del Puente, considered their roles adequate to their status, while the American Alwina Valleria, singing Micaëla at Her Majesty's, thought her part more suited to a standout from the chorus than to a leading soprano; eventually, however, all three were reconciled to accepting them.

Among later notable performers of the title role in the Victorian period (including at Covent Garden) was Marie Roze, who had turned down the chance to create the role when it was offered to her by the composer. Not all singers attracted to Carmen, however, made a success of her. Adelina Patti was one of the greatest vocal artists of her day, but she nevertheless experienced a disaster as Carmen at Covent Garden in 1885. 'Clever but colourless', said her supporter, the vocal authority Herman Klein, 'a skilful *tour de force*, nothing more. To the great regret of the audience that filled Covent Garden from floor to ceiling, the representation fell painfully flat.'[7]

The Austrian soprano Pauline Lucca and the American mezzo Zélie de Lussan were two interpreters widely admired at this period, but outshining them all internationally around the turn of the twentieth century was Emma Calvé. Klein wrote of her performance:

> It had the calm, easy assurance, the calculated dominating power of Galli-Marié's; it had the strong sensual suggestion and defiant resolution of Minnie Hauk's; it had the panther-like quality, the grace, the fatalism, the dangerous impudent coquetry of Pauline Lucca's; it had the sparkle and vim, the Spanish *insouciance* and piquancy of Zélie de Lussan's. That is to say, it combined them each and all in some degree; and the wonder of the *mélange*, added to exquisite singing, made Calvé's assumption from first to last superlative.[8]

Press comment at the time of the London premiere seems to have been less morally censorious than it had previously been in Paris. 'Although Carmen is an even less respectable personage than the heroine of *La traviata*,' judged the *Observer* on 30th June 1878, 'the plot of the opera is not openly offensive [...] The heroine commands no respect and little sympathy, but the character has been so skilfully drawn, and the wilfulness of the gay coquette is so piquantly painted, that the spectator is too much fascinated to inquire whether he is justified in giving her his smiles and his applause.'

Several of Bizet's leading contemporaries came to admire the piece, one of the most fervent being Tchaikovsky, who caught one of the

---

7 Herman Klein, *The Reign of Patti* (New York: The Century Co., 1920), p. 227.
8 Herman Klein, *The Golden Age of Opera* (London: Routledge, 1933), p. 159.

initial staging's later Opéra-Comique performances early in 1876. Two years later his brother recalled the composer's enthusiasm:

> Rarely have I seen my brother so deeply moved by a performance in the theatre. Though he was already familiar with the music of the opera, the fact that this was the occasion when he first became acquainted with the beauties of the scoring explains this [strong reaction]. In addition, Mme Galli-Marié's stunning performance of the part of Carmen proved to be a significant factor in making this impression. As a singer she was not outstanding, for her vocal equipment was far from first-class – but, on the other hand, as an actress she had the most compelling gifts. In her performance, Carmen, while retaining all the vitality of her type, was at the same time shrouded in a certain indescribable magic web of burning, unbridled passion and mystic fatalism.[9]

Melbourne witnessed the first *Carmen* in Australasia in 1879, also the year of its first performances in Naples (again with Galli-Marié). Hamburg, Berlin, Prague and Geneva followed in 1880; Zurich, Mexico, Rio de Janeiro, Malta, Barcelona and Buenos Aires in 1881. Operatic audiences in Riga and Santiago experienced *Carmen* in 1883, those in Lisbon in 1885. Within a decade the opera had convincingly established itself in the international repertory.

Back at the Opéra-Comique

Meanwhile the Opéra-Comique, where the indefatigable impresario Léon Carvalho had taken over the management from Du Locle in 1876, delayed the work's revival until 1883. Though widely supportive of Bizet during his lifetime, in the year of his appointment Carvalho had turned down Ludovic Halévy's suggestion of a *Carmen* revival and in 1878 he specifically rejected Galli-Marié as protagonist; in this view, at least, he seems to have had the support of both librettists, who

---

9   David Brown, *Tchaikovsky: The Crisis Years, 1874–1878* (London: Gollancz, 1982), p. 13.

claimed that while the singer may have played Mérimée's Carmen, she did not play theirs! Galli-Marié, by 1883 a renowned interpreter of the role internationally, also tried to enlist Geneviève Bizet's support, even offering to 'modify' her interpretation to make it more acceptable.

None of this was to any avail, and the belated first revival (21st April 1883) of the work at the Opéra-Comique took place without her or indeed any of the original principals. Adèle Isaac (previously the first exponent of Olympia, Antonia and Stella in Offenbach's posthumously premiered *Les Contes d'Hoffmann*) sang Carmen in a production that was widely regarded as both under-rehearsed and artistically compromised; Carvalho had been unhappy about his audiences recognizing the nature of Lillas Pastia's tavern, which he regarded as a thinly disguised bordello. Ironically, his muted revival attracted criticism for demeaning a work that Parisian critics now considered a masterpiece. Carvalho was forced to restage it and presented it again on 27th October 1883 with Galli-Marié now restored as heroine.

Carmen's reign at the Opéra-Comique began that night. The opera reached its five hundredth performance at the theatre on 21st October 1891, its thousandth on 23rd December 1904 (Emma Calvé sang the title role), its two thousandth on 29th June 1930, its 2,500th on 1st June 1947. It eventually attained a total of 2,942 performances at that theatre alone, before officially becoming part of the repertory of the Paris Opéra on 10th November 1959, when General de Gaulle attended; its second act had already been performed at a gala at the Opéra in 1900, while at another gala in 1907 it was performed complete for the first time at the venue. Its three thousandth Parisian performance took place at the Palais Garnier on 10th January 1960, though since its official move to the more august venue *Carmen* has latterly also enjoyed further performances at the Salle Favart.

Carmen's *Interpreters*

If stagings of the opera (indeed of all operas) have become over the decades ever more coherently the products of a single guiding *auteur*-like figure – the director – it would be a mistake to suppose that earlier productions were entirely lacking in dramatic viability any more than were their contemporary counterparts in the spoken theatre. But there was certainly greater room for the initiative of individual performers, who would have regarded themselves as not fulfilling their creative task if they had merely stood there and sung. From the first, Bizet's opera was seen as highly dramatic in nature, and performers of all four of its major roles have seized the opportunities it presents. Though any attempt even to list – let alone describe – the great interpreters of Carmen, Don José, Micaëla and Escamillo would stretch this article beyond any reasonable length, some of the most notable protagonists deserve at least a mention.

Emma Calvé was one of the first great exponents to record extracts from the title role, which she did between 1902 and 1920. Born in 1858 in a mining town in southern France, she was already a star – if a controversial one – when she first took on Carmen at the Opéra-Comique in 1892; some felt her highly studied interpretation exaggerated (she modelled her approach on the great Italian actress Eleonora Duse). In what Calvé expert Francisco L. Segalerva Cabello has called a 'study trip' made prior to her debut as Carmen, she visited San Sebastián, Madrid, Ávila and Granada, spending time observing 'the dances, lifestyle, psychology and costumes of the gypsies, until she decided that she had grasped [their] "inner truth"'.[10] Reviewing one of her subsequent Covent Garden performances, George Bernard Shaw noted in *The World* on 30th May 1894 some of her extraordinary qualities as an actress:

> Her death scene [...] is horribly real. The young lady Carmen is never so effectively alive as when she falls, stage dead, beneath José's cruel knife. But to see Calvé's Carmen changing from a live creature, with properly coordinated movements, into a reeling, staggering, flopping, disorganized thing, and finally tumble down a mere heap of carrion, is to get much the same sensation as might be given by the reality of a brutal murder. It is perhaps just as well that a great artist should, once in a way, give our opera-goers a glimpse of the truth about the things they play with so lightheartedly.

---

10 Francisco L. Segalerva Cabello, 'Emma Calvé', in *The Record Collector* Vol. 53, No. 4 (December 2008), p. 252.

Less renowned, though she enjoyed a successful career in her day, was Jeanne Marié de l'Isle, whose appearances at the Opéra-Comique began in 1896 and continued through to 1917. Her most famous role was Charlotte in Massenet's *Werther*, but her posthumous significance consists in her recording extracts in 1904–6 from both *Carmen* and *Mignon* – roles she had studied with their creator, Galli-Marié, who happened to be her aunt.

Born in Barcelona in 1876, the mezzo Maria Gay was one of the most prominent interpreters of the role internationally between 1905 and her retirement from the stage in 1926, often singing opposite her husband, the Italian tenor Giovanni Zenatello, who instituted the regular operatic seasons at the Verona Arena (the couple led performances of Bizet's opera there in 1914). She sang only one performance of the work at the Opéra-Comique (29th April 1906), though it was apparently memorable. 'In the last act,' wrote the critic of *Musical America* later, on 16th December 1911, 'the ebullient singer refused to die [...] The tenor, who was a rather small man [Thomas Salignac], brought her to earth only with the greatest difficulty and after repeated struggles. He gave chase, and round and round the stage they went quite madly. That innocent man came near to being really throttled. Carmen's mantilla was torn to shreds, her hair came tumbling, and the audience, catching the infection, or else realizing the genuineness of the skirmish, began to behave as if they were indeed at a bullfight. The papers next day said it was "*trop fort*".'

Gay did not tone down her no-holds-barred interpretation, even when singing opposite Enrico Caruso at the Met in 1908. Geraldine Farrar (later herself a famous Carmen, but singing Micaëla in this Toscanini-led production) recorded that this 'tempestuous daughter of Iberia [...] kicked and spat, till even the blasé New York dowagers were moved to raise their fans to shocked faces, to screen some of her more frank and realistic attempts at seduction. A shower of orange juice precipitated with accuracy toward the unfortunate hero surprised not only him, but the audience in general, to protest.'[11]

---

11 Geraldine Farrar, *Such Sweet Compulsion: The Autobiography of Geraldine Farrar* (New York, NY: The Greystone Press, 1938), p. 126.

Recordings made by Gay between 1903 and 1930 present her in the standard extracts, as well as in a terrifyingly over-the-top account of the final scene with Zenatello.

Gay was apparently also present in Rosa Ponselle's dressing room at the Met on the night of the American soprano's first Carmen (27th December 1935), and was even suspected of 'egging her on', as Danton Walker wrote the following day in the *New York Daily News*. Ponselle, the Met's leading soprano for nearly twenty years, had learnt the role with Albert Carré, a former director of the Opéra-Comique, and was choreographed by George Balanchine; but she nevertheless received some withering reviews, notably from the eminent Olin Downes in the *New York Times* on 28th December 1935:

> We have never heard Miss Ponselle sing so badly, and we have seldom seen the part enacted in such an artificial and generally unconvincing manner. Her first act was more carefully composed than what followed. It had less exaggeration, fewer mannerisms, some interesting detail and clean diction. She used a little of the spoken dialogue of the original version of the opera with good effect, but already showed a cheerful disregard of the laws of good singing for which she has won richly deserved eminence. She also played fast and loose with time and with rhythm, and this to an extent unnecessary for any genuinely expressive purpose.
>
> [...] Her dancing need not be dwelt upon, although in the inn scene it raised the question whether Spanish gypsies preferred the Charleston or the Black Bottom as models for their evolutions.

Such responses almost certainly contributed to Ponselle's retirement from the stage two years later following an out-of-town performance of Bizet's opera.

Another notable Carmen (and a Spanish one) sang her last performances of the role around this time: Conchita Supervía, who had been performing the gypsy heroine since her teens, and who finally offered it to Covent Garden audiences in the 1935 season, which would be her last, since she died in childbirth in London the following year. Her interpretation divided the critics on that occasion, though she had earlier triumphed in the role, notably at the Opéra-Comique in 1930.

Another Spanish singer to attempt the role of Carmen was the soprano Victoria de los Ángeles, who was already an acclaimed Micaëla when she recorded the title role in Paris in 1958–59 under Sir Thomas Beecham, but who waited another twenty years before making her stage debut as Carmen, with New Jersey State Opera in 1978, by which time she was fifty-five. In post-war France, Solange Michel claimed the rights to a role she sang more than 600 times, as well as setting down a celebrated recording with Opéra-Comique forces under André Cluytens in 1950. The wide-ranging Régine Crespin agreed to sing her first staged Carmen at the Met in October 1975, when *Newsday*'s critic Byron Belt thought her 'vocally a dream', her 'rich, ripe voice [...] seductive, playful or passionately expressive without ever losing its distinctive, exquisite timbre'.

The Spanish mezzo Teresa Berganza first sang the role at the Edinburgh Festival in 1977 in a famous production directed by Piero Faggioni, conducted by Claudio Abbado and co-starring Plácido Domingo – though as she herself admitted she had been preparing it for twenty years. After agreeing to perform it she – like Calvé – studied the Roma people: 'I went off to Granada and stayed in the Sacromonte [traditionally the *gitano* quarter of the city] to learn about today's gypsies – to see if they were like the gypsies of the past. Some of the women, including young ones, were dressed in black and wore shawls, in Eastern fashion; they didn't show any cleavage. I soaked all that up, then read Mérimée, underlining everything to do with Carmen's character traits.'[12] Experienced critic Harold Rosenthal, in the 1977 Festivals issue of *Opera*, was impressed with the resulting realization: 'Berganza, slight of figure, beautiful of face, was seductive, enchanting, almost aristocratic as Carmen – never vulgar, never a whore.' Berganza is one of a number of artists who have said in interview that they found the

---

12 From an interview with Rafael Banús included in Deutsche Grammophon's *Brava Berganza! A Birthday Tribute* (477 5489), a four-CD set issued in 2005.

experience of singing the role of Carmen extremely liberating in personal terms.[13]

Maria Ewing's feisty Carmen made a splash at Glyndebourne in 1985 in a production staged by her then husband, Peter Hall. 'An exciting performer in all that she undertakes', commented Rosenthal in the July 1985 *Opera*. '"Jolie-laide" she certainly is, but that helped to make her Carmen a truly fascinating creature. Some found her too much of a sex kitten, others too contrived, and maybe there is some truth in both these points of view. Nonetheless, whenever she was on stage she became the central figure, which is, after all, what Carmen is. Miss Ewing is also a controversial singer, at times indulging in almost Édith Piaf-like vocalism, at others opening up her rich, luscious voice to near-Verdian proportions. But whatever she does she remains a compelling performer.' Ewing would go on to perform the role at the Met in 1986 (when Hall's production, designed by John Bury, was restaged) and in 1991 at Covent Garden (in Núria Espert's production).

The gypsy offered by the Latvian mezzo Elīna Garanča to audiences at Covent Garden in 2009 (in Francesca Zambello's production) and to those at the Met in 2010 (in Richard Eyre's staging) succeeded in persuading them that Carmen need not be dark but could, indeed, be a blonde – at least beneath her brunette wig. For critic Kate Molleson in the December 2009 *Opera*, in London Garanča made 'a stunning Carmen [...] She doesn't try to do anything outlandish with the role, but nails the sexy, stroppy, powerful-yet-vulnerable-deep-down Latina. Her mezzo is extremely seductive but never crass – if anything she verges on musical understatement, which is a classy achievement in this opera and adds fresh refinement to those sing-along tunes that are so often over-sung. She looks gorgeous, too, and moves well.' Turning up in New York the following year, Garanča's Carmen met with some cavils on vocal grounds from Martin Bernheimer in the *Financial Times* on 4th January 2010, but he nevertheless found her

13 In her interview with Helena Matheopoulos in *Diva: Great Sopranos and Mezzos Discuss their Art* (London: Gollancz, 1991), Berganza goes so far as to state: 'At the same time I began to liberate myself from my own repression and self-imposed brakes, the first and greatest of which was my husband. Because of Carmen, through her honesty and uncompromising refusal to lie, which became part of me, too, I found the courage to separate from my husband.'

'beautiful and smart, sexy and gutsy [...] flashing a devastating smile and magnetizing attention even when standing still'.

Carmen remains a defining role for mezzo-sopranos (and – even today – numerous sopranos), and few are able to resist its temptation at some point in their career. Apart from the handful of interpreters discussed above, other artists who have made a considerable impression over the years include the French lyric soprano Ninon Vallin (who made her debut at the Opéra-Comique as Micaëla in 1912, going on to undertake Carmen for the first time in 1926); the German mezzo (and then soprano and subsequently again mezzo!) Martha Mödl; the Italian Giulietta Simionato; American mezzo Risë Stevens (who sang 124 performances with the Met, either in New York or on tour; Calvé alone exceeded her, with a total of 137); her compatriots Regina Resnik, Shirley Verrett and Denyce Graves; the Greek Agnes Baltsa; the Greek-Americans Maria Callas (on disc only)[14] and Tatiana Troyanos; and the Italian Anna Caterina Antonacci.

Each of the other three principal roles has acquired vast numbers of memorable exponents. Among many distinguished tenors to tackle Don José with notable success have been Jean de Reszke, Fernando de Lucia, Charles Dalmorès, Georges Thill, Raoul Jobin, Ramón Vinay, Franco Corelli, Nicolai Gedda, Jon Vickers, Plácido Domingo, José Carreras, José Cura, Roberto Alagna and Jonas Kaufmann. Micaëla has vied with her gypsy rival for the audience's attention in the shape of such artists such as Nellie Melba, Eide Norena, Martha Angelici, Solange Michel, Mirella Freni, Ileana Cotrubas, Barbara Hendricks, Kiri Te Kanawa and Angela Gheorghiu. Donning the bullfighter's suit-of-lights with appreciable impact have been baritones (or basses) including Marcel Journet, Ezio Pinza, Ruggero Raimondi, José van Dam, Ildebrando D'Arcangelo and Erwin Schrott.

---

14 Franco Zeffirelli's film *Callas Forever* (2002), co-written with Martin Sherman and starring Fanny Ardant, presents a fictional account of a belated attempt to persuade the Greek diva to come out of retirement to make a film of Bizet's opera by lip-synching to her 1964 recording. Callas never sang the role on stage.

Carmen *beyond the Opera House*

As its fame as a work of art steadily spread well beyond the bounds of its operatic origins, *Carmen* has frequently been recreated in other media, too, sometimes employing Mérimée as a secondary reference point but deriving principally from the work of Bizet and his librettists. Durable in the commercial theatre has been Oscar Hammerstein II's adaptation as the musical *Carmen Jones*, which opened at the Broadway Theatre, New York, on 2nd December 1943, initially running for 503 performances. Much of Bizet's score was retained, though in new arrangements (in the original production these were the work of Robert Russell Bennett) and with the locale moved to a US parachute factory and Chicago during the Second World War; Escamillo becomes the boxer Husky Miller. In the first cast Muriel Smith played Carmen opposite Luther Saxon as Jo, as José is renamed. (Smith would go on to sing Bizet's original at Covent Garden in 1956.) London audiences have seen revivals of *Carmen Jones* at the Old Vic in 1991 (directed by Simon Callow and starring Wilhelmenia Fernandez) and at the Southbank Centre in 2007 (directed by Jude Kelly). A film version dates from 1954, directed by Otto Preminger and starring Dorothy Dandridge and Harry Belafonte, though their singing voices were dubbed by Marilyn Horne and LeVern Hutcherson respectively.

In the cinema, *Carmen* first appeared in the silent era as far back as 1909 in a short made by Pathé and starring Vittoria Lepanto and Dante Cappelli, with the Edison studios responding the following year with *The Cigarette Maker of Seville*, starring Pilar Morin and Verner Clarges. More ambitious was Cecil B. De Mille's hour-long 1915 Lasky Paramount movie, which headlined star soprano Geraldine Farrar in the title role with Wallace Reid as Don José; a Fox version from the same year and featuring legendary screen vamp Theda Bara is now lost. Also in 1915, Chaplin played 'Darn Hosiery' opposite Edna Purviance's Carmen in a comic riposte, *A Burlesque on Carmen*.

Numerous other cinematic treatments followed in the silent era alone: Ernst Lubitsch's 1918 *Carmen* (retitled *Gypsy Blood* in the US) pitted Pola Negri against Harry Liedtke. Dolores del Río lured Victor McLaglen astray in Raoul Walsh's 1927 *The Loves of Carmen*; in the

1948 remake, directed by Charles Vidor, Rita Hayworth treated Glenn Ford in similar fashion. Even in silent versions, however, portions of Bizet's score could be heard played by theatre orchestras or eked out, in less well equipped cinemas, by a single organist or pianist. Jean-Luc Godard's 1984 *Prénom Carmen*, however, famously substitutes Beethoven string quartets.

This and other subsequent treatments, such as Radley Metzger's erotic *Carmen, Baby* (1967), wander a long way from the original narrative and setting. MTV's *Carmen: A Hip Hopera* (2001), directed by Robert Townsend, was a reworking giving the piece a contemporary, American urban setting in Philadelphia and Los Angeles, emulating what Hammerstein had done in his musical; Beyoncé Knowles tempted Mekhi Phifer as Police Officer Hill; Blaze, the Escamillo character, is a successful rapper. More recent films (out of a total of some seventy in all)[15] include Vicente Aranda's 2003 Spanish-language version, starring Paz Vega and Leonardo Sbaraglia, and based on Mérimée rather than Bizet, which even includes the French writer as a character; and Mark Dornford-May's directorial debut *U-Carmen eKhayelitsha* (2005), sung and acted in Xhosa and set in the modern South African township of Khayelitsha; Pauline Malefane and Andile Tshoni starred as Carmen and Jongikhaya (Don José).[16]

Carlos Saura's 1983 film *Carmen* employed flamenco as its chief expressive medium, utilizing a double plot in which the relationship as real performers between Antonio Gades's flamenco troupe leader Antonio and Laura del Sol's Carmen mirrors the relationship they are playing in their recreation of Mérimée's two main characters; Bizet's score is cut and pasted to fit the concept and interspersed with authentic flamenco. Gades and his company also provided the choreography for Francesco Rosi's 1984 film of the opera – one of the most ambitious and artistically satisfying ever made. Opera singers Julia Migenes-Johnson, Plácido Domingo, Faith Esham and Ruggero Raimondi both

---

15 For an overview, see Phil Powrie, Bruce Babington, Ann Davies and Chris Perriam, *'Carmen': A Cultural History on Film* (Bloomington: Indiana University Press, 2007).

16 Dornford-May's film had its origins in a staged production using a new English translation by Rory Bremner, though that was dropped and replaced by a Xhosa text once the South African cast began working on it.

sang and acted their roles and Lorin Maazel conducted the soundtrack. The location shooting, mainly in Ronda near Seville, is often stunning.

Purely balletic versions have included one choreographed by Roland Petit (1949) incorporating Bizet's score and garnering more than five thousand performances over its first fifty years alone. A more radical rewriting of Bizet was contained in the Russian Rodion Shchedrin's one-act ballet *Carmen Suite*, composed as a vehicle for his wife, the ballerina Maria Plisetskaya, and first performed in 1967.[17]

Maintaining its position as a scaled-down theatrical version of the opera has been Peter Brook's *La Tragédie de Carmen*, premiered at the Théâtre des Bouffes du Nord in Paris in 1981 and filmed two years later. Brook worked with the composer Marius Constant on his conception of the piece in which, it was claimed, 'everything is trimmed away to focus on the intense interaction, the tragedy of four people'. The orchestration is reduced to fifteen players, all of the choruses go, and there is some reordering of the remainder. One of Mérimée's other characters – Carmen's husband, García, who is murdered by Don José – is reintroduced.

A distinctive variation on the arena tradition, meanwhile, developed in southern France, where in Nîmes and Béziers performances of the opera (often in cut form) were interrupted by actual bullfights. At Nîmes, where bullfighting was first seen at the Roman Arena in 1853, the tradition of conjoined bullfight and opera was initiated on 12th May 1900, and thereafter continued on an occasional basis up to 1979. Régine Crespin sang Carmen during the final season, her matador being Nimenos II. Often the toreros were more famous than the singers. In 1962 it was Antonio Ordóñez, friend of Ernest Hemingway and Orson Welles, while in Béziers it was Alfonso Vásquez II. In 1964 the bullfighter Manuel Benítez, known as 'El Cordobés', replaced the singer of Escamillo in the final act, though it's not recorded whether he actually sang the vocal part; the highest-paid matador of his time, he also appeared as an actor in three films.

---

17 Shchedrin's score (in an expansion by composer Terry Davies) is also used as the basis for Matthew Bourne's dance work *The Car Man* (2000), though confusingly that derives from James M. Cain's 1934 novel *The Postman Always Rings Twice* and its film versions, not Bizet or Mérimée.

Directorial Interventions

Throughout the twentieth century and into the twenty-first *Carmen* has maintained its position within the schedules of opera companies just as it has acquired new and larger audiences when transferred to other media. Leading directors have continued to be attracted to its possibilities. Constantin Stanislavsky staged a production in Moscow in 1935. The highly influential East German director Walter Felsenstein introduced a version at the Komische Oper, Berlin in 1949. Many stagings have tended to remain traditional to the extent of keeping faith with the Spanish setting, if not necessarily the early-nineteenth-century period of the original; the Spanish Civil War, or the Franco regime, have become regular replacements, though there have been others.

The Romanian theatre director Lucian Pintilie's 1983 Welsh National Opera production, starring Jennifer Jones and Jacque Trussel, was set during a recent if unspecified South American revolution; its (disputable) premise held that after a social upheaval, *Carmen* is the first opera that gets performed. Critic William Mann, in the July 1983 *Opera*, considered the director's theatrical inventiveness 'the nearest thing to perpetual motion you could ever hope to see on the stage outside of a juggling robot', while others thought the show's revolutionary setting merely got in the way. Even Mann quoted Pintilie to demonstrate how the director made Micaëla into 'a prime target of [his] scorn: she is a "ridiculous cliché" whose music makes her "genuinely pathetic". So Helen Field enters dancing on point, mimicking the Rose Adagio with support from the soldiery at hand, and singing in a little-girl voice that is not her normal soprano. The rail-cart [in Act Three] brings up absurd, sentimental props to underline the topics of the music, and on it she eventually faints and is transported out of sight.'

Three years later David Pountney's *Carmen* hit the stage at the London Coliseum. Maria Bjørnson's designs made a permanent feature of what Rodney Milnes in the January 1987 *Opera* called 'a graveyard for wrecked cars, inhabited by a brightly costumed crowd of the "poorest of the poor" that might have made even Brecht blench

[...] From the moment the curtain rose on a brilliantly animated scene, an air of intolerable heat, of sleaziness, of real danger, of anarchy of every kind (not least from the soldiery) pervaded the scene: this was the sort of place where Micaëla might indeed suffer several fates worse than death were she not so nippy on her feet.' The show pitted Sally Burgess's 'unsettlingly, brazenly sexy' gypsy (which was subsequently seen at the Met) against John Treleaven's 'mentally unbalanced' Don José. Anthony Burgess's translation (or a version thereof) was sung.

Carmen has adapted well to even grander spaces than London's largest theatre – as a regular constituent of the programme at the Verona Arena, for instance. In June 1989 Steven Pimlott's production played before audiences of some 14,500 customers a night at London's Earls Court. Pimlott saw his challenge as to try to 'generate something of the excitement you get at a football match [...] it is a gladiatorial opera'. Rodney Milnes admired the spectacle in the August 1989 *Opera*: 'a real torchlight procession for Escamillo, abseiling smugglers at "Bel officier", a Bridge of San Luis Rey [in Stefanos Lazaridis's designs] swaying down in Act 3, a cast of thousands plus seven horses milling about in Act 4'. The production starred the 'alarmingly elemental' Maria Ewing with Trussel once more her nemesis.

As well as his flamenco film, Carlos Saura was responsible for a staging of the opera at the 1995 Spoleto Festival with set designs by Antonio Saura. These were unusual, as the critic Luigi Bellingardi noted in the 1995 Festivals issue of *Opera*, in containing no visual references to Spain, consisting merely of 'bare flats like pure outlines, which created geometrical shapes; lighting alone suggested the setting and mood of each scene'. The Spanish setting 'crept back in through [...] all the characters' costumes (designed by Bettina Marx in collaboration with Saura), and in Manolo Marin's choreography'. But Bellingardi noted some oddities: 'the cigarette girls didn't smoke, the inn's customers didn't drink, the third-act smugglers weren't carrying the slightest bit of illegal merchandise, and Escamillo was dressed as a torero even when he went into the mountains to look for Carmen.' Adria Firestone presented a protagonist 'somewhere between Linda Darnell and Rita Hayworth'.

Far more traditional in mode, though conceived and executed on a lavish scale, was Franco Zeffirelli's 1996 production for the Met. 'Zeffirelli's crowd scenes were marvellous,' enthused Martin Mayer in the February 1997 *Opera*, 'complete with horses and donkeys, every member of the chorus (which was great) with a character to express, but the soloists just didn't relate to each other.' This may have been due to the fact that the Don José, Plácido Domingo, had cancelled late in the day, and his replacement had had no stage rehearsal whatsoever. Mayer was even less impressed with Carmen. 'Our gypsy spitfire was Waltraud Meier, a distinguished artist whose sex appeal is of the Marlene Dietrich school, and it doesn't work. At all.'

Carmen is certainly a work that contains significant violence – an aspect that has been increasingly emphasized over recent years. Phyllida Lloyd's 1998 staging for Opera North was, for Martin Dreyer in the March 1999 *Opera*, 'the most violent Carmen imaginable [...] The fight director must have had a field day. Knives were brandished at every opportunity – Carmen all but had her throat cut in the tavern, while pinned back over the edge of a table – fists flew, groins were viciously kneed [...] The occupying army might as well have been in Kosovo, so brutish were its men: even the children were savagely treated.' Antoni Garfield Henry partnered Ruby Philogene in the central roles. But 'Spain was not seen', Dreyer complained – something that recurred in Opera North's next (2011) production of the work, by Daniel Kramer, which moved the opera out of Europe altogether, to Seville, Ohio (consequently for bullfight, read dogfight). At least by the start of Act Four of Sally Potter's 2007 *Carmen* for ENO, according to the programme book synopsis, 'the smugglers have reached Spain, where they have been invited to watch Escamillo in a bullfight' – which raised the question as to where they had spent the previous three acts. No answers could be obtained from the dialogue, all of which had been cut. Alice Coote occupied *terra incognita* in the company of Julian Gavin.

Violence again exceeded expectations in Martin Kušej's 2004 staging for the Berlin Staatsoper, a production in which Dorothea Röschmann's Micaëla was accidentally shot by Rolando Villazón's Don José, and which ended with his execution. Barry Emslie in the

March 2005 *Opera* admired Kušej's 'powerful, unsentimental drama of love and death' whose general feel, in Jens Kilian's designs, was 'not unlike one of those spaghetti westerns – which, one suddenly realizes, were filmed in Spain'. In Dmitry Bertman's 1996 staging for the Moscow Helikon Opera, meanwhile, it was Micaëla, not Don José, who killed Carmen.

Even less traditional in approach was Sebastian Baumgarten's 2011 staging for the Komische Oper, which took in numerous cuts, including the children's chorus, two entr'actes, half of the Micaëla-Don José duet and a chorus or two; the dialogue was also largely rewritten. Though the performance was nominally in German, Stella Doufexis's Carmen sang both the Habanera and the Séguedille in French, while José and Moralès occasionally spoke in English in what was nominally a contemporary Spanish setting. 'Micaëla,' reported Carlos Maria Solare in the May 2012 *Opera*, 'was a walking image of the Virgin Mary whose aria, staged as José's vision, reduced him to a thumb-sucking foetus.'

Many other productions – John Copley's (1970) and later Jonathan Miller's (1995), both for ENO, Zambello's for the Royal Opera (2006) and Richard Eyre's for the Met (2009) – have stuck more closely to the traditional narrative and setting. So, on the whole, have arena stagings such as those offered to audiences at the Royal Albert Hall by David Freeman for the first time in 2002, though that moved the action to the 1920s. Adrian Noble's 2009 staging for the Opéra-Comique was described by Hugh Canning in the October 2009 *Opera* as 'traditional in outline but entirely fresh, both musically and theatrically', and left him with the feeling of 'seeing *Carmen* for the first time'; period instruments undoubtedly helped, as did dropping Fritz Oeser's edition in favour of Richard Langham Smith's. Anna Caterina Antonacci impressed singing the title role opposite Andrew Richards under the baton of John Eliot Gardiner.

Salzburg's 2012 Easter Festival *Carmen*, which later transferred (with a change of orchestra) to the main summer event, was by Aletta Collins and conducted by Simon Rattle, whose wife, Magdalena Kožená, sang the title role. While John Allison, in the *Sunday Telegraph* on 22nd April 2012, liked Miriam Buether's 1970s designs, notably the 'peeling paint and white tiles of the cigarette factory's loading bay, with boxes coming off conveyor belts', Koženà seems to have been one of those distinguished artists unable to encompass the needs of Bizet's complex heroine, resembling instead 'a nice girl from Brno who got lost on the Sunday School trip to Seville'.

One of the most travelled stagings of recent years has been that by the Catalan director Calixto Bieito, which originated at the Peralada Festival in Spain in 1999 and has subsequently been seen, in various revisions and with different casts, in Dublin, Belgium, Holland, Barcelona, and more recently in Basle and Palermo (2011), as well as in Colombia, Venice, Turin and at English National Opera in London (2012). Bieito's dark but fascinating vision of the piece places it in the 1970s and on the fringes of Spanish territory – one of its former North African colonies may be intended. While hard-hitting, arguably to the point of excess, its concentrated focus on the central characters and their interactions has been regularly admired.

Though there's no sign of diminishing interest either in the opera or in its iconic protagonist, critical perceptions of the central characters and their relationships have necessarily altered over the last 138 years, and will presumably continue to do so; certainly the disgust aimed at Carmen herself by some of the opera's earliest critics has been modified or expunged as reactions to the figure of the *femme fatale* have shifted significantly.[18] *Carmen* clearly remains a major challenge to its interpreters and a work that fascinates connoisseurs as well as the broadest audiences; one can only speculate on how her presentation will evolve and in what medium she might turn up in next.

---

18 Changing attitudes have clearly impacted on and in turn been influenced by such feminist critiques as those of Nelly Furman, 'The Languages of Love in *Carmen*', in Arthur Groos and Roger Parker (eds.), *Reading Opera* (Princeton, NJ: Princeton University Press, 1988) and Susan McClary, *Georges Bizet: 'Carmen'* (Cambridge: Cambridge University Press, 1992).

Carmen's Early Lovers

Gary Kahn

Despite the considerable amount of hostile criticism that greeted the first performances of *Carmen* (see Lesley Wright's and George Hall's articles, pp. 48–51 and pp. 60–62), there were numerous other contemporary reactions to the work at its earliest appearances that bordered on the ecstatic. The diversity of these commentators is perhaps as interesting as their shared enthusiasm. Not all of these tributes, some of them frequently reprinted, can be fully substantiated. One supposedly favourable remark by Richard Wagner after seeing the opera at its first appearance in Vienna in 1875 ('Here at last is someone with ideas, thank God!') cannot be traced any further back than 1887 when Friedrich Wilhelm Langhans quotes it, without giving any source, in *Die Geschichte der Musik des 17., 18. und 19. Jahrhunderts,* vol. 2. Even less reliable and now exposed as a hoax is the quote attributed to Johannes Brahms by Andrew de Ternant in issue 65 of the venerable *Musical Times* in 1924, which recounts Brahms, after telling Claude Debussy that he had attended twenty performances of the work, saying that he 'would have gone to the ends of the earth to embrace the composer of *Carmen*'.[1]

However, there are expressions of admiration from many others during the early years of *Carmen* which are properly documented. These include several from fellow musicians in Paris at the time of the first performances. Jules Massenet wrote a note to Bizet in the early hours of the morning following the premiere saying,

---

1 See James F. Penrose, 'Inventing Claude Debussy' in *The New Criterion*, 1st June 2002.

'How happy you must be at this time. It's a great success. When I have the good fortune to see you, I shall tell you how happy you made me.'[2] Camille Saint-Saëns, who was unable to go to a performance until a week after the premiere, was similarly enthusiastic and wrote afterwards to Bizet, 'At last I have seen *Carmen*. I found it marvellous.'[3] Another prominent French composer, Vincent d'Indy, then an organ student at the Paris Conservatoire, who was also present at the first performance later wrote, 'I will always remember with emotion the feeling of a *new art* which overcame us from the beginning until the end of the piece.'[4]

Pyotr Ilyich Tchaikovsky saw the production at the Opéra-Comique with his brother Modest in January 1876, the year following its premiere, and found it overwhelming:

> In my opinion it is a *masterpiece* in the full meaning of the word – that is, one of those rare pieces which are destined to reflect most strongly the musical aspirations of an entire epoch. [...] And what a wonderful subject for an opera! I cannot play the last scene without weeping; on the one hand, the people enjoying themselves, and the coarse gaiety of the crowd watching the bullfight, on the other, the dreadful tragedy and death of two of the leading characters, whom an evil destiny, *fatum*, has brought together and driven, through a whole series of agonies, to their inescapable end.[5]

A little later, Friedrich Nietzsche famously used *Carmen* as the stick with which to beat his former idol, Richard Wagner, in *The Case of Wagner* (1888):

> Yesterday I heard – would you believe it? – Bizet's masterpiece for the twentieth time. [...] How such a work makes one perfect! One

---

2 Mina Curtiss: *Bizet and His World* (London: Secker & Warburg, 1959), pp. 395–96.
3 Ibid., p. 396.
4 D.C. Parker, *Georges Bizet: His Life and Works* (New York: Harper & Brothers, 1926), p. 86.
5 David Brown, *Tchaikovsky: The Crisis Years, 1874–1878* (London: Gollancz, 1982), p. 59.

becomes a 'masterpiece' oneself. [...] This music seems perfect to me. It approaches lightly, supplely, politely. It is pleasant, it does not *sweat*. [...] This music is evil, subtly fatalistic: at the same time it remains popular – its subtlety belongs to a race, not to an individual. It is rich. It is precise. It builds, organizes, finishes: thus it constitutes the opposite of the polyp in music, the 'infinite melody'. Have more painful tragic accents ever been heard on the stage? How are they achieved? Without grimaces. Without counterfeit. Without the *lie* of the great style.[6]

Giacomo Puccini saw a production in Milan as early as 1880 and wrote in 1904:

I adore Bizet, and *Carmen* is the most complete and most expressive opera which has been written in recent years.[7]

The popularity of *Carmen* has since spread rapidly everywhere and its position as a masterwork has now long been established. Unlike many other popular operas, it has never lost its place in the central repertory of the major opera companies of the world. By 1938, Reynaldo Hahn, the composer, conductor and music critic, could write:

Bizet has conquered the universe. He has conquered not only by his talent, but also by the sympathy, the warmth, the profoundly human quality of that talent. His soul showed through his music – that sensitive, loyal, generous soul; that spontaneous, kind, uncomplicated character that all those who knew Bizet enjoyed praising. And just because it is reflected so faithfully in his music, the resistance of which he was the victim is difficult to understand.[8]

---

6 Friedrich Nietzsche, *The Case of Wagner*, trans. Walter Kaufmann (New York: Random House, 1967), p. 157.
7 Léon Vallas, *Revue musicale de Lyon*, vol. 7 (1909), p. 464.
8 Reynaldo Hahn, article in *Le Figaro*, 1938, quoted by Frédéric Robert, *Georges Bizet, l'homme et son oeuvre* (Paris: Slatkine, 1981), p. 77.

Sources and Editions

Richard Langham Smith

Original Sources

There are several original sources for *Carmen* which remain on public access in libraries, and some others uncatalogued in private collections. Two main sources of the orchestral score survive in manuscript as well as orchestral parts, though these are incomplete. Bizet's original score survives in the Bibliothèque Nationale de France though it has been heavily tampered with and clearly used for conducting at some stage. Not only has it been used so heavily that the first twenty-six pages have had to be recopied, but it has Guiraud's recitatives pasted in, obscuring some original material.

A second copy, in another hand, entitled *Partition ayant servi à la première représentation* ('Score used at the first performance'), is an invaluable source since it contains rich stage directions and all kinds of markings giving an idea of changes made in rehearsal and during the first run, as well as musical alterations made as the piece was rehearsed and performed.

Complementing these are the printed vocal scores (*partitions chant et piano*). The first – extremely rare – was used for the first performances and categorizes the work as an *opéra-comique*. The second, called a *'nouvelle édition'* is cobbled together from the plates of the original edition with Guiraud's recitatives added and some amendments and cuts made. The piano reduction in these was expertly done by the composer himself and a few pages of proofs survive, meticulously corrected in Bizet's hand. In the second of these, ossias have been added to the parts of Carmen and José, mainly to avoid Carmen's very low notes and to raise José's tessitura.

The surviving orchestral parts, especially the string parts, are also of great interest since they contain markings giving us clues as to what was actually done in the performances of the work, especially regarding cuts. Some of the parts for the instruments which play only occasionally, for example the brass, have all kinds of additions to relieve the boredom of the players: calculations of earnings, caricatures of the conductor and other players, and even pornographic crosswords.

The first printed orchestral score is of interest but little use since it has little to do with the original and contains a ballet concocted from other works by Bizet.

Production materials relating to the first stagings are preserved in the Bibliothèque de l'Association de la Régie Théâtrale housed in the Bibliothèque Historique de la Ville de Paris.

Modern Performing Editions

There are many of these in various languages: principal publishers are Novello, Schirmer Cramer, Peters, Kalmus and Belwin Mills. These use various translations.

Modern Scholarly Edition with Performance Materials

Carmen: Kritische Neuausgabe nach den Quellen. Partitur, Klavierauszug und Bericht, Alkor-Edition, Kassel, 1964–65. Edited by Fritz Oeser. A separate *Vorlagenbericht* accompanies the main scores.

The first critical edition going back to original sources. First language for the text is German with French underneath. Both the main text and the *Bericht* include many variants, early versions, rejected material and the Opéra-Comique text as well as Guiraud's recitatives. It is left to the performer to find a way through all the variants presented.

CARMEN

Vocal and Orchestral Score by Robert Didion

Schott ED 7965, Mainz 2000; Orchestral Score published by Eulenburg without critical apparatus and a short preface (Edition Eulenburg No. 8062). Unfortunately, Didion died before completing this work but there is a substantial preface to the vocal score. First language for the text is French with German underneath.

'Performance Urtext' by Richard Langham Smith

New Peters Edition, London, 2013. Vocal Score first language French with English translation by David Parry underneath. Orchestral score in French only. Substantial prefatory and critical material in English and French. The only source to contain important extracts from the *mises-en-scène* mentioned in my article in this guide. See also Peters Edition website for this edition. An alternative translation made to fit this edition is by Rory Bremner: *Carmen* (London, Frankfurt, Leipzig, New York: Peters Edition, 2004).

Thematic Guide

Themes from the opera have been identified by the numbers in square brackets in the article on the music. These are also printed at corresponding points in the libretto, so that the words can be related to the musical themes.

CARMEN

[5] **ACT I CHORUS**
Allegretto moderato / *légèrement*

[6] **MORALÈS**
Allegretto mosso / *Léger, mais bien rythmé*

[7] *Air et Chœur*
Allegro moderato
Strs, Cls, Bns

[8] *Marche et Chœur des Gamins*
Allegretto moderato

[9] **CHORUS OF CIGARIÈRES**
Andantino

[10] *Entrée de Carmen*
Allegro moderato

THEMATIC GUIDE

[11] **CARMEN** *Habanera*
Allegretto, quasi andantino

[12] **MICAËLA** *(from duet with José)*
Andantino quasi allegretto / *simplement*

[13] **MICAËLA**
Allegro moderato / *espressivo*

[14] **JOSÉ**
Andantino moderato

[15] **CARMEN** / *Chanson*
Allegretto molto moderato (*murmuring to herself*)

CARMEN

[16] **CARMEN** / *Séguedille*
Allegretto

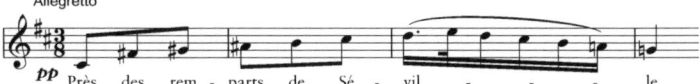

pp Près des rem - parts de Sé - vil - - - le,

[17] *Final*
Allegretto vivo
Vcs

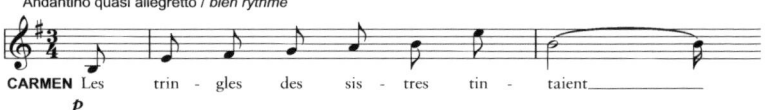

[18] Act II *Chanson bohème*
Andantino quasi allegretto / *bien rythmé*

CARMEN Les trin - gles des sis - tres tin - taient
p

[19] **ESCAMILLO** / *Couplets*
Allegro molto moderato / *rude et très rythmé*

f Vot - re toast, je peux vous le ren - dre

[20] *No. 15 Quintet (Dancaïre, Remendado, Carmen, Frasquita, Mercédès)*
Allegretto vivo

DANCAÏRE Nous a - vons en tête une af - fai - - - re
mf

[21] **JOSÉ** / *Chanson* (in the wings)
Allegretto moderato / *la voix très éloignée*

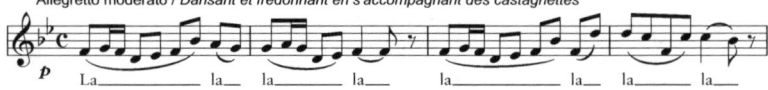

f Hal - te là! Qui va là? Dra - gon d'Al - ca - là!

[22] *Carmen's 'Romalis'*
Allegretto moderato / *Dansant et fredonnant en s'accompagnant des castagnettes*

p La la la la la la la la

CARMEN

[29] **FRASQUITA, MERCÉDÈS** / *Morceau d'ensemble*

[30] **MICAËLA** *Air (accompanied by four horns)*

[31] **JOSÉ, ESCAMILLO** *Fight with navajas*

[32] *Entr'acte*

[33] *Chœur*

[34] **ESCAMILLO, CARMEN** *Duo*

[35] **JOSÉ, CARMEN** *Duo*

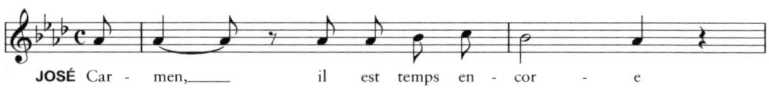

[36] *Carmen / Fate / Death motive*

Carmen

Note on the Libretto

Richard Langham Smith

Three principal sources have been consulted in the preparation of this libretto: first, the printed *livret*, undated, but available a little while before the premiere at the Opéra-Comique on 3rd March 1875. This was issued by the book publishers Calmann-Lévy. It was the norm for *opéras-comiques* to have printed the libretto separately from the vocal score (*chant-piano*) which only contained the cues (*répliques*) that immediately preceded the start of the musical numbers.

Second comes the vocal score itself, more reliable for the actual texts of the musical numbers, especially where words are repeated or recapitulated. In this case the rare first vocal score gives the piece roughly as it was first performed, although cuts were subsequently made. This was published by Choudens in 1875. Most important among these cuts was the removal of the '*Scène de l'Anglais*' or 'Englishman's Scene', eradicated from all subsequent scores before modern urtexts, probably just after Bizet's death.[1]

Third, and appended to the libretto in this guide, are the recitatives used to replace all the spoken dialogue, composed by Bizet's friend Ernest Guiraud some time after Bizet's death for the fully sung version. These are found in the second vocal score published by Choudens in 1877. A somewhat messy score, this used plates from the first vocal score, renumbered clumsily and often with the now redundant cues left in. Guiraud's recitatives, however, are clear from this score which was used for performances for many

---

1 It is included on pp. 108–113 of the libretto with a grey background [Ed.].

years, and which formed the basis of the majority of scores by other publishers.

Even this is not quite the end of the story since there is considerable disparity between the stage directions in the published libretto and those in the score. This is further confused by the manuscript performing score used at the Opéra-Comique. Stage directions in the fascinating production materials in the Bibliothèque Historique de la Ville de Paris are often even fuller, giving much more idea of the original stagings. Details of these can be found in the collection of the Association de la Régie théâtrale. My own vocal score of the piece (London: New Peters Edition, 2013) includes some of the richest material from these sources.

In the French libretto the original capitalization has been retained, since in the rhymed sections this clearly indicates the rhythmic schemes and separates these from the dialogue which is often in prose. The English translation does not aim either to rhyme or to retain the original stresses. Unlike many of the somewhat quaint translations found in scores with the English underlaid, the translation is driven by the aim of capturing the meaning.

It goes without saying that a lot of meanings and details are lost in the recitative version where swathes of dialogue are replaced by only a few bars. On the other hand, I have never heard an *opéra-comique* version with all the original spoken dialogue: a challenge usually beyond the capabilities of present-day international casts, and I am fairly confident in asserting that the piece has never been recorded complete in this way. However, a version performed at Manchester's Royal Northern College of Music in 2010 came fairly close, convincing in the way it gradually progressed from a combination of speech and song into through-composed music as the piece approached its final, terrible end.

There are many variants between the published libretto and the several scores mentioned above. The version published here follows the *livret* for the spoken dialogue but on the whole prefers the first vocal score for the words of the sung music. In particular, there are many significant repetitions in the music which are passed over in the separate libretto and the punctuation in the score is significantly

NOTE ON THE LIBRETTO

more continuous with the frequent replacement of full stops with ellipses. Guiraud's recitatives composed for the non-dialogue version are appended (following the later vocal score) and indications of when they replace the spoken text are included, as well as signalling where the music resumes. Cuts in the libretto which are not replaced by a recitative are also indicated.

Those wishing to follow a recording with the libretto are unlikely to find an exact tally: I know of no recording which uses the complete spoken dialogue, and there are many variants between printed editions and individual recordings.

Note the distinct numbering systems: the 'Scenes', i.e. the staged scenes, the 'numbers', which are the musical items within these scenes and the numbers in square brackets, which refer to the musical examples in the Thematic Guide (pp. 87–92).

THE CHARACTERS

CARMEN, *a gypsy*	mezzo-soprano
DON JOSÉ, *a corporal*	tenor
MICAËLA, *a country girl*	soprano
ESCAMILLO, *a bullfighter*	bass-baritone
FRASQUITA ⎱ *gypsies*	soprano
MERCÉDÈS ⎰	soprano
LE DANCAÏRE ⎱ *smugglers*	tenor/baritone
LE REMENDADO ⎰	tenor
ZUNIGA, *a lieutenant*	bass
MORALÈS, *a corporal*	baritone
LILLAS PASTIA, *an innkeeper*	spoken
A LIEUTENANT	spoken
GUIDE	spoken

Soldiers, young men, tobacco-factory girls, Escamillo's supporters, gypsies, merchants and orange-sellers, police, bullfighters, urchins

Spain – around 1820

Carmen

Opéra-comique in four acts
by Georges Bizet

Libretto by Henri Meilhac and Ludovic Halévy
after the novella by Prosper Mérimée

English translation by Richard Langham Smith

Carmen was first performed at the Opéra-Comique, Paris, on 3rd March 1875. It was first performed in Britain at Her Majesty's Theatre, London, on 22nd June 1878 (in Italian and with recitatives). The first performance in the United States was at the Academy of Music, New York, on 23rd November 1878 (also in Italian and with recitatives).

Prélude [1, 2, 3, 4]

PREMIER ACTE

Une place, à Séville. À droite, la porte de la manufacture de tabac. Au fond, face au public, pont praticable traversant la scène dans toute son étendue. De la scène on arrive à ce pont par un escalier tournant qui fait sa révolution à droite au-dessus de la porte de la manufacture de tabac. Le dessous du pont est praticable. À gauche, au premier plan, le corps de garde. Devant le corps de garde, une petite galerie couverte, exhaussée de deux ou trois marches ; près du corps de garde, dans un râtelier, les lances des dragons avec leurs banderoles jaunes et rouges.

Scène I

Moralès, Micaëla, soldats, passants

N° 1 Introduction

Au lever du rideau, une quinzaine de soldats (dragons du régiment d'Almanza) sont groupés devant le corps de garde. Les uns assis et fumant, les autres accoudés sur la balustrade de la galerie. Mouvement de passants sur la place. Des gens pressés, affairés, vont, viennent, se rencontrent, se saluent, se bousculent, etc.

SOLDATS [5]
 Sur la place
 Chacun passe,
 Chacun vient, chacun va ;
 Drôles de gens que ces gens-là !
 Drôles de gens ! Drôles de gens !

MORALÈS *(avec nonchalance)*
 À la porte du corps de garde,
 Pour tuer le temps,
 On fume, on jase, l'on regarde
 Passer les passants.

Prelude [1, 2, 3, 4]

ACT ONE

A square in Seville. On the right, the entrance to the tobacco factory. Backstage, facing the audience, a bridge crossing the entire stage, reached from a curved staircase which turns right above the entry to the tobacco factory. There is an entrance from under the bridge. On the left, in the foreground, is the guardroom. In front of this is a small covered gallery, accessed by two or three steps near the guardroom; in a rack are the lances of the dragoons with their yellow and red pennants.

Scene 1

Moralès, Micaëla, soldiers, passers-by

No. 1 Introduction

The curtain rises on fifteen or so soldiers (dragoons of the Almanza regiment) who have gathered outside the guardroom. Some are smoking, others lean on the balustrade of the gallery. Coming and going of people in the square. Those in a hurry, with business to do, come and go, meeting and greeting each other and bumping into each other, etc.

SOLDIERS [5]
   In the square
   everyone's there
   coming and going...
   What funny people those people are!
   Funny people! Funny people!

MORALÈS *(idly)*
   At the entrance to the guardroom,
   just to kill time
   we smoke, we chat, we watch
   the passers-by.

Sur la place
Chacun passe,
Chacun vient, chacun va...

SOLDATS
Sur la place
Chacun passe,
Chacun vient, chacun va ;
Drôles de gens que ces gens-là !
Drôles de gens ! Drôles de gens !

MORALÈS, SOLDATS
Drôles de gens !

(Depuis quelques minutes Micaëla est entrée. Jupe bleue, nattes tombant sur les épaules, hésitante, embarrassée, elle regarde les soldats, avance, recule, etc.)

MORALÈS *(aux soldats)*
Regardez donc cette petite
Qui semble vouloir nous parler...
Voyez ! voyez !... elle tourne... elle hésite...

SOLDATS
À son secours il faut aller !

MORALÈS *(à Micaëla, galamment)*
Que cherchez-vous, la belle ?

MICAËLA *(simplement)*
Moi, je cherche un brigadier.

MORALÈS *(avec emphase)*
Je suis là...
Voilà !

MICAËLA
Mon brigadier, à moi, s'appelle
Don José... le connaissez-vous ?

ACT ONE SCENE I

> In the square
> everyone's there
> coming and going...

SOLDIERS
> In the square
> everyone's there
> coming and going...
> What funny people they are!
> Funny people! Funny people!

MORALÈS, SOLDIERS
> Funny people!

(Micaëla has been on stage for a few minutes. She has a blue skirt and plaits falling over her shoulders. Hesitant and embarrassed she watches the soldiers, advances and withdraws, etc.)

MORALÈS *(to the soldiers)*
> Look at that nice little girl
> who seems to want to talk to us...
> Look! Look!... She's turning round, hesitating...

SOLDIERS
> We'd better go and help her!

MORALÈS *(to Micaëla, gallantly)*
> What are you looking for, my beauty?

MICAËLA *(simply)*
> I'm looking for a corporal.

MORALÈS *(emphatically)*
> Well here I am...
> Right here!

MICAËLA
> The one I'm looking for is called
> Don José... Do you know him?

MORALÈS
Don José ? Nous le connaissons tous.

MICAËLA *(avec joie)*
Vraiment ? Est-il avec vous, je vous prie ?

MORALÈS *(avec élégance)*
Il n'est pas brigadier dans notre compagnie.

MICAËLA *(désolée)*
Alors, il n'est pas là.

MORALÈS
Non, ma charmante, il n'est pas là.
Mais tout à l'heure il y sera,
Oui, tout à l'heure il y sera.
Il y sera quand la garde montante
Remplacera la garde descendante.

MORALÈS, SOLDATS
Il y sera quand la garde montante [6]
Remplacera la garde descendante.

MORALÈS *(très galant)*
Mais en attendant qu'il vienne
Voulez-vous, la belle enfant,
Voulez-vous prendre la peine
D'entrer chez nous un instant ?

MICAËLA
Chez vous ?

MORALÈS, SOLDATS
Chez nous ! Chez nous ! Chez nous !

MICAËLA *(finement)*
Non pas, non pas,
Grand merci, messieurs les soldats.

ACT ONE SCENE 1

MORALÈS
Don José? We all know him.

MICAËLA *(joyfully)*
Really? So is he with you, may I ask?

MORALÈS *(formally)*
He is not a corporal in our company.

MICAËLA *(disappointedly)*
Oh, so he's not here.

MORALÈS
No my lovely, he's not here.
But he will be soon,
yes, he will be soon.
He'll be here when the relief guard
replace those going off-duty.

MORALÈS, SOLDIERS
He'll be here when the relief guard [6]
replace those going off-duty.

MORALÈS *(very gallantly)*
But while you wait for him
my little one, wouldn't you
like to take the trouble
to come into our guardroom for a little while?

MICAËLA
In there?

MORALÈS, SOLDIERS
In here! In here! In here!

MICAËLA *(shrewdly)*
No I won't. I won't,
thanks all the same, soldiers.

MORALÈS
>Entrez sans crainte, mignonne,
>Je vous promets qu'on aura,
>Pour votre chère personne,
>Tous les égards qu'il faudra.

MICAËLA
>Je n'en doute pas, cependant je reviendrai,
>Je reviendrai, c'est plus prudent.

(reprenant en riant la phrase du sergent)
>Je reviendrai quand la garde montante
>Remplacera la garde descendante.

MORALÈS, SOLDATS
>Il faut rester, car la garde montante
>Va remplacer la garde descendante.

MORALÈS *(retenant Micaëla)*
>Vous resterez !

MICAËLA *(cherchant à se dégager)*
>Non pas, non pas !

MORALÈS, SOLDATS
>Vous resterez !

MICAËLA
>Non pas, non pas !
>Non ! non ! non ! non ! non !

MORALÈS, SOLDATS
>Vous resterez ! Vous resterez !
>Oui, vous resterez, vous resterez !

MICAËLA
>Au revoir, messieurs les soldats !

MORALÈS
> You can come in without fear, my sweet.
> I promise you
> we'll treat you
> with all proper respect.

MICAËLA
> I don't doubt it, I'll come back,
> yes I'll come back, it would be wiser.

(laughing and repeating the phrase the sergeant sang)

> I'll come back when the relief guard
> replaces those going off-duty.

MORALÈS, SOLDIERS
> You should stay, because the relief guard
> will replace those going off-duty.

MORALÈS *(holding back Micaëla)*
> You'll stay!

MICAËLA *(trying to break away)*
> I won't, I won't!

MORALÈS, SOLDIERS
> You'll stay!

MICAËLA
> Certainly not!
> No! no! no! no! no!

MORALÈS, SOLDIERS
> You'll stay! You'll stay!
> Yes you'll stay, you'll stay!

MICAËLA
> Goodbye, soldiers!

MORALÈS
L'oiseau s'envole,
On s'en console.
Reprenons notre passe-temps
Et regardons passer les gens.

(Elle s'échappe et se sauve en courant.)

SOLDATS
Sur la place, chacun passe,
Chacun vient, chacun va ;
Drôles de gens que ces gens-là !
Drôles de gens ! Drôles de gens !
Drôles de gens que ces gens-là !

MORALÈS, SOLDATS
Drôles de gens !

N° 1bis *Air et Chœur (Scène et Pantomime)*   [Scène de l'Anglais]

Le mouvement des passants qui avait cessé pendant la scène de Micaëla a repris avec une certaine animation. Parmi les gens qui vont et viennent, un vieux monsieur donnant le bras à une jeune dame. Le vieux monsieur voudrait continuer sa promenade, mais la jeune dame fait tout ce qu'elle peut pour le retenir sur la place. Elle paraît émue, inquiète. Elle regarde à droite, à gauche. Elle attend quelqu'un et ce quelqu'un ne vient pas. Cette pantomime doit cadrer très exactement avec le couplet suivant. [7]

MORALÈS *(presque parlé)*
Attention ! chut ! Attention !... taisons-nous !
Voici venir un vieil époux...
Œil soupçonneux ! mine jalouse !...
Il tient au bras sa jeune épouse...

MORALÈS, SOLDATS
L'amant, sans doute, n'est pas loin,
Il va sortir de quelque coin !

MORALÈS
>The bird flies away,
>but we'll get over it.
>Let's carry on what we were doing
>and watch everyone passing by.

(She breaks free and escapes by running away.)

SOLDIERS
>In the square, everyone's there
>coming and going…
>What funny people they are!
>Funny people! Funny people!
>What funny people they are!

MORALÈS, SOLDIERS
>Funny people!

No. 1b Air and Chorus (Scene and Pantomime) [Englishman's scene]

The movement of the passers-by now resumes with some vigour, having ceased during the scene with Micaëla. Among those coming and going is an elderly gentleman with a young lady on his arm. The old gentleman wants to continue his walk, but the young lady is doing everything she can to keep him in the square. She appears to be upset, anxious. She looks to the left and the right. She is waiting for someone who does not appear. The miming must coincide very precisely with the following lines. [7]

MORALÈS *(almost spoken)*
>Just look! Hush! Just look!… Let's be quiet!
>There's an ageing husband coming,
>with a mistrustful look in his eye, and a jealous expression!…
>On his arm is his young bride…

MORALÈS, SOLDIERS
>Her lover, no doubt, isn't far away,
>he'll come out from somewhere!

(En ce moment un jeune homme entre rapidement sur la place. Toute cette pantomime doit cadrer exactement avec le récit de Moralès qui en indique tous les mouvements.)

MORALÈS, SOLDATS *(riant)*
Ah ! ah ! ah ! ah !
Le voilà !

MORALÈS
Le voilà ! ah ! le voilà !
Oui, le voilà ! oui, le voilà !
Oui, le voilà ! ah ! ah ! Oui, le voilà !

MORALÈS, SOLDATS
Voyons, voyons comment ça tournera.

(Le second couplet continue et s'adapte fidèlement à la scène mimée par les trois personnages. Le jeune homme s'approche du vieux monsieur et de la jeune dame, salue et échange quelques mots à voix basse, etc.)

MORALÈS *(imitant le salut empressé du jeune homme)*
« Vous trouver ici, quel bonheur ! »

(prenant l'air rechigné du vieux mari)

« Je suis bien votre serviteur ! »

(reprenant l'air du jeune homme)

Il salue, il parle avec grâce !

(puis l'air du vieux mari)

Le vieux mari fait la grimace.

(imitant les mines souriantes de la dame)

Mais d'un air très encourageant
La dame accueille le galant.

(At this moment a young man comes hastily into the square. All this pantomime must be fitted exactly to Moralès's story, which indicates all the gestures.)

MORALÈS, SOLDIERS *(laughing)*
Ha! Ha! Ha! Ha!
Here he is!

MORALÈS
Here he is! Ah! Here he is!
Yes, here he is! Yes here he is!
Yes, here he is! Ha! Ha! Yes, here he is!

MORALÈS, SOLDIERS
Let's see how this is going to turn out.

(The second verse continues, faithfully fitting in with the scene as mimed by the three characters. The young man approaches the old gentleman and the young lady, greets them and exchanges several words in a whisper, etc.)

MORALÈS *(imitating the assiduous greeting of the young man)*
'How lovely to find you here!'

(imitating the sour-faced appearance of the old husband)

'I am your humble servant, sir!'

(imitating the young man again)

How gracefully he greets us and speaks to us!

(imitating the old man again)

How the old man grimaces!

(now imitating the smiles of the lady)

But how encouragingly
the lady welcomes the young gallant!

Le jeune homme à ce moment tire de sa poche un billet qu'il fait voir à la dame.

Le mari, la femme et le galant font tous les trois très lentement un petit tour sur la place. Le jeune homme cherchant à remettre son billet-doux à la dame.

> Ils font ensemble quelques pas...
> Notre amoureux, tendant le bras,
> Fait voir au mari quelque chose...
> Et le mari, toujours morose,
> Regarde en l'air...
> Le tour est fait ! Le tour est fait !
> Car la dame a pris le billet !
> La dame a pris le billet !

(Le jeune homme, d'une main, montre quelque chose en l'air au vieux monsieur et, de l'autre, passe le billet à la dame.)

> Et voilà ! Et voilà ! ah ! ah !

MORALÈS, SOLDATS
> On voit comment ça tournera,
> comment ça tournera !

Scène II

Les mêmes, Don José, le Lieutenant Zuniga

N° 2 Marche et Chœur des gamins

On entend au loin, très au loin, une marche militaire, clairons et fifres. C'est la garde montante qui arrive. Le vieux monsieur et le jeune homme échangent une cordiale poignée de main. Salut respectueux du jeune homme à la dame. Un officier sort du poste. Les soldats du poste vont prendre leurs lances et se rangent en ligne devant le corps de garde. Les passants à droite forment un groupe pour assister à la parade. La marche militaire se rapproche, se rapproche... La garde montante débouche enfin venant de la gauche et traverse le pont. Deux clairons et deux fifres d'abord. Puis une bande de petits gamins qui

(The young man at this moment takes a note out of his pocket and shows it to the lady.)

(The husband, the lady and the gallant together take a little walk around the square. The young man is trying to get the lady to take the billet-doux.)

> They're taking a few steps together...
> Our lover, holding out his arm,
> points out something to the husband...
> And the husband, still sour-faced,
> looks into the distance...
> The trick has worked! The trick has worked!
> The lady has taken the billet-doux!
> She's taken the billet-doux!

(The young man, with one hand, points out something to the old man, and with the other gives the billet-doux to the woman.)

> And there it is! There it is! Ah! Ha!

MORALÈS, SOLDIERS
> Now we can see how it's going to turn out,
> and what's going to happen!

Scene 2

The same, Don José, Lieutenant Zuniga

No. 2 March and Chorus of urchins

From the very far distance a military march with bugles and fifes is heard. The relief guard is arriving. The elderly gentleman and the young man exchange a cordial handshake. The young man respectfully takes his leave of the lady. An officer comes out of the guardhouse. The soldiers from the guardhouse pick up their lances and line up in front of it. The passers-by on the right form a group to watch the parade. The military march gets nearer and nearer... The relief guard finally appears from the left and crosses the bridge. At the head are two bugles and two fifes. Then a group of street urchins

s'efforcent de faire de grandes enjambées pour marcher au pas des dragons. Aussi petits que possible les enfants. Derrière les enfants, le lieutenant Zuniga et le brigadier Don José, puis les dragons avec leurs lances. [8]

CHŒUR DES GAMINS
    Avec la garde montante
    Nous arrivons, nous voilà !
    Sonne, trompette éclatante !
    Ta ra ta ta ta ra ta ta.
    Nous marchons, la tête haute
    Comme de petits soldats,
    Marquant, sans faire de faute,

(crié)

    Une, deux, marquant le pas.
    Les épaules en arrière
    Et la poitrine en dehors,
    Les bras de cette manière,
    Tombant tout le long du corps.
    Avec la garde montante
    Nous arrivons, nous voilà !
    Sonne, trompette éclatante !
    Ta ra ta ta ta ra ta ta.
    Nous marchons, la tête haute
    Comme de petits soldats,
    Marquant, sans faire de faute,

(crié)

    Une, deux, marquant le pas.
    Les épaules en arrière
    Et la poitrine en dehors,
    Les bras de cette manière,
    Tombant tout le long du corps.
    Nous arrivons ! Nous voilà !

appear imitating their long strides in an attempt to match the pace of the dragoons. The urchins should be as young as possible. Behind them come Lieutenant Zuniga and Corporal Don José, followed by the dragoons bearing their lances. [8]

CHORUS OF URCHINS
   With the relief guard
   we've arrived. Here we are!
   Sound, shining trumpet!
   Ta ra ta ta ta ra ta ta.
   Heads held high we march
   just like little soldiers,
   keeping step with no mistakes:

(shouted)

   One, two, marking time.
   Shoulders back,
   chest pushed out,
   arms held in this manner
   down our sides.
   With the relief guard
   we arrive. Here we are!
   Sound, shining trumpet!
   Ta ra ta ta ta ra ta ta.
   Heads held high we march
   just like little soldiers,
   keeping step with no mistakes,

(shouted)

   One, two, marking time.
   Shoulders back
   chest pushed out,
   arms held in this manner
   down our sides.
   We've arrived! Here we are!

Ta ra ta ta ra ta ta
Ra ta ta ta ta ra ta ta.

(La garde montante va se ranger à droite en face de la garde descendante. Dès que les petits gamins qui se sont arrêtés à droite devant les curieux ont fini de chanter, les officiers se saluent de l'épée et se mettent à causer à voix basse. On relève les sentinelles.)

ZUNIGA *(parlé)*
  Halte ! Repos !

Mélodrame [ou Récitatif 1, p. 338]

MORALÈS *(à Don José)*
  Il y a une jolie fille qui est venue te demander.
  Elle a dit qu'elle reviendrait...

DON JOSÉ
  Une jolie fille ?...

MORALÈS
  Oui, et gentiment habillée : une jupe bleue, des nattes tombant sur les épaules...

DON JOSÉ
  C'est Micaëla ! Ce ne peut être que Micaëla.

MORALÈS
  Elle n'a pas dit son nom.

LE LIEUTENANT DE LA GARDE DESCENDANTE
  Allons ! allons !

N° 2bis (Reprise du N° 2)

Les factionnaires sont relevés. Sonneries des clairons. La garde descendante passe devant la garde montante. Les gamins en troupe reprennent derrière les clairons et les fifres de la garde descendante la place qu'ils occupaient derrière les tambours et les fifres de la garde montante.

ACT ONE SCENE 2

Ta ra ta ta ra ta ta
ra ta ta ta ta ra ta ta.

(The relief guard lines up on the right, facing the guard going off duty. When the street urchins, who have halted on the right in front of the onlookers, have finished singing, the officers salute one another with their swords and begin to talk quietly together. The sentinels are relieved of their duty.)

ZUNIGA *(spoken)*
    Halt! At ease!

Melodrama [or Recitative 1, p. 339]

MORALÈS *(to Don José)*
    A pretty girl came to ask for you.
    She said she'd come back…

DON JOSÉ
    A pretty girl?…

MORALÈS
    Yes, and nicely dressed too, in a blue skirt, with plaits falling over her shoulders.

DON JOSÉ
    That's Micaëla! That can only be Micaëla.

MORALÈS
    She didn't give her name.

THE LIEUTENANT OF THE OFF-DUTY GUARD
    Let's go! Let's go!

No. 2b (Repeat of No. 2)

The sentries are changed. Bugles sound. The outgoing guard pass in front of the incoming guard. The pack of urchins re-form behind the bugles and fifes of the off-duty guard, taking the same place behind the fifes and drums of the relief guard.

CHŒUR DES GAMINS
>Et la garde descendante
>Rentre chez elle et s'en va.
>Sonne, trompette éclatante !
>Ta ra ta ta ta ra ta ta.
>Nous marchons, la tête haute
>Comme de petits soldats,
>Marquant, sans faire de faute,

(crié)

>Une, deux, marquant le pas.
>Les épaules en arrière
>Et la poitrine en dehors,
>Les bras de cette manière,
>Tombant tout le long du corps.
>Oui, la garde descendante
>Rentre chez elle et s'en va.
>Sonne, trompette éclatante !
>Ta ra ta ta ta ra ta ta.

(Les fifres et les clairons disparaissent. Les soldats sortent de scène peu à peu, les gamins disparaîtront sur la dernière note du chœur.)

(Soldats, gamins et curieux s'éloignent par le fond; chœur, fifres et clairons vont diminuant. L'officier de la garde montante, pendant ce temps, passe silencieusement l'inspection de ses hommes. Quand le chœur des gamins et les fifres ont cessé de se faire entendre, le lieutenant dit « Présentez lances ! Haut lances ! Rompez les rangs ! ». Les dragons vont tous déposer leurs lances dans le râtelier, puis ils rentrent dans le corps de garde. Don José et le lieutenant Zuniga restent seuls en scène.)

Scène III

Le lieutenant Zuniga, Don José

Dialogue [ou Récitatif 2, p. 338]

ZUNIGA
>Dites-moi, brigadier ?

CHORUS OF URCHINS
> There go the off-duty guard
> away back to their homes.
> Sound, shining trumpet!
> Ta ra ta ta ta ra ta ta.
> Heads held high we march
> just like little soldiers,
> keeping step with no mistakes:

(shouted)

> one, two, marking time.
> Shoulders back
> chest pushed out,
> arms held in this manner
> down our sides.
> Yes, the off-duty guard
> go away back to their homes.
> Sound, shining trumpet!
> Ta ra ta ta ra ta ta.

(The fifes and bugles disappear. The soldiers gradually leave the stage, the urchins will disappear on the last note of the chorus.)

(Soldiers, urchins and bystanders move off via the back of the stage; the fifes and bugles fade away. Meanwhile the officer of the relief guard silently inspects his men. When the chorus of urchins and the fifes can no longer be heard, the lieutenant orders 'Present arms! Raise lances! Break ranks!' The dragoons all deposit their lances in the rack, then go into the guardhouse. Don José and Lieutenant Zuniga remain alone on stage.)

Scene 3

Lieutenant Zuniga, Don José

Dialogue [or Recitative 2, p. 339]

ZUNIGA
> Tell me, Corporal?

DON JOSÉ *(se levant)*
   Mon lieutenant ?

ZUNIGA
   Je ne suis dans le régiment que depuis deux jours et jamais je n'étais venu à Séville. Qu'est-ce que c'est que ce grand bâtiment ?

DON JOSÉ
   C'est la manufacture de tabacs…

ZUNIGA
   Ce sont des femmes qui travaillent là ?…

DON JOSÉ
   Oui, mon lieutenant. Elles n'y sont pas maintenant ; tout à l'heure, après leur dîner, elles vont revenir. Et je vous réponds qu'alors il y aura du monde pour les voir passer.

ZUNIGA
   Elles sont beaucoup ?

DON JOSÉ
   Ma foi, elles sont bien quatre ou cinq cents qui roulent des cigares dans une grande salle…

ZUNIGA
   Ce doit être curieux.

DON JOSÉ
   Oui, mais les hommes ne peuvent pas entrer dans cette salle sans une permission…

ZUNIGA
   Ah !

DON JOSÉ
   Parce que, lorsqu'il fait chaud, ces ouvrières se mettent à leur aise, surtout les jeunes.

ZUNIGA
   Il y en a de jeunes ?

ACT ONE SCENE 3

DON JOSÉ *(standing up)*
Yes, Lieutenant?

ZUNIGA
I've only been in the regiment two days and I've never been to Seville before. What's that big building over there?

DON JOSÉ
It's the tobacco factory...

ZUNIGA
And is it women who work in there?...

DON JOSÉ
Yes, Lieutenant. They aren't there now, but they'll soon be coming back after their lunch break. And I can tell you there'll be plenty of people to watch them come past.

ZUNIGA
Are there lots of them?

DON JOSÉ
Lord yes, at least four or five hundred, rolling cigars in a large hall...

ZUNIGA
It must be quite a sight.

DON JOSÉ
Yes, but men aren't allowed into the hall without permission...

ZUNIGA
Ah!

DON JOSÉ
Because when it's hot in there the factory girls make themselves comfortable, especially the young ones.

ZUNIGA
There are young ones?

DON JOSÉ
  Mais oui, mon lieutenant.

ZUNIGA
  Et de jolies ?

DON JOSÉ *(en riant)*
  Je le suppose… Mais à vous dire vrai, et bien que j'aie été de garde ici plusieurs fois déjà, je n'en suis pas bien sûr, car je ne les ai jamais beaucoup regardées…

ZUNIGA
  Allons donc !…

DON JOSÉ
  Que voulez-vous ?… ces Andalouses me font peur. Je ne suis pas fait à leurs manières, toujours à railler… jamais un mot de raison…

ZUNIGA
  Et puis nous avons un faible pour les jupes bleues, et pour les nattes tombant sur les épaules…

DON JOSÉ *(riant)*
  Ah ! mon lieutenant a entendu ce que me disait Moralès ?…

ZUNIGA
  Oui…

DON JOSÉ
  Je ne le nierai pas… la jupe bleue, les nattes… c'est le costume de la Navarre… ça me rappelle le pays…

ZUNIGA
  Vous êtes Navarrais ?

DON JOSÉ
  Et vieux chrétien. Don José Lizzarabengoa, c'est mon nom… On voulait que je fusse d'église, et l'on m'a fait étudier. Mais je ne profitais guère, j'aimais trop jouer à la paume… Un jour que j'avais gagné, un gars de l'Alava me chercha querelle ; j'eus

DON JOSÉ
Oh yes, Lieutenant.

ZUNIGA
And pretty ones?

DON JOSÉ *(laughing)*
I suppose so... To tell you the truth, although I've already stood guard several times I'm not really sure, because I've never paid them much attention...

ZUNIGA
Well then!...

DON JOSÉ
What do you expect?... These Andalusian girls frighten me. I'm not used to their ways, always mocking... never a word of sense...

ZUNIGA
And then we've got a weakness for blue skirts and plaits falling over her shoulders...

DON JOSÉ *(laughing)*
Ah, Lieutenant, you heard what Moralès was telling me?

ZUNIGA
Yes...

DON JOSÉ
I can't deny it... A blue skirt and plaits, it's the costume of Navarre, it reminds me of my country...

ZUNIGA
You're from Navarre?

DON JOSÉ
Yes, from old Christian stock. Don José Lizzarabengoa, that's my name... They wanted me to go into the Church and sent me to study. But I didn't take to it, I was too fond of playing pelota... One day, when I'd won, a lad from Alava picked a

encore l'avantage, mais cela m'obligea de quitter le pays. Je me fis soldat ! Je n'avais plus mon père ; ma mère me suivit et vint s'établir à dix lieues de Séville... avec la petite Micaëla... c'est une orpheline que ma mère a recueillie, et qui n'a pas voulu se séparer d'elle...

ZUNIGA
Et quel âge a-t-elle, la petite Micaëla ?...

DON JOSÉ
Dix-sept ans...

ZUNIGA
Il fallait dire cela tout de suite ! Je comprends maintenant pourquoi vous ne pouvez pas me dire si les ouvrières de la manufacture sont jolies ou laides...

Scène IV

Don José, soldats, jeunes gens et cigarières

N° 3 Chœur et Scène

La cloche de la manufacture se fait entendre.

DON JOSÉ *(parlé)*
Voici la cloche qui sonne, mon lieutenant, et vous allez pouvoir juger par vous-même... Quant à moi je vais faire une chaîne pour attacher mon épinglette.

La place se remplit de jeunes gens qui viennent se placer sur le passage des cigarières. Les soldats sortent du poste. Don José s'assied et reste fort indifférent à toutes les allées et venues, le nez sur sa chaine. La cloche s'arrête.

JEUNES GENS
La cloche a sonné. Nous, des ouvrières,
Nous venons ici guetter le retour ;
Et nous vous suivrons, brunes cigarières,
En vous murmurant des propos d'amour !

fight with me; I got the better of him again, but had to leave the area. I joined the army! My father was dead, my mother followed me and set up house ten leagues away from Seville... with little Micaëla... she's an orphan my mother took in and who doesn't want to leave her...

ZUNIGA
And how old is little Micaëla?...

DON JOSÉ
Seventeen...

ZUNIGA
You should have said so straight away! Now I understand why you can't tell me whether the factory girls are pretty or ugly...

Scene 4

Don José, soldiers, youths and cigar girls

No. 3 Chorus and Scene

The factory bell is heard.

DON JOSÉ *(spoken)*
There's the bell ringing, Lieutenant, now you can judge for yourself... As for me, I'm going to make a chain to attach to my priming pin.

The square fills up with young people who have come to line the way for the cigar girls. The soldiers come out from their post. Don José sits down, impervious to all the comings and goings, engrossed with his chain. The bell stops.

YOUTHS
The bell's rung. We'll lie in wait
for your return, and follow you,
You dark-haired cigar girls,
while whispering proposals of love to you!

(À ce moment paraissent les cigarières, la cigarette aux lèvres. Elles passent sous le pont et descendent lentement en scène.)

LES SOLDATS
>Voyez-les ! regards impudents
>Mine coquette !
>Fumant toutes, du bout des dents,
>La cigarette.

LES CIGARIÈRES
>Dans l'air, nous suivons des yeux [9]
>La fumée, la fumée,
>Qui vers les cieux
>Monte, monte parfumée.
>Cela monte gentiment
>À la tête, à la tête,
>Tout doucement cela vous met
>L'âme en fête !

1rs DESSUS
>Le doux parler, le doux parler des amants !

2ds DESSUS
>C'est fumée !

1rs DESSUS
>Leurs transports, leurs transports et leurs serments !

2ds DESSUS
>C'est fumée !

CHŒUR
>Oui, c'est fumée, c'est fumée !

1rs ET 2ds DESSUS
>Dans l'air, nous suivons des yeux,
>La fumée ! La fumée, ah !

(At this moment the cigar girls appear smoking cigarettes. They go under the bridge and slowly come down onto the stage.)

THE SOLDIERS
>Look at them with their impudent look
>and their coquettish manner!
>Cigarettes between their lips
>All of them smoking!

CIGAR GIRLS
>We look up, following with our eyes [9]
>the smoke, the smoke
>rising up into the sky
>so fragrantly.
>It gently goes
>to your head, to your head,
>Quietly making you
>happy inside!

1ST SOPRANOS
>The gentle words, the gentle words of lovers!

2ND SOPRANOS
>It's smoke!

1ST SOPRANOS
>Their delights, their delights and their entreaties!

2ND SOPRANOS
>It's smoke!

CHORUS
>It's smoke! It's smoke!

1ST AND 2ND SOPRANOS
>We look up, following with our eyes,
>the smoke, the smoke! Ah!

CHŒUR
>Nous suivons la fumée
>Qui monte en tournant,
>En tournant vers les cieux !
>La fumée ! La fumée !

LES JEUNES GENS *(aux cigarières)*
>Sans faire les cruelles,
>Écoutez-nous les belles,
>Ô vous que nous adorons,
>Que nous idolâtrons !
>Sans faire les cruelles,
>Écoutez-nous les belles,
>Vous que nous adorons,
>Écoutez-nous les belles,
>Ô vous que nous idolâtrons !

LES CIGARIÈRES *(reprennent en riant)*
>Le doux parler des amants
>Et leurs transports et leur serments,

1^{rs} ET 2^{ds} DESSUS
>C'est fumée,

LES JEUNES GENS
>Ô vous que nous aimons, écoutez-nous les belles !
>Écoutez ! Écoutez! Écoutez-nous !
>Écoutez-nous les belles !

LES CIGARIÈRES
>Dans l'air nous suivons la fumée
>Qui monte en tournant,
>En tournant vers les cieux !
>La fumée ! La fumée !

ACT ONE SCENE 4

CHORUS
>We follow the smoke,
>rising and curling
>up into the sky!
>The smoke, the smoke!

YOUTHS *(to the cigar girls)*
>Don't be heartless!
>Listen to us, lovely ones,
>us who adore you
>who idolize you!
>Don't be heartless,
>listen to us, lovely ones,
>us who adore you,
>listen to us, lovely ones,
>oh you whom we idolize!

CIGAR GIRLS *(laughing, beginning again)*
>The gentle words of lovers,
>their delights and their entreaties,

1ST AND 2ND SOPRANOS
>It's smoke,

YOUTHS
>Oh you whom we love, listen to us, lovely ones!
>Listen! Listen! Listen to us!
>Listen to us, lovely ones!

CIGAR GIRLS
>In the air we follow the smoke,
>rising and curling
>up into the sky!
>The smoke, the smoke!

Scène V

Les mêmes, Carmen

SOLDATS
Mais nous ne voyons pas la Carmencita !

Entrée de Carmen [10]

JEUNES GENS, SOLDATS
La voilà !

CHŒUR
La voilà, voilà la Carmencita !

(Entre Carmen. Absolument le costume et l'entrée indiqués par Mérimée. Elle a un bouquet de cassie à son corsage et une fleur de cassie dans le coin de la bouche. Trois ou quatre jeunes gens entrent avec Carmen. Ils la suivent, l'entourent, lui parlent. Elle minaude et caquette avec eux. Don José lève la tête. Il regarde Carmen, puis se remet à travailler à son épinglette.)

LES JEUNES GENS *(entrés avec Carmen)*
Carmen ! sur tes pas nous nous pressons tous !
Carmen ! sois gentille, au moins réponds-nous,
Et dis-nous quel jour tu nous aimeras !

CARMEN *(les regardant gaiment)*
Quand je vous aimerai ? Ma foi, je ne sais pas…
Peut-être jamais !… peut-être demain !…

(résolument)

Mais pas aujourd'hui… c'est certain.

N° 4 Havanaise

CARMEN
L'amour est un oiseau rebelle [11]
Que nul ne peut apprivoiser,
Et c'est bien en vain qu'on l'appelle,
S'il lui convient de refuser !

Scene 5

The same, Carmen

SOLDIERS
  But we can't see Carmencita!

Carmen's entry [10]

YOUTHS, SOLDIERS
  There she is!

CHORUS
  There she is, there's Carmencita!

(Carmen enters. Her entrance and costume should be exactly as described by Mérimée. She has a spray of cassia flowers in her bodice and one in the corner of her mouth. Three or four young men enter with Carmen. They follow her, surround her and speak to her. She simpers and flirts with them. Don José looks up, then quietly resumes polishing his priming pin.)

THE YOUTHS *(who entered with Carmen)*
  Carmen! We all follow eagerly in your steps!
  Carmen! Be kind, at least reply to us,
  and tell us which day we can hope for your love!

CARMEN *(looking at them cheerfully)*
  When will I love you? I can't say, I'm sure…
  Perhaps never!… Perhaps tomorrow!

(resolutely)

  But not today… that's for sure.

No. 4 Habanera

CARMEN
  Love is like a wild bird [11]
  which no one knows how to tame,
  and there's no use calling it
  if it doesn't want to come!

Rien n'y fait, menace ou prière,
L'un parle bien, l'autre se tait ;
Et c'est l'autre que je préfère,
Il n'a rien dit, mais il me plaît.

CHŒUR DES CIGARIÈRES ET JEUNES GENS
L'amour est un oiseau rebelle
Que nul ne peut apprivoiser,
Et c'est bien en vain qu'on l'appelle,
S'il lui convient de refuser !

CARMEN
L'amour ! l'amour ! l'amour ! l'amour !

CARMEN
L'amour est enfant de Bohème,
Il n'a jamais, jamais connu de loi,
Si tu ne m'aimes pas, je t'aime,
Si je t'aime, prends garde à toi !

CHŒUR (CIGARIÈRES, JEUNES GENS ET SOLDATS)
Prends garde à toi !

CARMEN
Si tu ne m'aimes pas,
Si tu ne m'aimes pas, je t'aime !

CHŒUR
Prends garde à toi !

CARMEN
Mais si je t'aime,
Si je t'aime, prends garde à toi !

CIGARIÈRES ET JEUNES GENS
L'amour est enfant de Bohème,
Il n'a jamais, jamais connu de loi,
Si tu ne m'aimes pas, je t'aime,
Si je t'aime, prends garde à toi !

ACT ONE SCENE 5

> Nothing at all will tempt it, neither threat nor prayer:
> one will try charm, the other says nothing,
> and it's that last one I prefer,
> he hasn't said a word, but I like him.

CHORUS OF CIGAR GIRLS AND YOUTHS
> Love is like a wild bird
> which no one knows how to tame,
> and it's no use calling him
> if he doesn't want to come!

CARMEN
> Love! Love! Love! Love!

CARMEN
> Love was born to gypsy life
> and has never obeyed any law,
> if you don't love me, I'll love you,
> if I love you, beware!

CHORUS (CIGAR GIRLS, YOUTHS AND SOLDIERS)
> Beware!

CARMEN
> If you don't love me,
> if you don't love me, I'll love you!

CHORUS
> Beware!

CARMEN
> But if I love you,
> if I love you, beware!

CIGAR GIRLS AND YOUTHS
> Love was born to gypsy life
> and has never obeyed any law,
> if you don't love me, I'll love you,
> if I love you, beware!

JEUNES GENS ET SOLDATS
L'amour est enfant de Bohème !

CHŒUR
Prends garde à toi !

CARMEN
Si tu ne m'aimes pas,
Si tu ne m'aimes pas, je t'aime !

CHŒUR
Prends garde à toi !

CARMEN
L'oiseau que tu croyais surprendre
Battit de l'aile et s'envola ;
L'amour est loin, tu peux l'attendre,
Tu ne l'attends plus, il est là.
Tout autour de toi, vite, vite,
Il vient, s'en va, puis il revient ;
Tu crois le tenir, il t'évite,
Tu crois l'éviter, il te tient !

CIGARIÈRES ET JEUNES GENS
Tout autour de toi, vite, vite,
Il vient, s'en va, puis il revient ;
Tu crois le tenir, il t'évite,
Tu crois l'éviter, il te tient !

CARMEN
L'amour ! l'amour ! l'amour ! l'amour !

CARMEN
L'amour est enfant de Bohème,
Il n'a jamais, jamais connu de loi,
Si tu ne m'aimes pas, je t'aime,
Si je t'aime, prends garde à toi !

CHŒUR (CIGARIÈRES, JEUNES GENS ET SOLDATS)
Prends garde à toi !

YOUTHS AND SOLDIERS
Love was born to gypsy life!

CHORUS
Beware!

CARMEN
If you don't love me,
If you don't love me, I'll love you!

CHORUS
Beware!

CARMEN
The bird you hoped to surprise
flapped its wings and flew away;
when love seems far away, you wait,
and when you're not waiting, it's there.
All around you suddenly, suddenly
it arrives, goes away and then comes back;
you think you've trapped it, but it escapes,
you think you've escaped, and it catches you!

CIGAR GIRLS AND YOUTHS
All around you suddenly, suddenly,
it arrives, goes away and then comes back;
you think you've trapped it, but it escapes,
you think you've escaped, and it catches you!

CARMEN
Love! Love! Love! Love!

CARMEN
Love was born to gypsy life
and has never obeyed any law,
if you don't love me, I'll love you,
if I love you, beware!

CHORUS (CIGAR GIRLS, YOUTHS AND SOLDIERS)
Beware!

CIGARIÈRES ET JEUNES GENS
L'amour est enfant de Bohème,
Il n'a jamais, jamais connu de loi,
Si tu ne m'aimes pas, je t'aime,
Si je t'aime, prends garde à toi !

JEUNES GENS ET SOLDATS
L'amour est enfant de Bohème !

CHŒUR
Prends garde à toi !

N° 5 Scène

LES JEUNES GENS
Carmen ! sur tes pas nous nous pressons tous !
Carmen ! sois gentille, au moins réponds-nous !
Réponds-nous, ô Carmen !
Sois gentille, au moins réponds-nous !

(Moment de silence. Les jeunes gens entourent Carmen, celle-ci les regarde l'un après l'autre, sort du cercle qu'ils forment autour d'elle et s'en va droit à Don José, qui est toujours occupé de son épinglette.)

Mélodrame

CARMEN
Eh ! compère, qu'est-ce que tu fais là ?…

DON JOSÉ
Je fais une chaîne du fil de laiton, une chaîne pour attacher mon épinglette.

CARMEN *(riant)*
Ton épinglette, vraiment ! Ton épinglette… épinglier de mon âme…

(Elle arrache de son corsage la fleur de cassie et la lance à Don José. Il se lève brusquement. La fleur de cassie est tombée à ses pieds. Éclat

ACT ONE SCENE 5

CIGAR GIRLS AND YOUTHS
> Love was born to gypsy life
> and has never obeyed any law,
> if you don't love me, I'll love you,
> if I love you, beware!

YOUTHS AND SOLDIERS
> Love was born to gypsy life!

CHORUS
> Beware!

No. 5 Scene

YOUTHS
> Carmen! We all follow eagerly in your steps!
> Carmen! Be kind, at least reply to us!
> Reply to us, oh Carmen!
> Be kind, at least reply to us!

(Moment of silence. The youths surround Carmen, who looks at them one by one, escapes from the circle that they have formed around her and goes straight up to Don José, who is still busy with his priming pin.)

Melodrama

CARMEN
> Hey, friend! What is it that you are doing there?...

DON JOSÉ
> I'm making a brass-wire chain to attach to my priming pin.

CARMEN *(laughing)*
> Your priming-pin! Really! Your priming pin. Pin-maker of my soul...

(She rips the cassia flower from her bodice and throws it to Don José. He quickly gets up. The cassia flower has fallen at his feet. General

de rire général ; la cloche de la manufacture sonne une deuxième fois. Sortie des ouvrières et des jeunes gens sur la reprise de :)

CIGARIÈRES (*riant entre elles*)
L'amour est enfant de Bohème,
Il n'a jamais, jamais connu de loi,
Si tu ne m'aimes pas, je t'aime,
Si je t'aime, prends garde à toi !

(Carmen sort la première en courant et elle entre dans la manufacture. Les jeunes gens sortent à droite et à gauche. Le lieutenant Zuniga, qui, pendant cette scène, bavardait avec deux ou trois ouvrières, les quitte et rentre dans le poste après que les soldats y sont rentrés. Don José reste seul.)

Scène VI

Don José

Dialogue [ou Récitatif 3, p. 340]

DON JOSÉ
Qu'est-ce que cela veut dire, ces façons-là ?... Quelle effronterie !...

(en souriant)

Tout ça parce que je ne faisais pas attention à elle !... Alors, suivant l'usage des femmes et des chats qui ne viennent pas quand on les appelle et qui viennent quand on ne les appelle pas, elle est venue...

(Il regarde la fleur de cassie qui est par terre à ses pieds. Il la ramasse.)

Avec quelle adresse elle me l'a lancée, cette fleur ! Là, juste entre les deux yeux... ça m'a fait l'effet d'une balle qui m'arrivait...

(Il respire le parfum de la fleur.)

Comme c'est fort !... Certainement s'il y a des sorcières, cette fille-là en est une.

laughter; the factory bell rings for a second time. Exit the workers and youths at the reprise of:)

CIGAR GIRLS *(laughing among themselves)*
    Love was born to gypsy life
    and has never obeyed any law,
    if you don't love me, I'll love you,
    if I love you, beware!

(Carmen is the first to exit, running into the factory. The youths exit from both sides. Lieutenant Zuniga, who has been chatting with one or two of the cigar girls during this scene, leaves them and returns to the guard post, following the soldiers. Don José remains alone.)

Scene 6

Don José

Dialogue [or Recitative 3, p. 341]

DON JOSÉ
    Well, what sort of behaviour is that, then?... What cheek!...

(smiling)

    And all because I didn't pay any attention to her!... So, just like women and cats who don't come when you call them and come when you don't call them, she came up...

(He looks at the cassia flower on the ground by his feet. He picks it up.)

    How expertly she threw it to me, that flower! There, right between the eyes... it seemed as if I'd been hit by a bullet...

(He breathes in its fragrance.)

    How strong it smells!... If witches really do exist, that girl's one of them.

Entre Micaëla.

Scène VII

Don José, Micaëla

MICAËLA
   Monsieur le brigadier ?

DON JOSÉ *(cachant précipitamment la fleur de cassie)*
   Quoi ?... Qu'est-ce que c'est ?... Micaëla !...
   c'est toi...

MICAËLA
   C'est moi !

DON JOSÉ
   Et tu viens de là-bas ?...

MICAËLA
   Et je viens de là-bas... c'est votre mère qui m'envoie...

DON JOSÉ
   Ma mère...

N° 7 Duo

DON JOSÉ *(ému)*
   Parle-moi de ma mère !

MICAËLA *(simplement)*
   J'apporte de sa part, fidèle messagère, [12]
   cette lettre...

DON JOSÉ *(joyeux, regardant la lettre)*
   Une lettre !

MICAËLA
   Et puis un peu d'argent,

(Elle lui remet une petite bourse.)

(Enter Micaëla.)

Scene 7

Don José, Micaëla

MICAËLA
Corporal?

DON JOSÉ *(quickly hiding the cassia flower)*
What?... What's this?... Micaëla!...
It's you...

MICAËLA
It's me!

DON JOSÉ
And you've come from back home?...

MICAËLA
I've come from back home... It's your mother who sent me...

DON JOSÉ
My mother...

No. 7 Duo

DON JOSÉ *(moved)*
Tell me about my mother!

MICAËLA *(simply)*
I bring as the faithful messenger, [12]
this letter...

DON JOSÉ *(thrilled, looking at the letter)*
A letter!

MICAËLA
And then a little money,

(She hands him a small purse.)

pour ajouter à votre traitement.
Et puis...

DON JOSÉ
Et puis ?...

MICAËLA
Et puis... vraiment je n'ose...
Et puis... encore une autre chose
Qui vaut mieux que l'argent !
Et qui, pour un bon fils
Aura sans doute plus de prix.

DON JOSÉ
Cette autre chose, quelle est-elle ?
Parle donc...

MICAËLA
Oui, je parlerai.
Ce que l'on m'a donné, je vous le donnerai.
Votre mère avec moi sortait de la chapelle,
Et c'est alors qu'en m'embrassant :
« Tu vas, m'a-t-elle dit, t'en aller à la ville ;
La route n'est pas longue; une fois à Séville,
Tu chercheras mon fils, mon José, mon enfant !
Et tu lui diras que sa mère [13]
Songe nuit et jour à l'absent,
Qu'elle regrette et qu'elle espère,
Qu'elle pardonne et qu'elle attend.
Tout cela, n'est-ce pas, mignonne,
De ma part tu le lui diras ;
Et ce baiser que je te donne,
De ma part tu le lui rendras. »

DON JOSÉ *(très ému)*
Un baiser de ma mère !

MICAËLA
Un baiser pour son fils !...

ACT ONE SCENE 7

that you can add to what they're paying you.
And then...

DON JOSÉ
What else?...

MICAËLA
And then... really I daren't tell you...
and well, something else as well,
more valuable than money!
And which for a loving son
would be worth much more.

DON JOSÉ
This other thing, what can it be?
Tell me...

MICAËLA
Yes, I'll tell you.
What she gave me, I'll give to you.
Your mother and I were coming out of the chapel,
and it was then, kissing me,
she told me to come to town and that it wasn't far by road;
once in Seville, she told me:
'Find my son, my José, my child!
And tell him that his mother [13]
thinks of her absent son night and day,
that she misses him and hopes for him,
that she forgives him and waits for him.
All that, sweet one,
is to be said on my part;
and this kiss I give to you,
you pass on to him on my behalf.'

DON JOSÉ *(very moved)*
A kiss from my mother!

MICAËLA
A kiss for her son!...

DON JOSÉ
   Un baiser de ma mère !

MICAËLA
   Un baiser pour son fils !…
   José, je vous le rends comme je l'ai promis !

(Micaëla se hausse un peu sur la pointe des pieds et donne à Don José un baiser bien franc, bien maternel. Don José, très ému, la laisse faire. Il la regarde bien dans les yeux. Un moment de silence.)

DON JOSÉ *(continuant de regarder Micaëla)*
   Ma mère, je la vois !… oui, je revois mon village ! [14]
   Ô souvenirs d'autrefois ! doux souvenirs du pays !
   Doux souvenirs du pays ! Ô souvenirs chéris !
   Ô souvenirs ! Ô souvenirs chéris,
   Vous remplissez mon cœur de force et de courage !
   Ô souvenirs chéris ! Ma mère, je la vois,
   Je revois mon village !

MICAËLA
   Sa mère, il la revoit ! Il revoit son village !
   Ô souvenirs d'autrefois ! Souvenirs du pays !
   Vous remplissez son cœur de force et de courage !
   Ô souvenirs chéris ! Sa mère, il la revoit,
   Il revoit son village !

DON JOSÉ *(les yeux fixés sur la manufacture)*

(à lui-même)

   Qui sait de quel démon j'allais être la proie !

(recueilli)

   Même de loin, ma mère me défend,
   Et ce baiser qu'elle m'envoie,

(avec élan)

ACT ONE SCENE 7

DON JOSÉ
A kiss from my mother!

MICAËLA
A kiss for her son!...
José, I pass it on to you just as I promised!

(Micaëla raises herself up a little on tiptoe and gives Don José a very simple kiss, very motherly. Don José, deeply moved, lets her do it, looking her straight in the eyes. A moment of silence.)

DON JOSÉ *(still looking at Micaëla)*
My mother, I can picture her... yes, I can see my village! [14]
Oh memories of yesteryear! Fond memories of home!
Fond memories of home! Oh fond memories!
Oh memories! Oh fond memories!
You fill my heart with strength and courage!
Oh fond memories! My mother, I can picture her... yes,
I can see my own village!

MICAËLA
His mother, he can picture her! He can see his own village!
Oh memories of yesteryear! Memories of home!
You fill his heart with strength and courage!
Oh fond memories! His mother, he can picture her,
he can see his own village!

DON JOSÉ *(his eyes fixed on the factory)*

(to himself)

Who knows to what demon I was going to be prey!

(reverently)

But even from afar, my mother protects me,
and this kiss she has sent me,

(confidently)

Ce baiser qu'elle m'envoie,
Écarte le péril et sauve son enfant !

MICAËLA *(vivement)*
Quel démon ? Quel péril ? Je ne comprends pas bien...
Que veut dire cela ?

DON JOSÉ
Rien ! Rien !
Parlons de toi, la messagère ;
Tu vas retourner au pays ?

MICAËLA
Oui, ce soir même... demain je verrai votre mère.

DON JOSÉ *(vivement)*
Tu la verras ! Eh bien ! tu lui diras
Que son fils l'aime et la vénère
Et qu'il se repent aujourd'hui.
Il veut que là-bas sa mère
Soit contente de lui !
Tout cela, n'est-ce pas, mignonne,
De ma part, tu le lui diras !
Et ce baiser que je te donne,
De ma part, tu le lui rendras !

(Il l'embrasse.)

MICAËLA *(simplement)*
Oui, je vous le promets... de la part de son fils,
José, je le rendrai, comme je l'ai promis.

DON JOSÉ
Ma mère, je la vois !... oui, je revois mon village !
Ô souvenirs d'autrefois ! doux souvenirs du pays !
Doux souvenirs du pays ! Ô souvenirs chéris !
Ô souvenirs ! Ô souvenirs chéris,
Vous remplissez mon cœur de force et de courage !
Ô souvenirs chéris ! Ma mère, je la vois,

this kiss she has sent me,
will drive away the peril and save her child!

MICAËLA *(sharply)*
What demon? What peril? I don't understand at all…
What is he talking about?

DON JOSÉ
Nothing! Nothing!
Let's talk about you, messenger;
are you going back home?

MICAËLA
Yes this very evening… tomorrow I'll see your mother.

DON JOSÉ *(brightly)*
You'll see her! Ah good! You tell her
that her son loves her and worships her
and he is now repentant.
He hopes that back there
his mother will be pleased with him!
All that, my sweet, is
from me: you say it to her!
And this kiss which I give you,
pass it on to her, from me!

(He kisses her.)

MICAËLA *(simply)*
Yes, I promise you… on behalf of her son,
José, I'll pass it on, just as I've promised.

DON JOSÉ
My mother, I can picture her… yes, I can see my village!
Oh memories of yesteryear! Fond memories of home!
Fond memories of home! Oh fond memories!
Oh memories! Oh fond memories!
You fill my heart with strength and courage!
Oh fond memories! My mother, I can picture her…

Je revois mon village !
Je te revois, ô mon village !
Doux souvenirs, souvenirs du pays !
Vous remplissez mon cœur de courage,
Ô souvenirs, ô souvenirs chéris !

MICAËLA
Sa mère, il la revoit ! Il revoit son village !
Ô souvenirs d'autrefois ! souvenirs du pays !
Vous remplissez son cœur de force et de courage !
Ô souvenirs chéris ! Sa mère, il la revoit,
Il revoit son village !
Il te revoit, ô mon village !
Doux souvenirs, souvenirs du pays !
Vous remplissez son cœur de courage,
Ô souvenirs, ô souvenirs chéris !

DON JOSÉ
Je revois mon village !

MICAËLA
Ô souvenirs chéris ! Il revoit son village !

DON JOSÉ
Ô souvenirs chéris !
Vous me rendez tout mon courage,
Ô souvenirs du pays !

MICAËLA
Vous lui rendez tout son courage,
Ô souvenirs du pays !

Dialogue [ou Récitatif 4, p. 340]

DON JOSÉ
Attends un peu maintenant... je vais lire sa lettre...

MICAËLA
J'attendrai, monsieur le brigadier, j'attendrai...

ACT ONE SCENE 7

I can see my own village!
I can see you, oh my village!
Oh fond memories, memories of home!
You fill my heart with strength and courage!
Oh memories, oh fond memories.

MICAËLA
His mother, he can picture her... He can see his own village!
Oh memories of the past! Oh memories of the country!
You fill his heart with strength and courage!
Oh fond memories! His mother, he can picture her...
He can see his own village!
He can see you, oh my own village!
Fond memories, memories of home!
You fill his heart with strength and courage,
oh memories, oh fond memories !

DON JOSÉ
I can see my village!

MICAËLA
Oh fond memories! He can see his village!

DON JOSÉ
Oh fond memories!
You fill my heart with strength and courage,
oh memories of home!

MICAËLA
You fill his heart with strength and courage!
Oh memories of home!

Dialogue [or Recitative 4, p. 341]

DON JOSÉ
Wait a moment now... I'm going to read her letter...

MICAËLA
I'll wait, Corporal, I'll wait...

DON JOSÉ *(embrassant la lettre avant de commencer à lire)*
Ah ! *(lisant)*
« Continue à te bien conduire, mon enfant ! L'on t'a promis de te faire maréchal-des-logis. Peut-être alors pourrais-tu quitter le service, te faire donner une petite place et revenir près de moi. Je commence à me faire bien vieille. Tu reviendrais près de moi et tu te marierais, nous n'aurions pas, je pense, grand peine à te trouver une femme, et je sais bien, quant à moi, celle que je te conseillerais de choisir : c'est tout justement celle qui te porte ma lettre… Il n'y en a pas de plus sage ni de plus gentille… »

MICAËLA *(l'interrompant)*
Il vaut mieux que je ne sois pas là !…

DON JOSÉ
Pourquoi donc ?…

MICAËLA *(troublée)*
Je viens de me rappeler que votre mère m'a chargée de quelques petits achats : je vais m'en occuper tout de suite.

DON JOSÉ
Attends un peu, j'ai fini…

MICAËLA
Vous finirez quand je ne serai plus là…

DON JOSÉ
Mais la réponse ?…

MICAËLA
Je viendrai la prendre avant mon départ et je la porterai à votre mère… Adieu.

DON JOSÉ
Micaëla !

ACT ONE SCENE 7

DON JOSÉ *(putting his lips to the letter before he begins to read)*
Ah! *(reading)*
'Keep behaving yourself, my child! They promised to make you a quartermaster. Perhaps then you could leave the services, find yourself a little place and come back near to me. I'm beginning to get quite old. You come back near to me, and get married; we wouldn't have any trouble finding you a wife, I think; as for me, I know which one I'd advise you to choose: it is the very person who has brought you this letter... There is no one kinder or nicer...'

MICAËLA *(interrupting him)*
It would be better if I weren't here!...

DON JOSÉ
Why's that?...

MICAËLA *(worried)*
I've just remembered that your mother asked me to buy a few things for her; I'd better do it straight away.

DON JOSÉ
Wait a moment, I've finished...

MICAËLA
You can finish when I've gone...

DON JOSÉ
But what about the reply?...

MICAËLA
I'll come and get it before I leave and I'll take it to your mother... Goodbye.

DON JOSÉ
Micaëla!

MICAËLA
Non, non... je reviendrai, j'aime mieux cela, je reviendrai, je reviendrai...

(Elle sort.)

Scène VIII

Don José, puis les ouvrières, le Lieutenant Zuniga, Soldats

DON JOSÉ *(lisant)*
« Il n'y en a pas de plus sage ni de plus gentille... il n'y en a pas surtout qui t'aime davantage... et si tu voulais... » Oui, ma mère, oui, je ferai ce que tu désires... j'épouserai Micaëla, et quant à cette bohémienne, avec ses fleurs qui ensorcellent...

(Au moment où il va arracher les fleurs de sa veste, grande rumeur dans l'intérieur de la manufacture.)

N° 8 *Chœur*

CHŒUR DES CIGARIÈRES, 2^{ds} DESSUS *(dans la coulisse)*
Au secours !

CHŒUR DES CIGARIÈRES, 1^{rs} DESSUS *(dans la coulisse)*
Au secours !

(Entre Zuniga suivi des soldats.)

ZUNIGA *(parlé)*
Eh bien, eh bien, qu'est-ce qui arrive ?

(Les ouvrières sortent rapidement et en désordre.)

CHŒUR DES CIGARIÈRES, 1^{rs} DESSUS
Au secours ! au secours ! n'entendez-vous pas ?

CHŒUR DES CIGARIÈRES, 2^{ds} DESSUS
Au secours ! au secours ! messieurs les soldats !

ACT ONE SCENE 8

MICAËLA
No, no! I'll come back, I'd prefer that. I'll come back, I'll come back...

(She leaves.)

Scene 8

Don José, then the cigar girls, Lieutenant Zuniga, soldiers

DON JOSÉ *(reading)*
'There is no one kinder or nicer... there is no one, moreover, who loves you more... and if you wanted...' Yes. Mother, yes, I'll do as you wish... I'll marry Micaëla, and as for that gypsy with her bewitching flowers...

(Just as he is about to tear the flowers from his tunic a great commotion is heard from inside the factory.)

No. 8 Chorus

CIGAR GIRLS, 2ND SOPRANOS *(in the wings)*
Help!

CIGAR GIRLS, 1ST SOPRANOS *(in the wings)*
Help!

(Zuniga enters, accompanied by soldiers.)

ZUNIGA *(spoken)*
Well, well, what's going on here?

(The cigar girls come out in a disorderly fashion.)

CIGAR GIRLS, 1ST SOPRANOS
Help! Help! Can't you hear?

CIGAR GIRLS, 2ND SOPRANOS
Help! Help! Soldier men!

PREMIER GROUPE DE FEMMES
C'est la Carmencita !

DEUXIÈME GROUPE DE FEMMES
Non, non, ce n'est pas elle !

PREMIER GROUPE
C'est la Carmencita !

DEUXIÈME GROUPE
Non, non, ce n'est pas elle !

PREMIER GROUPE
C'est elle ! Si fait, si fait, c'est elle ! Elle a porté les premiers coups !

DEUXIÈME GROUPE *(entourant le lieutenant)*
Ne les écoutez pas !

PREMIER GROUPE *(entourant le lieutenant)*
Ne les écoutez pas !
Monsieur, écoutez-nous !

DEUXIÈME GROUPE
Écoutez-nous, monsieur !

PREMIER GROUPE
Écoutez-nous, monsieur !

TOUTES LES FEMMES
Monsieur, écoutez-nous !

2^{ds} DESSUS *(tirent l'officier de leur côté)*
La Manuelita disait
Et répétait à voix haute,
Qu'elle achèterait sans faute
Un âne qui lui plaisait.

1^{rs} DESSUS *(même jeu)*
Alors la Carmencita,
Railleuse à son ordinaire,

ACT ONE SCENE 8

FIRST GROUP OF WOMEN
    It was Carmencita!

SECOND GROUP OF WOMEN
    No, no, it wasn't her!

FIRST GROUP
    It was Carmencita!

SECOND GROUP
    No, no, it wasn't her!

FIRST GROUP
    It was her! It was definitely her!
    She started it!

SECOND GROUP *(surrounding the lieutenant)*
    Don't listen to them!

FIRST GROUP *(surrounding the lieutenant)*
    Don't listen to them!
    Sir, listen to us!

SECOND GROUP
    Monsieur, listen to us!

FIRST GROUP
    Monsieur, listen to us!

ALL THE WOMEN
    Monsieur, listen to us!

2ND SOPRANOS *(taking the officer aside)*
    Manuelita said,
    and repeated it in a loud voice,
    that she could buy a good donkey
    which would give her pleasure.

1ST SOPRANOS *(in a similar way)*
    So Carmencita replied,
    mockingly, as usual,

Dit: « Un âne, pour quoi faire ?
Un balai te suffira. »

2^{ds} DESSUS

Manuelita riposte
Et dit à sa camarade:
« Pour certaine promenade,
Mon âne te servira ! »

1^{rs} DESSUS

« Et ce jour-là tu pourras
à bon droit faire la fière !
Deux laquais suivront derrière,
t'émouchant à tour de bras. »

TOUTES LES FEMMES

Là-dessus, toutes les deux
Se sont prises aux cheveux,
Toutes les deux, toutes les deux
Se sont prises aux cheveux !

ZUNIGA *(avec humeur)*

Au diable tout ce bavardage !
Au diable tout ce bavardage !

(à Don José)

Prenez, José, deux hommes avec vous
et voyez là-dedans qui cause ce tapage !

(Don José prend deux hommes avec lui. Les soldats entrent dans la manufacture. Pendant ce temps les femmes se pressent, se disputent entre elles.)

PREMIER GROUPE

C'est la Carmencita !

DEUXIÈME GROUPE

Non, non, ce n'est pas elle !

ACT ONE SCENE 8

>said: 'A donkey? What for?
>A broom would satisfy you!'

2ND SOPRANOS
>Manuelita replied
>and said to her friend:
>'For a certain type of walk
>my donkey would be perfect!'

1ST SOPRANOS
>'So on that day
>you'd have a right to be proud!
>Two lackeys would be following
>swatting off the flies.'

ALL THE WOMEN
>At that, both of them started pulling
>each other's hair,
>both of them, both of them
>pulling their hair!

ZUNIGA *(annoyed)*
>To hell with all this gossip!
>To hell with all this gossip!

(to Don José)

>Take two men with you, José,
>and go inside to see who's caused this row!

(Don José takes two men with him, and the soldiers go into the factory. Meanwhile the women crowd together, quarrelling among themselves.)

FIRST GROUP
>It was Carmencita!

SECOND GROUP
>No, no, it wasn't her!

PREMIER GROUPE
   Si fait, si fait; c'est elle !

DEUXIÈME GROUPE
   Pas du tout !

PREMIER GROUPE
   Elle a porté les premiers coups !

ZUNIGA *(assourdi, aux soldats)*
   Holà !
   Éloignez-moi toutes ces femmes-là !

CHŒUR DES CIGARIÈRES
   Monsieur !

SOLDATS *(repoussent les femmes et les écartent)*
   Tout doux !

CHŒUR DES CIGARIÈRES
   Monsieur !

SOLDATS
   Éloignez-vous !

CHŒUR DES CIGARIÈRES
   Monsieur !

SOLDATS
   Et taisez-vous !

CHŒUR DES CIGARIÈRES
   Monsieur !

CHŒUR DES CIGARIÈRES
   Ne les écoutez pas !

SOLDATS
   Tout doux ! Éloignez-vous !

CHŒUR DES CIGARIÈRES
   Monsieur, écoutez-nous !

ACT ONE SCENE 8

FIRST GROUP
Yes, yes; it was definitely her!

SECOND GROUP
No it wasn't!

FIRST GROUP
She started it!

ZUNIGA *(deafened, to the soldiers)*
Hey!
Get these women out of my way!

CIGAR GIRLS
Monsieur!

SOLDIERS *(pushing the women back and separating them)*
Quietly, quietly!

CIGAR GIRLS
Sir!

SOLDIERS
Get back!

CIGAR GIRLS
Sir!

SOLDIERS
And shut up!

CIGAR GIRLS
Sir!

CIGAR GIRLS
Don't listen to them!

SOLDIERS
Quietly please, and get back!

CIGAR GIRLS
Sir, listen!

SOLDATS
Éloignez-vous !

CHŒUR DES CIGARIÈRES
Écoutez-nous !

SOLDATS
Éloignez-vous !

CHŒUR DES CIGARIÈRES
Écoutez-nous !
Écoutez-nous, monsieur !

SOLDATS
Éloignez-vous
Et taisez-vous !

CHŒUR DES CIGARIÈRES
Écoutez-nous, monsieur !

SOLDATS
Tout doux, éloignez-vous !

(Les cigarières glissent entre les mains des soldats qui cherchent à les écarter. Elles se précipitent sur Zuniga et reprennent le chœur.)

ZUNIGA
Holà ! Soldats !

(Les soldats réussissent enfin à repousser les cigarières. Les femmes sont maintenues à distance autour de la place par une haie de dragons. Carmen paraît sur la porte de la manufacture amenée par Don José et suivie par deux dragons.)

1ʳˢ DESSUS
C'est la Carmencita
Qui porta les premiers coups !

SOLDIERS
    Get back!

CIGAR GIRLS
    Listen to us!

SOLDIERS
    Get back!

CIGAR GIRLS
    Listen to us!
    Listen to us, sir!

SOLDIERS
    Get back!
    And shut up!

CIGAR GIRLS
    Listen to us, sir!

SOLDIERS
    Quietly! Get back!

(The cigar girls slip through the hands of the soldiers, who are trying to push them away. They hurl themselves on Zuniga and resume their chorus.)

ZUNIGA
    Hey! Soldiers!

(The soldiers finally succeed in pushing back the cigar girls. The women are held at a distance around the square by a line of dragoons. Carmen appears at the factory gates escorted by Don José and followed by two dragoons.)

1ST SOPRANOS
    It was Carmencita
    who struck the first blows!

2ds DESSUS
  C'est la Manuelita
  Qui porta les premiers coups !

1rs DESSUS
  La Carmencita !

2ds DESSUS
  La Manuelita !

1rs DESSUS
  Si !

2ds DESSUS
  Non !

1rs DESSUS
  Si ! Si ! Si ! Si !

2ds DESSUS
  Non ! Non ! Non !

CHUŒR DES CIGARIÈRES
  Elle a porté les premiers coups !

SOLDATS
  Tout doux ! Tout doux ! Éloignez-vous !
  Éloignez-vous et taisez-vous !

1rs DESSUS
  C'est la Carmencita !

2ds DESSUS
  C'est la Manuelita !

SOLDATS
  Éloignez-vous !

1rs DESSUS
  C'est la Carmencita !

ACT ONE SCENE 8

2ND SOPRANOS
> It was Manuelita
> who struck the first blows!

1ST SOPRANOS
> Carmencita!

2ND SOPRANOS
> Manuelita!

1ST SOPRANOS
> Yes!

2ND SOPRANOS
> No!

1ST SOPRANOS
> Yes! Yes! Yes! Yes!

2ND SOPRANOS
> No! No! No!

CIGAR GIRLS
> She struck the first blows!

SOLDIERS
> Quietly! Quietly! Get back!
> Get back and shut up!

1ST SOPRANOS
> It was Carmencita!

2ND SOPRANOS
> It was Manuelita!

SOLDIERS
> Get back!

1ST SOPRANOS
> It was Carmencita!

2ds DESSUS
>   C'est la Manuelita !

SOLDATS
>   Éloignez-vous
>   Et taisez-vous, taisez-vous !
>   Éloignez-vous !

1rs DESSUS
>   C'est la Carmencita ! Carmencita !

2ds DESSUS
>   Manuelita ! Manuelita !

(La place est enfin dégagée. Les femmes sont maintenues à distance.)

Scène IX

Les mêmes, Carmen

Dialogue [ou Récitatif 5, p. 342]

ZUNIGA
>   Voyons, brigadier… Maintenant que nous avons un peu de silence… qu'est-ce que vous avez trouvé là-dedans ?…

DON JOSÉ
>   J'ai d'abord trouvé trois cents femmes, criant, hurlant, gesticulant, faisant un tapage à ne pas entendre Dieu tonner… D'un côté il y en avait une, les quatre fers en l'air, qui criait: Confession ! confession ! je suis morte… Elle avait sur la figure un X qu'on venait de lui marquer en deux coups de couteau… en face de la blessée j'ai vu…

(Il s'arrête sur un regard de Carmen.)

ZUNIGA
>   Eh bien ?…

DON JOSÉ
>   J'ai vu Mademoiselle…

2ND SOPRANOS
It was Manuelita!

SOLDIERS
Get back
and shut up, shut up!
Get back!

1ST SOPRANOS
It was Carmencita! Carmencita!

2ND SOPRANOS
Manuelita! Manuelita!

(The square is finally cleared. The women are kept at a distance.)

Scene 9

The same, Carmen

Dialogue [or Recitative 5, p. 343]

ZUNIGA
Let's see, Corporal... Now we've got some quiet... what did you find in there?

DON JOSÉ
First I found three hundred women shouting, screaming, waving their arms about and making such a row you couldn't have heard a thunderbolt from God himself... On one side there was one of them lying on her back screaming 'Get me a priest, get me a priest!... I'm dying!'... Someone had just carved an X on her face with two knife slashes... Opposite the wounded woman I saw...

(He hesitates at a look from Carmen.)

ZUNIGA
Well?...

DON JOSÉ
I saw the Señorita...

ZUNIGA
Mademoiselle Carmencita ?

DON JOSÉ
Oui, mon lieutenant…

ZUNIGA
Et qu'est-ce qu'elle disait, Mademoiselle Carmencita ?

DON JOSÉ
Elle ne disait rien, mon lieutenant, elle serrait les dents et roulait des yeux comme un caméléon.

CARMEN
On m'avait provoquée… je n'ai fait que me défendre… Monsieur le brigadier vous le dira…

(à Don José)

N'est-ce pas, monsieur le brigadier ?

DON JOSÉ *(après un moment d'hésitation)*
Tout ce que j'ai pu comprendre au milieu du bruit, c'est qu'une discussion s'était élevée entre ces deux dames, et qu'à la suite de cette discussion, mademoiselle, avec le couteau dont elle coupait le bout des cigares, avait commencé à dessiner des croix de saint André sur le visage de sa camarade…

(Zuniga regarde Carmen: celle-ci, après un regard à Don José et un très léger haussement d'épaules, est redevenue impassible.)

Le cas m'a paru clair. J'ai prié Mademoiselle de me suivre… Elle a d'abord fait un mouvement comme pour résister… puis elle s'est résignée… et m'a suivi, douce comme un mouton !

ZUNIGA
Et la blessure de l'autre femme ?

DON JOSÉ
Très légère, mon lieutenant, deux balafres à fleur de peau.

ACT ONE SCENE 9

ZUNIGA
Señorita Carmencita?

DON JOSÉ
Yes, Lieutenant...

ZUNIGA
And what did Señorita Carmencita have to say for herself?

DON JOSÉ
Nothing, Lieutenant, she just ground her teeth and rolled her eyes like a chameleon.

CARMEN
I was provoked... I was just acting in self-defence... The corporal will tell you...

(to Don José)

That's right, isn't it, Corporal?

DON JOSÉ *(after a moment's hesitation)*
All I could make out in the middle of that row was that a quarrel had broken out between the two ladies. At the end of it, the Señorita took the knife she was using to cut off the ends of the cigars and started drawing St Andrew's crosses on her companion's face...

(Zuniga looks at Carmen who, after a glance at Don José and a slight shrug of the shoulders, becomes impassive again.)

It seemed clear to me. I asked the Señorita to follow me... At first she tried to resist... Then she came quietly... and she followed me out as gently as a lamb.

ZUNIGA
And the other woman's wound?

DON JOSÉ
Nothing serious, Lieutenant, just two light scratches on her skin.

ZUNIGA *(à Carmen)*
Eh bien, la belle, vous avez entendu le brigadier ?...

(à Don José)

Je n'ai pas besoin de vous demander si vous avez dit la vérité.

DON JOSÉ
Foi de Navarrais, mon lieutenant !

(Carmen se retourne brusquement et regarde encore une fois Don José.)

ZUNIGA *(à Carmen)*
Eh bien... vous avez entendu ?...

N° 9 *Chanson et Mélodrame*

ZUNIGA *(parlé)*
Avez-vous quelque chose à répondre ?... Parlez, j'attends !

(Carmen, au lieu de répondre, se met à fredonner.)

CARMEN *(chantant)*
Tra la, la, la, la, la, la, la, [15]
Coupe-moi, brûle-moi,
Je ne te dirai rien !
Tra la, la, la, la, la, la, la,
Je brave tout, le feu,
Le fer et le ciel même !

ZUNIGA *(parlé) [ou Récitatif 6, p. 344]*
Ce ne sont pas des chansons que je te demande, c'est une réponse.

CARMEN *(chantant)*
Tra la, la, la, la, la, la, la,
Mon secret, je le garde
Et je le garde bien !
Tra la, la, la, la, la, la, la,
J'aime un autre et meurs
En disant que je l'aime !

ACT ONE SCENE 9

ZUNIGA *(to Carmen)*
   Well, you beauty, you heard what the corporal said?...

(to Don José)

   I don't need to ask if you're telling the truth.

DON JOSÉ
   On the word of a Navarrese, Lieutenant!

(Carmen suddenly turns to stare again at Don José.)

ZUNIGA *(to Carmen)*
   All right... You heard?...

No. 9 Song and Melodrama

ZUNIGA *(spoken)*
   Have you got anything to say?... Come on, I'm waiting!

(Instead of answering, Carmen starts humming.)

CARMEN *(singing)*
   Tra la, la, la, la, la, la, la,   [15]
   cut me, burn me,
   I won't say a thing!
   Tra la, la, la, la, la, la, la,
   I can brave anything, fire,
   iron, even the wrath of heaven itself!

ZUNIGA *(spoken) [or Recitative 6, p. 345]*
   It's not a song I want. It's a reply.

CARMEN *(singing)*
   Tra la, la, la, la, la, la, la,
   I'll keep my secret
   and I'll keep it well!
   Tra la, la, la, la, la, la, la,
   there's someone I love,
   but I would die rather than say who!

ZUNIGA *(parlé) [ou Récitatif 7, p. 344]*
   Ah ! ah ! nous le prenons sur ce ton-là !...

(à Don José)

   Ce qui est sûr, n'est-ce pas, c'est qu'il y a eu des coups de couteau et que c'est elle qui les a donnés !

(En ce moment, cinq ou six femmes à droite réussissent à forcer la ligne des factionnaires et se précipitent sur la scène en criant: « Oui, oui, c'est elle! » Une de ces femmes se trouve près de Carmen. Celle-ci lève la main et veut se jeter sur la femme. Don José arrête Carmen. Les soldats écartent les femmes et les repoussent cette fois tout à fait hors de la scène. Quelques sentinelles continuent à rester en vue gardant les abords de la place.)

ZUNIGA *(à Carmen, parlé) [ou Récitatif 8, p. 344]*
   Eh ! eh ! Vous avez la main leste décidément.

(aux soldats)

   Trouvez-moi une corde.

(Moment de silence pendant lequel Carmen se remet à fredonner de la façon la plus impertinente en regardant l'officier.)

CARMEN
   Tra la, la, la, la, la, la, etc.

UN SOLDAT *(apportant une corde, parlé)*
   Voilà, mon lieutenant.

ZUNIGA *(à Don José, parlé) [ou Récitatif 9, p. 344]*
   Prenez, et attachez-moi ces deux jolies mains.

(Carmen, sans faire la moindre résistance, tend en souriant ses deux mains à Don José.)

   C'est dommage vraiment, car elle est gentille... Mais si gentille que vous soyez, vous n'en irez pas moins faire un tour à la prison. Vous pourrez y chanter vos chansons de bohémienne. Le porte-clefs vous dira ce qu'il en pense.

ACT ONE SCENE 9

ZUNIGA *(spoken) [or Recitative 7, p. 345]*
   Aha! So that's the way you're taking it.

(to Don José)

   One thing's sure, isn't it? Someone got slashed with a knife, and she was the one who did it!

(At this point five or six women on the right manage to break through the line of soldiers and run onto the stage shouting 'Yes, yes, it was her!' One of these women gets close to Carmen, who raises her hand and is about to attack her. Don José restrains Carmen. The soldiers get the women away, this time pushing them completely offstage. A few sentries remain in sight guarding the entrances to the square.)

ZUNIGA *(to Carmen, spoken) [or Recitative 8, p. 345]*
   Well, well! What a quick hand you've got.

(to the soldiers)

   Get me a rope.

(A moment of silence, during which Carmen starts singing again in the most impertinent manner, looking straight at the officer.)

CARMEN
   Tra la, la, la, la, la, la, la, etc.

A SOLDIER *(bringing a rope, spoken)*
   Here you are, Lieutenant.

ZUNIGA *(to Don José, spoken) [or Recitative 9, p. 345]*
   Take it and tie those pretty hands together for me.

(Carmen, without the least resistance, holds her hands out to Don José with a smile.)

   It's a shame, really, she's a pretty girl. But pretty as you are, you are still going to spend a while in prison. You can sing your gypsy songs there. The jailer will tell you what he thinks of them.

(Les mains de Carmen sont liées. On la fait asseoir sur un escabeau devant le corps de garde. Elle reste là, immobile, les yeux à terre.)

Je vais écrire l'ordre.

(à Don José)

C'est vous qui la conduirez…

(Il sort.)

Scène X

Carmen, Don José

Un petit moment de silence. Carmen lève les yeux et regarde Don José. Celui-ci se détourne, s'éloigne de quelques pas, puis revient à Carmen, qui le regarde toujours.

Dialogue

CARMEN
 Où me conduirez-vous ?

DON JOSÉ
 À la prison, ma pauvre enfant…

CARMEN
 Hélas ! que deviendrai-je ? Seigneur officier, ayez pitié de moi !… Vous êtes si jeune, si gentil !…

(Don José ne répond pas, s'éloigne et revient, toujours sous le regard de Carmen.)

Cette corde, comme vous l'avez serrée, cette corde… j'ai les poignets brisés.

DON JOSÉ *(s'approchant de Carmen)*
 Si elle vous blesse, je puis la desserrer… Le lieutenant m'a dit de vous attacher les mains… il ne m'a pas dit…

(Il desserre la corde.)

(Carmen's hands are tied. She is made to sit down on a bench in front of the guardhouse. She sits motionless, staring at the ground.)

I'll go and write out the warrant.

(to Don José)

You can take her there yourself...

(He exits.)

Scene 10

Carmen, Don José

A moment of silence. Carmen raises her eyes and gazes at Don José, who turns away, walks off a few paces, then turns back to her. Carmen continues to gaze at him.

Dialogue

CARMEN
Where are you going to take me?

DON JOSÉ
To prison, my poor child...

CARMEN
Alas, what's to become of me? Officer, take pity on me... You're so young, so nice!...

(Don José does not answer; he moves away and returns, still closely watched by Carmen.)

This rope, you've tied it so tightly... it's breaking my wrists.

DON JOSÉ *(approaching Carmen)*
If it's hurting you I can loosen it... The lieutenant told me to bind your hands, he didn't tell me to...

(He loosens the rope.)

CARMEN *(bas)*
Laisse-moi m'échapper, je te donnerai un morceau de la bar lachi, une petite pierre qui te fera aimer de toutes les femmes.

DON JOSÉ *(s'éloignant)*
Nous ne sommes pas ici pour dire des balivernes... il faut aller à la prison. C'est la consigne, et il n'y a pas de remèdes.

(Silence)

CARMEN
Tout à l'heure vous avez dit : « foi de Navarrais... » Vous êtes des Provinces ?...

DON JOSÉ
Je suis d'Elizondo...

CARMEN
Et moi d'Etchalar...

DON JOSÉ *(s'arrêtant)*
D'Etchalar !... c'est à quatre heures d'Elizondo, Etchalar.

CARMEN
Oui, c'est là que je suis née... J'ai été emmenée par des bohémiens à Séville. Je travaillais à la manufacture pour gagner de quoi retourner en Navarre, près de ma pauvre mère qui n'a que moi pour soutien... On m'a insultée parce que je ne suis pas de ce pays de filous, de marchands d'oranges pourries, et ces coquines se sont mises toutes contre moi parce que je leur ai dit que tous leurs Jacques de Séville avec leurs couteaux ne feraient pas peur à un gars de chez nous avec son béret bleu et son maquila. Camarade, mon ami, ne ferez-vous rien pour une payse ?

DON JOSÉ
Vous êtes Navarraise, vous ?...

CARMEN
Sans doute.

CARMEN *(softly)*
> Let me escape and I'll give you a piece of *bar lachi* – it's a little stone that'll make all women fall in love with you.

DON JOSÉ *(moving away)*
> We're not here to talk nonsense... You've got to go to prison. Those are my orders, and there's nothing I can do about it.

(Silence)

CARMEN
> Just now you said, 'On the word of a Navarrese...' So you come from the Provinces?...

DON JOSÉ
> I'm from Elizondo...

CARMEN
> And I'm from Echalar...

DON JOSÉ *(coming to a halt)*
> Echalar!... Echalar's just four hours away from Elizondo.

CARMEN
> Yes, that's where I was born... Some gypsies brought me to Seville. I've been working at the factory to earn enough to get back to Navarre, to my poor mother, who's only got me to support her. I've been insulted because I'm not from this land of crooks and sellers of rotten oranges, and those stupid women ganged up against me because I told them that all their Seville lads swaggering round with knives wouldn't frighten any boy from our parts with his blue beret and *maquila*. Comrade... my friend, won't you help a fellow countrywoman?

DON JOSÉ
> So you really come from Navarre?...

CARMEN
> Of course I do.

DON JOSÉ
Allons donc... il n'y a pas un mot de vrai... vos yeux seuls, votre bouche, votre teint... Tout vous dit bohémienne...

CARMEN
Bohémienne, tu crois ?

DON JOSÉ
J'en suis sûr...

CARMEN
Au fait, je suis bien bonne de me donner la peine de mentir... Oui, je suis bohémienne, mais tu n'en feras moins ce que je te demande... Tu le feras parce que tu m'aimes...

DON JOSÉ
Moi ?

CARMEN
Eh ! oui, tu m'aimes... ne me dis pas non, je m'y connais ! Tes regards, la façon dont tu me parles. Et cette fleur que tu as gardée. Oh ! tu peux la jeter maintenant... cela n'y fera rien. Elle est restée assez de temps sur ton cœur ; le charme a opéré...

DON JOSÉ *(avec colère)*
Ne me parle plus, tu entends, je te défends de me parler...

CARMEN
C'est très bien, seigneur officier, c'est très bien. Vous me défendez de parler, je ne parlerai plus...

(Elle regarde Don José qui recule.)

N° 10 Chanson et Duo

CARMEN *(avec intention, en regardant souvent Don José qui se rapproche peu à peu)*
Près des remparts de Séville, [16]
Chez mon ami Lillas Pastia,
J'irai danser la séguedille

ACT ONE SCENE 10

DON JOSÉ
> Come on, I don't believe a word of it... Your eyes, your mouth, your skin... Everything about you says you're a gypsy...

CARMEN
> You think I'm a gypsy?

DON JOSÉ
> I'm sure of it...

CARMEN
> All right, so I needn't have gone to the trouble of telling lies... Yes, I'm a gypsy, but all the same, you're going to do what I ask you... You'll do it because you're in love with me...

DON JOSÉ
> Me?

CARMEN
> Oh yes, you're in love with me... don't tell me you're not, I know what I'm talking about! The way you look, the way you talk to me. And that flower you kept. Oh you can throw it away now... it won't make a difference. It's been close to your heart long enough, the spell is working...

DON JOSÉ *(angrily)*
> Don't speak to me again, do you hear? I forbid you to speak to me...

CARMEN
> Very well, officer, very well. If you forbid me to speak, I won't say any more...

(She looks at Don José, who steps back.)

No. 10 Song and Duet

CARMEN *(meaningfully, and glancing frequently at Don José, who gradually comes nearer)*
> Close by the ramparts of Seville [16]
> at my friend Lillas Pastia's
> I'll go to dance the seguidilla

Et boire du Manzanilla,
J'irai chez mon ami Lillas Pastia.
Oui, mais toute seule on s'ennuie,
Et les vrais plaisirs sont à deux ;
Donc, pour me tenir compagnie,
J'amènerai mon amoureux !
Mon amoureux !... il est au diable !
Je l'ai mis à la porte hier !
Mon pauvre cœur, très consolable,
Mon cœur est libre comme l'air !
J'ai des galants à la douzaine ;
Mais ils ne sont pas à mon gré.
Voici la fin de la semaine :
Qui veut m'aimer ? Je l'aimerai !
Qui veut mon âme ? Elle est à prendre !
Vous arrivez au bon moment !
Je n'ai guère le temps d'attendre,
Car avec mon nouvel amant
Près des remparts de Séville,
Chez mon ami Lillas Pastia,
J'irai danser la séguedille
Et boire du Manzanilla,
Oui, j'irai chez mon ami Pastia !

DON JOSÉ
Tais-toi, je t'avais dit de ne pas me parler !

CARMEN *(simplement)*
Je ne te parle pas, je chante pour moi-même,
Je chante pour moi-même !
Et je pense ! Il n'est pas défendu de penser !
Je pense à certain officier,
Qui m'aime
Et qu'à mon tour, oui, qu'à mon tour
Je pourrais bien aimer !

DON JOSÉ *(ému)*
Carmen !

and drink some Manzanilla,
I'll go to my friend Lillas Pastia's.
Yes, but going alone's not much fun:
it's better when you are two;
so just to keep me company
I'll take my lover along!
My lover!... He can go to hell!
I showed him the door yesterday!
My poor heart is quite consolable,
it's really as free as the air!
I've got admirers by the dozen,
but they're not really to my taste.
The weekend's coming:
who wants to be my lover? I'll love him!
Who wants my soul? It's there for the taking!
You've come along just at the right time!
I'll hardly have to wait at all,
for with my new lover
close by the ramparts of Seville,
at my friend's Lillas Pastia's,
I'll go and dance the seguidilla
and drink some Manzanilla,
yes, I'll go to my friend Lillas Pastia's!

DON JOSÉ
Be quiet, I told you not to talk to me!

CARMEN *(simply)*
I'm not speaking to you, I'm singing to myself!
I'm singing to myself!
And I'm thinking! There's no law against thinking!
I'm thinking of a certain officer
who is in love with me
and whose love I could myself
quite well return!

DON JOSÉ *(moved)*
Carmen!

CARMEN
>   Mon officier n'est pas un capitaine,
>   Pas même un lieutenant, il n'est que brigadier ;
>   Mais c'est assez pour une bohémienne
>   Et je daigne m'en contenter !

DON JOSÉ *(déliant la corde qui attache les mains de Carmen)*
>   Carmen, je suis comme un homme ivre,
>   Si je cède, si je me livre,
>   Ta promesse, tu la tiendras,
>   Ah ! si je t'aime, Carmen, Carmen, tu m'aimeras !

CARMEN
>   Oui.

DON JOSÉ
>   Chez Lillas Pastia,

CARMEN
>   Nous danserons

DON JOSÉ
>   Tu le promets !

CARMEN
>   La séguedille

DON JOSÉ
>   Carmen…

CARMEN
>   En buvant du Manzanilla,

DON JOSÉ
>   Tu le promets…

CARMEN *(à peine chanté, murmuré)*
>   Ah ! Près des remparts de Séville,
>   Chez mon ami Lillas Pastia,
>   Nous danserons la séguedille
>   Et boirons du Manzanilla.

CARMEN
> The officer I'm thinking of isn't a captain,
> nor even a lieutenant: he's only a corporal;
> but for a gypsy that's quite sufficient,
> and I'm resigned to make do with him!

DON JOSÉ *(untying the rope that binds Carmen's hands)*
> Carmen, I'm like a drunken man,
> if I give in, if I surrender,
> you'll keep your promise.
> Ah! If I love you, Carmen, Carmen, you'll love me!

CARMEN
> Yes.

DON JOSÉ
> At Lillas Pastia's

CARMEN
> We'll dance

DON JOSÉ
> You promise!

CARMEN
> The seguidilla

DON JOSÉ
> Carmen...

CARMEN
> Drinking Manzanilla,

DON JOSÉ
> You promise...

CARMEN *(hardly sung, murmured)*
> Ah! Close by the ramparts of Seville,
> at my friend Lillas Pastia's,
> we'll dance the Seguidilla
> and drink some Manzanilla.

Tra la la la la la la la la la la
Tra la la la la la la la la la la.

Scène XI

Les mêmes, le lieutenant Zuniga, puis les ouvrières, les soldats, les bourgeois

N° 11 Final [17]

DON JOSÉ *(parlé)*
Le lieutenant !... Prenez garde !

(Carmen va se replacer sur son escabeau, les mains derrière le dos. Rentre le lieutenant Zuniga.)

ZUNIGA *(à Don José)*
Voici l'ordre ; partez, et faites bonne garde.

CARMEN *(bas à Don José)*
En chemin je te pousserai,
Je te pousserai aussi fort que je le pourrai ;
Laisse-toi renverser... le reste me regarde !

(Elle se place entre les deux dragons. Don José à côté d'elle. Les femmes et les bourgeois pendant ce temps sont rentrés en scène toujours maintenus à distance par les dragons... Carmen traverse la scène de gauche à droite allant vers le pont...)

CARMEN *(fredonnant et riant au nez de Zuniga)*
L'amour est enfant de Bohème,
Il n'a jamais, jamais connu de loi ;
Si tu ne m'aimes pas, je t'aime ;
Si je t'aime, prends garde à toi !

(En arrivant à l'entrée du pont à droite, Carmen pousse Don José qui se laisse renverser. Confusion, désordre, Carmen s'enfuit. Arrivée au milieu du pont, elle s'arrête un instant, jette sa corde à la volée par-dessus le parapet du pont, et se sauve pendant que sur la scène, avec de grands éclats de rire, les cigarières entourent Zuniga.)

Tra la la la la la la la la la
tra la la la la la la la la la la.

Scene 11

The same, Lieutenant Zuniga, then the factory girls, the soldiers and the townspeople

No. 11 Finale [17]

DON JOSÉ *(spoken)*
It's the lieutenant!... Watch out!

(Carmen gets back onto the bench, her hands behind her back. Lieutenant Zuniga comes back in.)

ZUNIGA *(to Don José)*
Here's the warrant, off you go and guard her well.

CARMEN *(under her breath to Don José)*
When we're on the road I'll push you,
I'll push you as hard as I can.
Let yourself fall over... and leave the rest to me!

(She takes her place between the two dragoons. Don José is at her side. The women and the townspeople are back on stage but held at a distance by the dragoons... Carmen crosses the stage from left to right going towards the bridge...)

CARMEN *(singing and laughing right in Zuniga's face)*
Love was born to gypsy life
and has never obeyed any law,
if you don't love me, I'll love you;
If I love you, beware!

(When they have reached the entrance to the bridge on the right, Carmen pushes Don José, who lets himself fall backwards. Confusion, disorder, Carmen escapes. When she reaches the middle of the bridge she hesitates for a moment, throws the rope over the parapet of the bridge and escapes, while on the stage the cigar girls surround Zuniga in fits of laughter.)

DEUXIÈME ACTE

Scène I

Carmen, le lieutenant Zuniga, Moralès, officiers et bohémiennes

La taverne de Lillas Pastia. Tables à droite et à gauche. Carmen, Mercédès, Frasquita, le lieutenant Zuniga, Moralès et un lieutenant. C'est la fin d'un dîner. La table est en désordre. Les officiers et les bohémiennes fument des cigarettes. Deux bohémiens raclent de la guitare dans un coin de la taverne et deux bohémiennes, au milieu de la scène, dansent. Carmen est assise regardant danser les bohémiennes, le lieutenant Zuniga lui parle bas, mais elle ne fait aucune attention à lui. Elle se lève tout à coup et se met à chanter.

N° 11 *Chanson*

CARMEN
    Les tringles des sistres tintaient, [18]
    Avec un éclat métallique,
    Et sur cette étrange musique
    Les zingarellas se levaient.
    Tambours de basque allaient leur train,
    Et les guitares forcenées
    Grinçaient sous des mains obstinées,
    Même chanson, même refrain.
    Tra la la la
    Tra la la la
    Tra la la la la la la la.

(Sur ce refrain les bohémiennes dansent.)

FRASQUITA, MERCÉDÈS, CARMEN
    Tra la la la *etc.*

ACT TWO

Scene 1

Carmen, Lieutenant Zuniga, Moralès, officers and gypsies

Lillas Pastia's tavern. Tables to the right and left. Carmen, Mercédès, Frasquita, Lieutenant Zuniga, Moralès and another lieutenant. Dinner is coming to an end. The table is in disarray. Both officers and gypsies are smoking cigarettes. Two gypsy men are strumming guitars in a corner of the tavern and two gypsy women, in the centre of the stage, are dancing. Carmen is sitting down, watching the gypsies dance; Lieutenant Zuniga is speaking quietly to her, but she pays no attention to him. Suddenly she gets up and begins to sing.

No. 11 Song

CARMEN
    The jingling sistrums rattled   [18]
    with a metallic ring
    and at this strange sound
    the gypsy girls got to their feet.
    The tambourines began their rhythm
    while mad guitars
    ground away under relentless hands,
    the same song and the same refrain.
    Tra la la
    tra la la la
    tra la la la la la la la.

(At the sound of this refrain the gypsies dance.)

FRASQUITA, MERCÉDÈS, CARMEN
    Tra la la la *etc.*

CARMEN
>   Les anneaux de cuivre et d'argent
>   Reluisaient sur les peaux bistrées ;
>   D'orange ou de rouge zébrées
>   Les étoffes flottaient au vent.
>   La danse au chant se mariait,
>   D'abord indécise et timide,
>   Plus vive ensuite et plus rapide…
>   Cela montait, montait, montait, montait !
>   Tra la la la
>   tra la la la *etc.*

FRASQUITA, MERCÉDÈS, CARMEN
>   Tra la la la *etc.*

CARMEN
>   Les bohémiens, à tour de bras,
>   De leurs instruments faisaient rage,
>   Et cet éblouissant tapage
>   Ensorcelait les zingaras
>   Sous le rythme de la chanson,
>   Ardentes, folles, enfiévrées,
>   Elles se laissaient, enivrées,
>   Emporter par le tourbillon !
>   Tra la la la *etc.*

FRASQUITA, MERCÉDÈS, CARMEN
>   Tra la la la *etc.*

(Mouvement de danse très rapide, très violent. Carmen elle-même danse et vient, avec les dernières notes de l'orchestre, tomber haletante sur un banc de la taverne. Après la danse, Lillas Pastia se met à tourner autour des officiers d'un air embarrassé.)

Dialogue [ou Récitatif 10, p. 346]

ZUNIGA
>   Vous avez quelque chose à nous dire, maître Lillas Pastia ?

CARMEN

    The copper and silver of the rings
    shone out against the dusky skins;
    the orange and red stripes
    of their fabrics swirled in the wind.
    The dance and the song were wedded,
    at first a little vague and shy,
    and then livelier and faster...
    And louder and louder and louder still!
    Tra la la la
    tra la la la *etc.*

FRASQUITA, MERCÉDÈS, CARMEN

    Tra la la la *etc.*

CARMEN

    The gypsies with forceful arms
    beat on their instruments wildly,
    and the deafening din
    bewitched the gypsy girls
    carried away by the rhythm of the song,
    ardent, mad and feverish,
    they let themselves be prey
    to the whirlwind!
    Tra la la la *etc.*

FRASQUITA, MERCÉDÈS, CARMEN

    Tra la la la *etc.*

(A dance which is both very fast and very violent. Carmen herself dances, and at the last notes of the orchestral music falls onto one of the benches in the tavern, out of breath. After the dance Lillas Pastia begins to circle round the officers awkwardly.)

Dialogue [or Recitative 10, p. 347]

ZUNIGA

    Are you trying to tell us something, Master Lillas Pastia?

PASTIA
Mon Dieu, messieurs...

MORALÈS
Parle, voyons...

PASTIA
Il commence à se faire tard... et je suis, plus que personne, obligé d'observer les règlements. Monsieur le corrégidor étant assez mal disposé à mon égard... je ne sais pas pourquoi il est mal disposé...

ZUNIGA
Je le sais très bien, moi. C'est parce que ton auberge est le rendez-vous ordinaire de tous les contrebandiers de la province.

PASTIA
Que ce soit pour cette raison ou pour une autre, je suis obligé de prendre garde... or, je vous le répète, il commence à se faire tard.

MORALÈS
Cela veut dire que tu nous mets à la porte !...

PASTIA
Oh ! Non, messieurs les officiers, oh ! non ! Je vous fais seulement observer que mon auberge devrait être fermée depuis dix minutes...

ZUNIGA
Dieu sait ce qui s'y passe dans ton auberge une fois qu'elle est fermée...

PASTIA
Oh ! mon lieutenant...

ZUNIGA
Enfin ! nous avons encore, avant l'appel, le temps d'aller passer une heure au théâtre. Vous y viendrez avec nous, n'est-ce pas, les belles ?

(Pastia fait signe aux bohémiennes de refuser.)

FRASQUITA
Non, messieurs les officiers, non, nous restons ici, nous.

ACT TWO SCENE I

PASTIA
For heaven's sake, gentlemen...

MORALÈS
Out with it, come on...

PASTIA
It's getting late... And I've got to obey the regulations more carefully than anyone else. The corregidor's got something against me. I can't imagine what it is...

ZUNIGA
I myself know perfectly well what it is. It's because your inn is the regular haunt of every smuggler in the province.

PASTIA
Whether that's the reason or whether it's something else, I've got to be careful... so, let me repeat, it's getting late.

MORALÈS
Does that mean you're throwing us out?...

PASTIA
Oh no, officers, oh no! I'm just saying that my inn should have been closed ten minutes ago...

ZUNIGA
God alone knows what goes on in your inn after closing time...

PASTIA
Oh! Lieutenant...

ZUNIGA
Oh well, we've still got time to spend an hour at the theatre before roll-call. You'll come with us, won't you girls?

(Pastia signals to the gypsy girls to refuse.)

FRASQUITA
No, officers, we won't, we're going to stay here.

ZUNIGA
   Comment, vous ne viendrez pas...

MERCÉDÈS
   C'est impossible...

MORALÈS
   Mercédès !

MERCÉDÈS
   Je regrette...

MORALÈS
   Frasquita !

FRASQUITA
   Je suis désolée...

ZUNIGA
   Mais toi, Carmen, je suis bien sûr que tu ne refuseras pas...

CARMEN
   C'est ce qui vous trompe, mon lieutenant... je refuse et encore plus nettement qu'elles deux, si c'est possible...

(Pendant que le lieutenant Zuniga parle à Carmen, Moralès et les deux autres lieutenants essaient de fléchir Frasquita et Mercédès.)

ZUNIGA
   Tu m'en veux ?

CARMEN
   Pourquoi vous en voudrais-je ?

ZUNIGA
   Parce qu'il y a un mois j'ai eu la cruauté de t'envoyer à la prison.

CARMEN *(comme si elle ne se rappelait pas)*
   À la prison ?

ACT TWO SCENE I

ZUNIGA
What, you won't come?

MERCÉDÈS
We can't...

MORALÈS
Mercédès!

MERCÉDÈS
Forgive me...

MORALÈS
Frasquita!

FRASQUITA
I'm very sorry...

ZUNIGA
How about you, Carmen, I'm sure you won't refuse...

CARMEN
That's where you're wrong, Lieutenant... I refuse too, and even more firmly than those two, if that's possible...

(While Lieutenant Zuniga speaks to Carmen, Moralès and the other two lieutenants are trying to make Frasquita and Mercédès change their minds.)

ZUNIGA
Are you angry with me?

CARMEN
Why should I be?

ZUNIGA
Because I was cruel enough to send you to prison last month.

CARMEN *(as if she can't remember)*
To prison?

ZUNIGA
J'étais de service, je ne pouvais pas faire autrement.

CARMEN *(même jeu)*
À la prison ?... je ne me souviens pas d'être allée à la prison.

ZUNIGA
Je sais pardieu bien que tu n'y es pas allée... le brigadier qui était chargé de te conduire ayant jugé à propos de te laisser échapper... et de se faire dégrader et emprisonner pour cela...

CARMEN *(sérieuse)*
Dégrader et emprisonner ?...

ZUNIGA
Mon Dieu oui... on n'a pas voulu admettre qu'une aussi petite main ait été assez forte pour renverser un homme...

CARMEN
Oh !

ZUNIGA
Cela n'a pas paru naturel...

CARMEN
Et ce pauvre garçon est redevenu simple soldat ?...

ZUNIGA
Oui et il a passé un mois en prison.

CARMEN
Mais il en est sorti ?

ZUNIGA
Depuis hier seulement !

CARMEN *(faisant claquer ses castagnettes)*
Tout est bien puisqu'il en est sorti, tout est bien.

ZUNIGA
À la bonne heure, tu te consoles vite...

ACT TWO SCENE I

ZUNIGA
I was on duty, I had no choice.

CARMEN *(as before)*
To prison? I don't remember going to prison.

ZUNIGA
I know damned well you didn't go… The corporal who was assigned to take you there thought fit to let you escape… And he was demoted and imprisoned for it…

CARMEN *(gravely)*
Demoted and imprisoned?

ZUNIGA
Heavens, yes. No one believed that such a tiny hand was strong enough to knock a man over…

CARMEN
Oh!

ZUNIGA
It didn't look convincing…

CARMEN
And that poor boy is back in the ranks?

ZUNIGA
Yes, and he's spent a month in prison.

CARMEN
Is he out now?

ZUNIGA
Only since yesterday!

CARMEN *(clicking her castanets)*
That's all right if he's out now, that's all right.

ZUNIGA
Well, I must say, you get over things quickly enough…

CARMEN *(à part)*
　Et j'ai raison…

(haut)

　Si vous m'en croyez, vous ferez comme moi… vous voulez nous emmener, nous ne voulons pas vous suivre… vous vous consolerez…

MORALÈS
　Il faudra bien.

(La scène est interrompue par un chœur chanté dans la coulisse.)

N° 12 Chœur et Ensemble

CHŒUR DES AMIS D'ESCAMILLO *(derrière la scène)*
　Vivat ! vivat le torero !
　Vivat ! vivat Escamillo !
　Vivat ! vivat ! vivat !

ZUNIGA *(parlé) [ou Récitatif 11, p. 348]*
　Qu'est-ce que c'est que ça ?

MERCÉDÈS *(parlé)*
　Une promenade aux flambeaux…

MORALÈS *(parlé)*
　Et qui promène-t-on ?

CHŒUR
　Vivat ! vivat le torero !
　Vivat ! vivat Escamillo !
　Vivat ! vivat ! vivat !

FRASQUITA *(parlé)*
　[supprimé dans la version avec récitatifs, suivi directement par le N° 13, p. 198]
　Je le reconnais…

CHŒUR
　Vivat !

CARMEN *(aside)*
>And I'm right...

(aloud)

>If you follow my advice, you'd do as I do... you want to take us off, we don't want to follow you... you'll get over it...

MORALÈS
>That's the way.

(The scene is interrupted by a chorus singing offstage.)

No. 12 Chorus and Ensemble

CHORUS OF ESCAMILLO'S FRIENDS *(behind the stage)*
>Long live the bullfighter!
>Long live Escamillo!
>Vivat! Vivat! Vivat!

ZUNIGA *(spoken) [or Recitative 11, p. 349]*
>What's going on?

MERCÉDÈS *(spoken)*
>A torchlight procession...

MORALÈS *(spoken)*
>And who's being honoured?

CHORUS
>Long live the bullfighter!
>Long live Escamillo!
>Vivat! Vivat! Vivat!

FRASQUITA *(spoken)*
>*[omitted in recitative version, cut to No. 13, p. 199]*
>I recognize him...

CHORUS
>Vivat!

FRASQUITA *(parlé)*
   C'est Escamillo... un torero qui s'est fait remarquer aux dernières courses de Grenade et qui promet d'égaler la gloire de Montes et de Pepe Illo...

MORALÈS
   Pardieu, il faut le faire venir ! Nous boirons en son honneur !

ZUNIGA
   C'est cela, je vais l'inviter.

(Il va à la fenêtre.)

   Monsieur le torero... voulez-vous nous faire l'amitié de monter ici ? Vous y trouverez des gens qui aiment fort tous ceux qui, comme vous, ont de l'adresse et du courage...

(quittant la fenêtre)

   Il vient...

PASTIA *(suppliant)*
   Messieurs, les officiers, je vous avais dit...

ZUNIGA
   Ayez la bonté de nous laisser tranquille, maître Lillas Pastia, et faites-nous apporter de quoi boire...

(Entrée d'Escamillo et de ses amis.)

ZUNIGA, CHŒUR (OFFICIERS et AMIS D'ESCAMILLO)
   Vivat ! vivat le torero !

FRASQUITA, MERCÉDÈS, CARMEN, MORALÈS, ZUNIGA, CHŒUR
   Vivat ! vivat le torero !

ZUNIGA, CHŒUR
   Vivat ! vivat Escamillo !

ACT TWO SCENE 1

FRASQUITA *(spoken)*
It's Escamillo... He's a bullfighter who made his name at the recent corrida in Granada; he'll probably become as famous as Montes and Pepe Illo...

MORALÈS
Good Lord, we'd better have him in here! We'll drink to him.

ZUNIGA
That's right, I'll invite him in.

(He goes to the window.)

Torero! Will you do us the honour of coming up? You'll find people here who admire those like you who show skill and courage...

(leaving the window)

He's coming...

PASTIA *(begging them)*
Officers, I've told you...

ZUNIGA
Be good enough to leave us in peace, Master Lillas Pastia, and bring us something to drink...

(Enter Escamillo and his friends.)

ZUNIGA, CHORUS (OFFICERS and FRIENDS OF ESCAMILLO)
Long live the bullfighter!

FRASQUITA, MERCÉDÈS, CARMEN, MORALÈS, ZUNIGA, CHORUS
Long live the bullfighter!

ZUNIGA, CHORUS
Long live Escamillo!

FRASQUITA, MERCÉDÈS, CARMEN, ANDRÈS, ZUNIGA, CHŒUR
Vivat ! vivat Escamillo !
Vivat ! vivat !

(Paraît Escamillo.)

Scène II

Les mêmes, Escamillo

Dialogue [supprimé dans la version avec récitatifs]

ZUNIGA
Ces dames et nous, vous remercions d'avoir accepté notre invitation ; nous n'avons pas voulu vous laisser passer sans boire avec vous au grand art de la tauromachie…

ESCAMILLO
Messieurs les officiers, je vous remercie.

N° 13 Couplets

ESCAMILLO
Votre toast, je peux vous le rendre, [19]
Señors, señors, car avec les soldats
Oui, les toreros peuvent s'entendre ;
Pour plaisirs, pour plaisirs,
Ils ont les combats !
Le cirque est plein, c'est jour de fête !
Le cirque est plein du haut en bas ;
Les spectateurs perdant la tête,
Les spectateurs s'interpellent à grands fracas !
Apostrophes, cris et tapage
Poussés jusques à la fureur !
Car c'est la fête du courage !
C'est la fête des gens de cœur !
Allons ! en garde !
Allons ! allons ! ah !

ACT TWO SCENE 2

FRASQUITA, MERCÉDÈS, CARMEN, ANDRÈS, ZUNIGA, CHORUS
Long live Escamillo!
Vivat! Vivat!

(Escamillo appears.)

Scene 2

The same, Escamillo

Dialogue [omitted in recitative version]

ZUNIGA
These ladies and ourselves thank you for accepting our invitation. We didn't want to let you pass by without drinking to the great art of bullfighting with you...

ESCAMILLO
Gentlemen, I thank you.

No. 13 Couplets

ESCAMILLO
I can return your toast, [19]
señors, señors, for with soldiers
bullfighters can get on very well:
their pleasures, their pleasures
are in fighting!
The ring is full, it's the day of the fiesta!
The ring is full from top to bottom;
the crowd are beside themselves,
yelling noisily!
Protests, shouts and uproar
approach the frontiers of fury!
For this fiesta celebrates courage!
It's the fiesta of the heartiest men!
Let's go! On guard!
Let's go! Let's go! Ah!

(légèrement, avec fatuité)

> Toréador, en garde !
> Toréador ! Toréador !
> Et songe bien, oui, songe en combattant,
> Qu'un œil noir te regarde
> Et que l'amour t'attend,
> Toréador, l'amour, l'amour t'attend !

TOUS
> Toréador, en garde !
> Toréador ! Toréador !

ESCAMILLO
> Et songe bien, oui, songe en combattant,
> Qu'un œil noir te regarde et que l'amour t'attend,
> Toréador, l'amour, l'amour t'attend !

CARMEN
> En combattant, songe
> Qu'un œil noir te regarde
> Et que l'amour, l'amour, l'amour t'attend !

MORALÈS, ZUNIGA
> En combattant, oui, songe
> Que l'amour, l'amour, l'amour t'attend !

CHŒUR, FRASQUITA, MERCÉDÈS
> En combattant, oui, songe que l'amour t'attend !
> Et songe bien, oui, songe en combattant
> Qu'un œil noir te regarde
> Et que l'amour t'attend,
> Oui, l'amour t'attend !

(Entre les deux couplets, Carmen remplit le verre d'Escamillo.)

ESCAMILLO
> Tout d'un coup, on fait silence, on fait silence...
> Ah ! que se passe-t-il ?
> Plus de cris, c'est l'instant !

(lightly and smugly)

> Toreador, on guard!
> Toreador! Toreador!
> And bear in mind, yes, bear in mind while fighting,
> that dark eyes are fixed on you
> and that love awaits you,
> Toreador, love, yes, love awaits you!

ALL
> Toreador, on guard!
> Toreador! Toreador!

ESCAMILLO
> And bear in mind, yes bear in mind while fighting,
> that dark eyes are fixed on you, and that love awaits you,
> Toreador, love, yes love awaits you!

CARMEN
> Bear in mind while fighting,
> that dark eyes are fixed on you
> and that love awaits you!

MORALÈS, ZUNIGA
> While fighting, remember
> that love, yes, love awaits you!

CHORUS, FRASQUITA, MERCÉDÈS
> While fighting, remember that love awaits you!
> Bear in mind, while fighting,
> that dark eyes are fixed on you
> and that love awaits you!
> Yes, love awaits you!

(Between the two verses Carmen tops up Escamillo's glass.)

ESCAMILLO
> Suddenly everyone is quiet, everyone is silent…
> Ah! What's going on?
> No more shouting: the moment has come!

Le taureau s'élance
En bondissant hors du toril !
Il s'élance, il entre, il frappe !... un cheval roule,
En entraînant un picador.
« Ah ! Bravo ! Toro ! » hurle la foule ;
Le taureau va... il vient... il vient et frappe encor !
En secouant ses banderilles,
Plein de fureur, il court !...
Le cirque est plein de sang !
On se sauve on franchit les grilles !...
C'est ton tour maintenant !
Allons ! en garde !
Allons ! allons ! ah !

(légèrement, avec fatuité)

Toréador, en garde !
Toréador ! Toréador !
Et songe bien, oui,
Songe en combattant
Qu'un œil noir te regarde
Et que l'amour t'attend,
Toréador, l'amour, l'amour t'attend !

TOUS

Toréador, en garde !
Toréador ! Toréador !
Et songe bien, oui, songe en combattant,
Qu'un œil noir te regarde
Et que l'amour t'attend,
Toréador, l'amour, l'amour t'attend !

(On boit, on échange des poignées de main avec le torero.)

Dialogue [ou Récitatif 12, p. 350]

PASTIA

Messieurs les officiers, je vous en prie.

ACT TWO SCENE 2

The bull charges
bounding out of its pen!
He charges! Coming in he strikes! A horse falls over
and his picador with him.
'Bravo to the bull!' shouts the crowd,
the bull moves back and forth and strikes again!
Shaking the banderillas,
mad with fury he charges!
The ring runs with blood!
Everyone gets out of the way, getting behind the fences!…
It's your turn now!
Come on, on guard!
Come on, ah!

(lightly and smugly)

Toreador, on guard!
Toreador! Toreador!
And bear in mind, yes,
bear in mind, while fighting,
that dark eyes are fixed on you
and that love awaits you,
Toreador, love, yes, love awaits you!

ALL
Toreador, on guard!
Toreador! Toreador!
And bear in mind, yes bear in mind while fighting,
that dark eyes are fixed on you
and that love awaits you,
Toreador, love, yes, love awaits you!

(Everyone drinks and shakes the torero's hand.)

Dialogue [or Recitative 12, p. 351]

PASTIA
Officers, please!

ZUNIGA
C'est bien, c'est bien, nous partons.

(Les officiers commencent à se préparer à partir. Escamillo se trouve près de Carmen.)

ESCAMILLO
Dis-moi ton nom, et la première fois que je frapperai le taureau, ce sera ton nom que je prononcerai.

CARMEN
Je m'appelle la Carmencita.

ESCAMILLO
La Carmencita ?

CARMEN
Carmen, la Carmencita, comme tu voudras.

ESCAMILLO
Et bien, Carmen, ou la Carmencita, si je m'avisais de t'aimer et de vouloir être aimé de toi, qu'est-ce que tu me répondrais ?

CARMEN
Je répondrais que tu peux m'aimer tout à ton aise, mais que quant à être aimé de moi pour le moment, il n'y faut pas songer !

ESCAMILLO
Ah !

CARMEN
C'est comme ça.

ESCAMILLO
J'attendrai alors et je me contenterai d'espérer…

CARMEN
Il n'est pas défendu d'attendre et il est toujours agréable d'espérer.

MORALÈS *(à Frasquita et Mercédès)*
Vous ne venez pas décidément ?

ACT TWO SCENE 2

ZUNIGA
All right, all right, we're going!

(The officers prepare to leave. Escamillo finds himself close to Carmen.)

ESCAMILLO
Tell me your name, and it will be your name that I'll utter as I kill the first bull.

CARMEN
I'm called Carmencita.

ESCAMILLO
Carmencita?

CARMEN
Carmen, Carmencita, as you like.

ESCAMILLO
All right, Carmen, or Carmencita, if I were inclined to fall in love with you and wanted you to return my love, what would you say?

CARMEN
I would reply that you're perfectly free to love me, but that at the moment you can't hope to be loved by me!

ESCAMILLO
Ah!

CARMEN
That's how it is.

ESCAMILLO
In that case I'll wait and will content myself with hoping...

CARMEN
It's not forbidden to wait, and always nice to hope.

MORALÈS *(to Frasquita and Mercédès)*
Are you definitely not coming?

MERCÉDÈS ET FRASQUITA *(sur un nouveau signe de Pastia)*
Mais non, mais non…

MORALÈS *(à Zuniga)*
Mauvaise campagne.

ZUNIGA
Bah ! la bataille n'est pas encore perdue…

(bas à Carmen)

Écoute-moi, Carmen, puisque tu ne veux pas venir avec nous, c'est moi qui dans une heure reviendrai ici…

CARMEN
Ici ?…

ZUNIGA
Oui, dans une heure… après l'appel.

CARMEN
Je ne vous conseille pas de revenir…

ZUNIGA *(riant)*
Je reviendrai tout de même.

(haut)

Nous partons avec vous, torero, et nous nous joindrons au cortège qui vous accompagne.

ESCAMILLO
C'est un grand honneur pour moi, je tâcherai de ne pas m'en montrer indigne lorsque je combattrai sous vos yeux.

N° 13bis Chœur [orchestre seul dans la version avec récitatifs]

CHŒUR DES AMIS D'ESCAMILLO
Toréador, en garde !
Toréador ! Toréador !
Et songe bien, oui, songe en combattant
Qu'un œil noir te regarde

ACT TWO SCENE 2

MERCÉDÈS AND FRASQUITA *(again at a sign from Pastia)*
Definitely not, definitely not...

MORALÈS *(to Zuniga)*
Your campaign's not going too well.

ZUNIGA
Bah! Well, the battle's not lost yet...

(softly to Carmen)

Listen, Carmen, since you don't want to come with us, I'll come back here in an hour...

CARMEN
Here?

ZUNIGA
Yes, in an hour... after roll-call.

CARMEN
I'd advise you not to come back...

ZUNIGA *(laughing)*
All the same I'm coming back.

(out loud)

We'll come with you, torero, and we'll join the procession which will accompany you.

ESCAMILLO
That's a great honour for me, I'll do my best not to show myself as unworthy when I fight with you all watching.

No. 13b Chorus [orchestra only in recitative version]

CHORUS OF ESCAMILLO'S FRIENDS
Toreador, on guard!
Toreador! Toreador!
And bear in mind, while fighting,
that dark eyes are fixed on you

Et que l'amour t'attend,
Toréador ! l'amour, l'amour t'attend !

(Tout le monde sort, excepté Carmen, Frasquita, Mercédès et Lillas Pastia.)

Scène III

Carmen, Frasquita, Mercédès, Pastia

Dialogue [ou Récitatif 13, p. 352]

FRASQUITA *(à Pastia)*
Pourquoi étais-tu si pressé de les faire partir et pourquoi nous as-tu fait signe de ne pas les suivre ?...

PASTIA
Le Dancaïre et le Remendado viennent d'arriver... ils ont à vous parler de vos affaires, des affaires d'Égypte.

CARMEN
Le Dancaïre et le Remendado ?...

PASTIA *(ouvrant une porte et appelant du geste)*
Oui, les voici... tenez...

(Entrent Le Dancaïre et Le Remendado. Pastia ferme les portes, met les volets, etc., etc.)

Scène IV

Carmen, Frasquita, Mercédès, Le Dancaïre, Le Remendado

FRASQUITA
Eh bien, les nouvelles ?

LE DANCAÏRE
Pas trop mauvaises les nouvelles, nous arrivons de Gibraltar...

LE REMENDADO
Jolie ville, Gibraltar !... on y voit des Anglais, beaucoup d'Anglais, de jolis hommes les Anglais : un peu froids, mais distingués.

ACT TWO SCENE 3

and that love awaits you!
Toreador! Love, yes, love awaits you!

(Exeunt all, except Carmen, Frasquita, Mercédès et Lillas Pastia.)

Scene 3

Carmen, Frasquita, Mercédès, Pastia

Dialogue [or Recitative 13, p. 353]

FRASQUITA *(to Pastia)*
   Why were you so keen to get rid of them, and why did you signal to us not to go with them?

PASTIA
   Dancaïre and Remendado have just arrived... they have some business to talk to you about, Egyptian business.

CARMEN
   Dancaïre and Remendado?

PASTIA *(opening a door and signalling them to enter)*
   Yes, they're here... come on...

(Enter Dancaïre and Remendado. Pastia shuts the doors and pulls down the shutters, etc., etc.)

Scene 4

Carmen, Frasquita, Mercédès, Dancaïre, Remendado

FRASQUITA
   So what's the news?

DANCAÏRE
   Not bad, we've just come back from Gibraltar...

REMENDADO
   Nice town, Gibraltar! You see the English there, lots of them. Nice fellows the English: a bit cold, but distinguished.

LE DANCAÏRE
Remendado !...

LE REMENDADO
Patron.

LE DANCAÏRE *(mettant la main sur son couteau)*
Vous comprenez ?

LE REMENDADO
Parfaitement, patron...

LE DANCAÏRE
Taisez-vous alors. Nous arrivons de Gibraltar, nous avons arrangé avec un patron de navire l'embarquement de marchandises anglaises. Nous irons les attendre près de la côte, nous en cacherons une partie dans la montagne et nous ferons passer le reste. Tous nos camarades ont été prévenus... ils sont ici, cachés, mais c'est de vous trois surtout que nous avons besoin... vous allez partir avec nous...

CARMEN *(riant)*
Pour quoi faire ? pour vous aider à porter les ballots ?...

LE REMENDADO
Oh ! non faire porter des ballots à des dames... ça ne serait pas distingué.

LE DANCAÏRE *(menaçant)*
Remendado ?

LE REMENDADO
Oui, patron.

LE DANCAÏRE
Nous ne vous ferons pas porter des ballots, mais nous aurons besoin de vous pour autre chose.

N° 14 *Quintette*

LE DANCAÏRE
Nous avons en tête une affaire ! [20]

ACT TWO SCENE 4

DANCAÏRE
Remendado!

REMENDADO
Boss.

DANCAÏRE *(putting his hand on his knife)*
Understand?

REMENDADO
Perfectly, boss...

DANCAÏRE
Well then, listen. We've just come back from Gibraltar, we've arranged with a ship's captain to unload some English goods. We're going to wait for them by the coast and hide some in the mountains and bring the rest through. All our comrades have been warned... they're here, hidden, but it's you three we need... so you're going to come with us...

CARMEN *(laughing)*
To do what? To help you carry the packages?

REMENDADO
Oh no! Making women carry the packages... that wouldn't be very proper.

DANCAÏRE *(threateningly)*
Remendado?

REMENDADO
Yes, boss.

DANCAÏRE
It'll be us who'll carry the packages; we need you for other purposes.

No. 14 Quintet

DANCAÏRE
We've got some business in mind! [20]

FRASQUITA, MERCÉDÈS
Est-elle bonne, dites-nous ?

LE DANCAÏRE
Elle est admirable, ma chère ;
Mais nous avons besoin de vous.

LE REMENDADO
Oui, nous avons besoin de vous.

CARMEN
De nous ?

LE DANCAÏRE
De vous !

MERCÉDÈS
De nous ?

LE REMENDADO
De vous !

FRASQUITA
De nous ?

LE REMENDADO, LE DANCAÏRE
De vous !

FRASQUITA, MERCÉDÈS, CARMEN
De nous ?
Quoi, vous avez besoin de nous ?

LE REMENDADO, LE DANCAÏRE
Oui, nous avons besoin de vous !

CARMEN
De nous ?

LE DANCAÏRE
De vous !

ACT TWO SCENE 4

FRASQUITA, MERCÉDÈS
Is it a good plan? Do tell us!

DANCAÏRE
It's a good plan, my dear,
but we need you.

REMENDADO
Yes, we need you.

CARMEN
Us?

DANCAÏRE
You!

MERCÉDÈS
Us?

REMENDADO
You!

FRASQUITA
Us?

REMENDADO, DANCAÏRE
You!

FRASQUITA, MERCÉDÈS, CARMEN
Us?
What, you need us?

REMENDADO, DANCAÏRE
Yes, we need you!

CARMEN
Us?

DANCAÏRE
You!

MERCÉDÈS
　De nous ?

LE REMENDADO
　De vous !

FRASQUITA
　De nous ?

LE DANCAÏRE
　De vous !

FRASQUITA, MERCÉDÈS, CARMEN
　De nous ?

LE REMENDADO, LE DANCAÏRE
　De vous !

FRASQUITA, MERCÉDÈS, CARMEN
　Quoi, vous avez besoin de nous ?

LE REMENDADO, LE DANCAÏRE
　Oui, nous avons besoin de vous !
　Car nous l'avouons humblement
　Et fort respectueusement,
　Oui, nous l'avouons humblement :
　Quand il s'agit de tromperie,
　De duperie,
　De volerie,
　Il est toujours bon, sur ma foi,
　D'avoir les femmes avec soi.
　Et sans elles,
　Mes toutes belles,
　On ne fait jamais rien
　De bien !

FRASQUITA, MERCÉDÈS, CARMEN
　Quoi, sans nous jamais rien
　De bien ?

ACT TWO SCENE 4

MERCÉDÈS
  Us?

REMENDADO
  You!

FRASQUITA
  Us?

DANCAÏRE
  You!

FRASQUITA, MERCÉDÈS, CARMEN
  Us?

REMENDADO, DANCAÏRE
  You!

FRASQUITA, MERCÉDÈS, CARMEN
  What, you need us?

REMENDADO, DANCAÏRE
  Yes, we need you!
  Because we admit to you with humility
  and the utmost respect,
  yes, with the utmost humility,
  that when it comes to deceit,
  trickery
  and theft,
  it's always good, believe me,
  to have women with you.
  And without them,
  my beauties,
  it never works out
  for the best!

FRASQUITA, MERCÉDÈS, CARMEN
  What, without us it never works out
  for the best?

LE REMENDADO, LE DANCAÏRE
> N'êtes-vous pas de cet avis ?

FRASQUITA, MERCÉDÈS, CARMEN
> Si fait, je suis
> De cet avis.

LE REMENDADO, LE DANCAÏRE
> N'êtes-vous pas de cet avis ?

FRASQUITA, MERCÉDÈS, CARMEN
> Si fait, je suis
> De cet avis.

LE REMENDADO, LE DANCAÏRE
> Vraiment, n'êtes-vous pas de cet avis ?

FRASQUITA, LE REMENDADO, LE DANCAÏRE
> Quand il s'agit de volerie,

MERCÉDÈS, CARMEN
> Quand il s'agit de tromperie,
> De duperie,
> De volerie,

TOUS LES CINQ
> Il est toujours bon, sur ma foi,
> D'avoir les femmes avec soi.
> Et sans elles,
> Les toutes belles,
> On ne fait jamais rien
> De bien !

FRASQUITA
> Oui, sur ma foi,

MERCÉDÈS, CARMEN, LE REMENDADO, LE DANCAÏRE
> Sur ma foi, sur ma foi,

ACT TWO SCENE 4

REMENDADO, DANCAÏRE
   Don't you agree?

FRASQUITA, MERCÉDÈS, CARMEN
   Yes absolutely,
   I entirely agree.

REMENDADO, DANCAÏRE
   Don't you agree?

FRASQUITA, MERCÉDÈS, CARMEN
   Yes absolutely,
   I entirely agree.

REMENDADO, DANCAÏRE
   Really, don't you agree?

FRASQUITA, REMENDADO, DANCAÏRE
   When it's theft,

MERCÉDÈS, CARMEN
   When it's deceit,
   trickery
   or theft,

ALL FIVE
   It's always good, believe me,
   to have women with you.
   And without them,
   all the beauties,
   it never works out
   for the best!

FRASQUITA
   Yes, believe me,

MERCÉDÈS, CARMEN, REMENDADO, DANCAÏRE
   Believe me, believe me,

TOUS LES CINQ
>Oui, sur ma foi, il est toujours bon d'avoir
>Les femmes avec soi !

LE DANCAÏRE
>C'est dit, alors ; vous partirez ?

MERCÉDÈS, FRASQUITA
>Quand vous voudrez.

LE DANCAÏRE
>Mais... tout de suite...

CARMEN
>Ah ! permettez, permettez !

(à Mercédès et à Frasquita)

>S'il vous plaît de partir... partez !
>Mais je ne suis pas du voyage.
>Je ne pars pas... je ne pars pas !

LE DANCAÏRE, LE REMENDADO
>Carmen, mon amour, tu viendras,
>Et tu n'auras pas le courage
>De nous laisser dans l'embarras !

FRASQUITA, MERCÉDÈS
>Ah ! Ma Carmen, tu viendras !

CARMEN
>Je ne pars pas, je ne pars pas !

LE DANCAÏRE
>Mais au moins la raison, Carmen, tu la diras.

FRASQUITA, MERCÉDÈS, LE REMENDADO, LE DANCAÏRE
>La raison !

CARMEN
>Je la dirai certainement...

ACT TWO SCENE 4

ALL FIVE
Yes, believe me, it's always good to have women with you!

DANCAÏRE
Well, we've said our bit; are you coming?

MERCÉDÈS, FRASQUITA
When you're ready.

DANCAÏRE
Well... straight away...

CARMEN
Ah! If you don't mind!...

(to Mercédès and Frasquita)

If you want to go... you go!
But I'm not coming on this trip.
I'm not leaving, I'm not leaving!

DANCAÏRE, REMENDADO
Carmen, my love, you will come.
Surely you wouldn't have the heart
to leave us in the lurch!

FRASQUITA, MERCÉDÈS
Ah! Carmen, you will come!

CARMEN
No, I'm not going, I'm not going!

DANCAÏRE
But Carmen, at least tell us the reason why?

FRASQUITA, MERCÉDÈS, REMENDADO, DANCAÏRE
The reason why!

CARMEN
I can definitely tell you that...

LE DANCAÏRE, LE REMENDADO, MERCÉDÈS, FRASQUITA
  Voyons ! Eh bien ?

CARMEN
  La raison, c'est qu'en ce moment...

LE REMENDADO, LE DANCAÏRE, FRASQUITA, MERCÉDÈS
  Eh bien ?

CARMEN
  Je suis amoureuse !

LE REMENDADO, LE DANCAÏRE *(stupéfaits)*
  Qu'a-t-elle dit ?

FRASQUITA, MERCÉDÈS
  Elle dit qu'elle est amoureuse !

LE REMENDADO, LE DANCAÏRE
  Amoureuse !

FRASQUITA, MERCÉDÈS, LE REMENDADO, LE DANCAÏRE
  Amoureuse !

CARMEN
  Oui, amoureuse !

LE DANCAÏRE
  Voyons, Carmen, sois sérieuse.

CARMEN
  Amoureuse à perdre l'esprit !

LE REMENDADO, LE DANCAÏRE *(un peu ironique)*
  La chose, certes, nous étonne,
  Mais ce n'est pas le premier jour
  Où vous aurez su, ma mignonne,
  Faire marcher de front le devoir, et l'amour...

ACT TWO SCENE 4

DANCAÏRE, REMENDADO, MERCÉDÈS, FRASQUITA
Come on, well then?

CARMEN
The reason is because at the moment...

REMENDADO, DANCAÏRE, FRASQUITA, MERCÉDÈS
Well then?

CARMEN
I'm in love!

REMENDADO, DANCAÏRE *(astonished)*
What was that she said?

FRASQUITA, MERCÉDÈS
She said she was in love!

REMENDADO, DANCAÏRE
In love!

FRASQUITA, MERCÉDÈS, REMENDADO, DANCAÏRE
In love!

CARMEN
Yes, in love!

DANCAÏRE
Come on, Carmen, be serious!

CARMEN
Madly in love!

REMENDADO, DANCAÏRE *(somewhat ironically)*
Well, we are certainly stunned,
but it's not the first time, my sweet,
that you've managed to bring duty
and love into line...

CARMEN *(franchement)*
>Mes amis, je serais fort aise
>De partir avec vous ce soir ;
>Mais cette fois, ne vous déplaise,
>Il faudra que l'amour passe avant le devoir…

LE DANCAÏRE
>Ce n'est pas là ton dernier mot ?

CARMEN
>Absolument !

LE REMENDADO
>Il faut que tu te laisses attendrir !

FRASQUITA, MERCÉDÈS, LE REMENDADO, LE DANCAÏRE
>Il faut venir, Carmen, il faut venir !
>Pour notre affaire,
>C'est nécessaire ;
>Car entre nous …

CARMEN
>Quant à cela, j'admets bien avec vous :

TOUS LES CINQ
>Quand il s'agit de tromperie,
>De duperie,
>De volerie,
>Il est toujours bon, sur ma foi,
>D'avoir les femmes avec soi.
>Et sans elles,
>Les toutes belles,
>On ne fait jamais rien
>De bien !

ACT TWO SCENE 4

CARMEN *(frankly)*
>My friends, I would very willingly
>leave with you this evening;
>but this time, don't be offended,
>love has to come before duty...

DANCAÏRE
>That can't be her last word?

CARMEN
>It certainly is!

REMENDADO
>You must let yourself be persuaded!

FRASQUITA, MERCÉDÈS, REMENDADO, DANCAÏRE
>You must come, Carmen, you must!
>For our business
>we need you;
>for between us...

CARMEN
>As for that I quite agree:

ALL FIVE
>When it comes to deceit,
>trickery
>and theft,
>it's always good, believe me,
>to have women with you.
>And without them,
>all the beauties,
>it never works out
>for the best!

Dialogue [ou Récitatif 14, p. 352]

LE DANCAÏRE
En voilà assez ; je t'ai dit qu'il fallait venir, et tu viendras... je suis le chef...

CARMEN
Comment dis-tu ça ?

LE DANCAÏRE
Je te dis que je suis le chef...

CARMEN
Et tu crois que je t'obéirai ?...

LE DANCAÏRE *(furieux)*
Carmen !...

CARMEN *(très calme)*
Eh bien !...

LE REMENDADO *(se jetant entre Le Dancaïre et Carmen)*
Je vous en prie... des personnes si distinguées...

LE DANCAÏRE *(envoyant un coup de pied que Le Remendado évite)*
Attrape ça, toi...

LE REMENDADO *(se redressant)*
Patron...

LE DANCAÏRE
Qu'est-ce que c'est ?

LE REMENDADO
Rien, patron !

LE DANCAÏRE
Amoureuse... ce n'est pas une raison, cela.

LE REMENDADO
Le fait est que ce n'en est pas une... moi aussi je suis amoureux et ça ne m'empêche pas de me rendre utile.

ACT TWO SCENE 4

Dialogue [or Recitative 14, p. 353]

DANCAÏRE
That's quite enough of that; I've told you that you must come, and you will come... I'm the boss...

CARMEN
How can you say that?

DANCAÏRE
I can say it because I'm the boss...

CARMEN
And you think I'll obey you?

DANCAÏRE *(furious)*
Carmen!

CARMEN *(very calmly)*
All right!

REMENDADO *(throwing himself between Dancaïre and Carmen)*
Please... for such distinguished people...

DANCAÏRE *(aiming a kick, which Remendado avoids)*
Take that, you...

REMENDADO *(pulling himself together)*
Boss...

DANCAÏRE
What is it?

REMENDADO
Nothing, boss!

DANCAÏRE
Being in love... well, that's certainly no excuse.

REMENDADO
The fact is that there are no excuses... I'm in love myself, but that doesn't prevent me from making myself useful.

CARMEN
> Partez sans moi... j'irai vous rejoindre demain... mais pour ce soir je reste...

FRASQUITA
> Je ne t'ai jamais vue comme cela ; qui attends-tu, donc ?...

CARMEN
> Un pauvre diable de soldat qui m'a rendu service...

MERCÉDÈS
> Ce soldat qui était en prison ?

CARMEN
> Oui !...

FRASQUITA
> Et à qui, il y a quinze jours, le geôlier a remis de ta part un pain dans lequel il y avait une pièce d'or et une lime ?

CARMEN *(remontant vers la fenêtre)*
> Oui.

LE DANCAÏRE
> Il s'en est servi de cette lime ?...

CARMEN
> Non.

LE DANCAÏRE
> Tu vois bien ! ton soldat aura eu peur d'être puni plus rudement qu'il ne l'avait été ; ce soir encore il aura peur... tu auras beau entr'ouvrir les volets et regarder s'il vient, je parierais qu'il ne viendra pas.

CARMEN
> Ne parie pas, tu perdrais...

(On entend dans le lointain la voix de Don José.)

CARMEN
> Leave without me... I'll catch you up tomorrow... but tonight I'm staying here...

FRASQUITA
> I've never seen you like this; who is it you're waiting for then?

CARMEN
> Some poor devil of a soldier who did me a good turn...

MERCÉDÈS
> What, that soldier who's been in prison?

CARMEN
> Yes!

FRASQUITA
> And to whom, a fortnight ago, the jailer gave a loaf in which you'd hidden a gold coin and a file?

CARMEN (*going back towards the window*)
> Yes.

DANCAÏRE
> And did he make use of the file?

CARMEN
> No.

DANCAÏRE
> You see! Your soldier boy was frightened that he'd be punished even more severely than he had been... he'll be frightened tonight too... even if you open the shutters and watch for him, I bet he won't come.

CARMEN
> I wouldn't bet on it, you'll lose...

(*The voice of Don José is heard in the distance.*)

N° 15 *Chanson*

DON JOSÉ *(la voix très éloigné)*
    Halte-là ! [21]
    Qui va là ?
    Dragon d'Alcala !
    Où t'en vas-tu par là,
    Dragon d'Alcala ?
    Moi, je m'en vais faire,
    Mordre la poussière
    À mon adversaire.
    S'il en est ainsi,
    Passez, mon ami.
    Affaire d'honneur,
    Affaire de cœur,
    Pour nous tout est là,
    Dragons d'Alcala !

Dialogue [ou Récitatif 15, p. 352]

(La musique n'arrête pas. Carmen, Le Dancaïre, Le Remendado, Mercédès et Frasquita, par les volets entr'ouverts, regardent venir Don José.)

MERCÉDÈS
    C'est un dragon, ma foi.

FRASQUITA
    Et un beau dragon.

LE DANCAÏRE *(à Carmen)*
    Eh bien, puisque tu ne veux pas venir que demain, sais-tu au moins ce que tu devrais faire ?

CARMEN
    Qu'est-ce que je devrais faire ?…

LE DANCAÏRE
    Tu devrais décider ton dragon à venir avec toi et à se joindre à nous.

ACT TWO SCENE 4

No. 15 Song

DON JOSÉ *(his voice very far away)*
>Halt there! [21]
>Who is there?
>Dragoon from Alcala!
>Where is it you're going,
>dragoon from Alcala?
>Me, I'm going to make
>the enemy
>bite the dust.
>If that's what you're doing,
>pass by, my friend.
>For honourable
>and amorous quests
>are all we live for,
>we dragoons from Alcala.

Dialogue [or Recitative 15, p. 353]

(The music continues. Carmen, Dancaïre, Remendado, Mercédès and Frasquita watch Don José's arrival through the half-open shutters.)

MERCÉDÈS
>Upon my word, it's a dragoon.

FRASQUITA
>And quite a handsome one.

DANCAÏRE *(to Carmen)*
>Well, since you're not coming until tomorrow, at least you should know what it is you need to do?

CARMEN
>And what is it that I've got to do?

DANCAÏRE
>You've got to persuade your dragoon to come with you and join us.

CARMEN
Ah !… si cela se pouvait !… Mais il n'y faut pas penser… ce sont des bêtises… il est trop niais.

LE DANCAÏRE
Pourquoi l'aimes-tu puisque tu conviens toi-même ?

CARMEN
Parce qu'il est joli garçon donc et qu'il me plaît.

LE REMENDADO *(avec fatuité)*
Le patron ne comprend pas ça, lui qu'il suffise d'être joli garçon pour plaire aux femmes…

LE DANCAÏRE
Attends un peu, toi, attends un peu…

(Le Remendado se sauve et sort. Le Dancaïre le poursuit et sort à son tour, entraînant Mercédès et Frasquita qui essaient de le calmer.)

Chanson

DON JOSÉ *(la voix beaucoup plus rapprochée, la voix se rapproche peu à peu)*
Halte-là !
Qui va là ?
Dragon d'Alcala !
Où t'en vas-tu par là,
Dragon d'Alcala ?
Exact et fidèle,
Je vais où m'appelle
L'amour de ma belle !
S'il en est ainsi,
Passez, mon ami.
Affaire d'honneur,
Affaire de cœur,
Pour nous tout est là,
Dragons d'Alcala !

(Entre Don José.)

ACT TWO SCENE 4

CARMEN
Ah, if only!... You can put that out of your mind... that's just nonsense... he's too stupid.

DANCAÏRE
Why do you love him if that's what you think?

CARMEN
Because he's a nice boy and I like him.

REMENDADO *(flippantly)*
The boss wouldn't understand that... that all a boy needs is to be handsome to be attractive to women...

DANCAÏRE
Just wait, just wait and see...

(Remendado makes his escape. Dancaïre follows him and takes with him Mercédès and Frasquita, who attempt to calm him.)

Song

DON JOSÉ *(his voice much nearer now, gradually getting closer and closer)*
Halt there!
Who is there?
Dragoon from Alcala!
Where is it you're going,
dragoon from Alcala?
On time and faithful
I go to where I'm called
by the love of my beauty!
If that's what you're doing
pass by, my friend.
For honourable
and amorous quests
are all we live for,
we dragoons from Alcala.

(Enter Don José.)

Scène V

Don José, Carmen

Dialogue [ou Récitatif 16, p. 354]

CARMEN
Enfin... te voilà... C'est bien heureux !

DON JOSÉ
Il y a deux heures seulement que je suis sorti de prison.

CARMEN
Qui t'empêchait de sortir plus tôt ? Je t'avais envoyé une lime et une pièce d'or... avec la lime il fallait scier le plus gros barreau de ta prison... avec la pièce d'or il fallait, chez le premier fripier venu, changer ton uniforme pour un habit bourgeois.

DON JOSÉ
En effet, tout cela était possible.

CARMEN
Pourquoi ne l'as-tu pas fait ?

DON JOSÉ
Que veux-tu ? j'ai encore mon honneur de soldat, et déserter me semblerait un grand crime... Oh ! je ne t'en suis pas moins reconnaissant... Tu m'as envoyé une lime et une pièce d'or. La lime me servira pour affiler ma lance et je la garde comme souvenir de toi.

(lui tendant la pièce d'or)

Quant à l'argent...

CARMEN
Tiens, il l'a gardé !... ça se trouve à merveille...

(criant et frappant)

Holà !... Lillas Pastia, holà !... nous mangerons tout... tu me régales... holà ! holà !...

Scene 5

Don José, Carmen

Dialogue [or Recitative 16, p. 355]

CARMEN
> At last... here you are... How very nice!

DON JOSÉ
> It's only two hours since I got out of prison.

CARMEN
> Who stopped you from getting out sooner? I sent you a file and a gold coin... with the file you were meant to saw through the bars of the prison... with the gold coin you were meant to buy civilian clothes from the first rag-dealer you could find.

DON JOSÉ
> I suppose all that would have been possible.

CARMEN
> So why didn't you do it?

DON JOSÉ
> What do you want? I've still got my honour as a soldier, and to desert seems to me a serious crime... Not that I'm any the less grateful... You sent me a file and a gold coin. Well, I can use the file to sharpen my lance, and I'll keep it as a souvenir of you.

(handing her the gold coin)

> And as for the money...

CARMEN
> Hey! He kept it! That's wonderful...

(shouting and clapping)

> Hey there! Lillas Pastia, hey there! We'll eat everything... you can spoil me... Hey! Hey!

(Entre Pastia.)

PASTIA *(l'empêchant de crier)*
   Prenez donc garde…

CARMEN *(lui jetant la pièce)*
   Tiens, attrape… et apporte-nous des fruits confits ; apporte-nous des bonbons, apporte-nous des oranges, apporte-nous du Manzanilla… apporte-nous de tout ce que tu as, de tout…

PASTIA
   Tout de suite, mademoiselle Carmencita.

(Il sort.)

CARMEN *(à Don José)*
   Tu m'en veux alors et tu regrettes de t'être fait mettre en prison pour mes beaux yeux ?

DON JOSÉ
   Quant à cela non, par exemple.

CARMEN
   Vraiment.

DON JOSÉ
   L'on m'a mis en prison, l'on m'a ôté mon grade, mais ça m'est égal.

CARMEN
   Parce que tu m'aimes ?

DON JOSÉ
   Oui, parce que je t'aime, parce que je t'adore.

CARMEN *(mettant ses deux mains dans les mains de Don José)*
   Je paie mes dettes… c'est notre loi à nous autres bohémiennes… Je paie mes dettes…

(Rentre Lillas Pastia apportant sur un plateau des oranges, des bonbons, des fruits confits, du Manzanilla.)

   Mets tout cela ici… d'un seul coup, n'aie pas peur…

(Enter Pastia.)

PASTIA *(stopping her from shouting)*
    Be careful...

CARMEN *(throwing him the coin)*
    Here you are, catch... and bring us some candied fruits; bring us sweets, bring us some oranges, bring us some Manzanilla... bring us everything you have, everything...

PASTIA
    At once, Señorita Carmencita.

(He exits.)

CARMEN *(to Don José)*
    Are you angry with me and are you sorry to have been put in prison because of my beautiful eyes?

DON JOSÉ
    Not particularly for that.

CARMEN
    Really.

DON JOSÉ
    I was put in prison, I was demoted, but I don't really care.

CARMEN
    Because you love me?

DON JOSÉ
    Yes, because I love you and because I adore you.

CARMEN *(putting her two hands in Don José's)*
    I pay my debts... for us gypsies that's the law... I pay my debts...

(Re-enter Lillas Pastia bringing a tray of oranges, sweets, candied fruits and Manzanilla.)

    Put everything here... tip it out all in one... don't be afraid...

(Pastia obéit et la moitié des objets roule par terre.)

Ça ne fait rien, nous ramasserons tout ça nous-mêmes... sauve-toi maintenant, sauve-toi.

(Pastia sort.)

Mets-toi là et mangeons de tout ! de tout !

(Elle est assise ; Don José s'assied en face d'elle.)

DON JOSÉ
Tu croques les bonbons comme un enfant de six ans...

CARMEN
C'est que je les aime. Ton lieutenant était ici tout à l'heure, avec d'autres officiers ; ils nous ont fait danser la Romalis...

DON JOSÉ
Tu as dansé ?

CARMEN
Oui ; et quand j'ai eu dansé, ton lieutenant s'est permis de me dire qu'il m'adorait...

DON JOSÉ
Carmen !...

CARMEN
Qu'est-ce que tu as ?.... Est-ce que tu serais jaloux, par hasard ?...

DON JOSÉ
Mais certainement, je suis jaloux...

CARMEN
Ah bien !... Canari, va !... tu es un vrai canari d'habit et de caractère... allons, ne te fâche pas... pourquoi es-tu jaloux ? parce que j'ai dansé tout à l'heure pour ces officiers... Eh bien, si tu le veux, je danserai pour toi maintenant, pour toi tout seul.

DON JOSÉ
Si je le veux, je crois bien que je le veux...

ACT TWO SCENE 5

(Pastia obeys and half of it goes on the floor.)

Never mind, we can pick it up ourselves... off you go now, off you go...

(Exit Pastia.)

Settle yourself over there, and we'll eat the lot! The lot!

(She sits down and Don José sits opposite her.)

DON JOSÉ
You scoff sweets as if you were a child of six...

CARMEN
That's because I like them... Your lieutenant was here a little while ago with some other officers; they made us dance the Romalis...

DON JOSÉ
You danced?

CARMEN
Yes, and when I'd finished, your lieutenant allowed himself to confess that he adored me...

DON JOSÉ
Carmen!

CARMEN
What's up with you? You're not jealous, are you, by any chance?

DON JOSÉ
Yes, I certainly am jealous...

CARMEN
Oh I see! You canary! You really are a canary, both in how you dress and in your character... Don't be angry... Why are you jealous? Just because I danced in front of your officers... Well, if you want I'll dance for you, just for you alone.

DON JOSÉ
If I want? I'm quite sure I do...

CARMEN
>   Où sont mes castagnettes… qu'est-ce que j'ai fait de mes castagnettes ?

(en riant)

>   C'est toi qui me les a prises, mes castagnettes ?

DON JOSÉ
>   Mais non !

CARMEN *(tendrement)*
>   Mais si, mais si… je suis sûr que c'est toi ah ! bah ! en voilà des castagnettes…

(Elle casse une assiette, avec deux morceaux de faïence, se fait des castagnettes et les essaie.)

>   Ah ! ça ne vaudra jamais mes castagnettes… Où sont-elles donc ?

DON JOSÉ *(trouvant les castagnettes sur la table à droite)*
>   Tiens, les voici…

CARMEN *(riant)*
>   Ah ! tu vois bien c'est toi qui les avais prises !

DON JOSÉ
>   Ah ! que je t'aime Carmen, que je t'aime !

CARMEN
>   Je l'espère bien.

N° 16 Duo

CARMEN *(avec une solennité comique)*
>   Je vais danser en votre honneur ;
>   Et vous verrez, seigneur,
>   Comment je fais claquer ces morceaux de faïence !
>   [ou : Comment je sais moi-même accompagner ma danse !]
>   Mettez-vous là, Don José ; je commence !

ACT TWO SCENE 5

CARMEN
Where are my castanets... what have I done with my castanets?

(laughing)

Have you taken my castanets?

DON JOSÉ
Not me!

CARMEN *(tenderly)*
Yes, yes! I'm sure it's you... Oh well, this'll do for castanets...

(She breaks a plate, and with two pieces of china makes a couple of castanets and tries them out.)

Oh! these will never be as good as my castanets... Where can they be?

DON JOSÉ *(finding the castanets on the table on the right)*
Here you are, they're here...

CARMEN *(laughing)*
Ah! You see, it was you who took them!

DON JOSÉ
Ah! Carmen, how much I love you!

CARMEN
I should hope so.

No. 16 Duet

CARMEN *(with a comic solemnity)*
I'll dance in your honour
and you'll see, Sir,
how well I click these pieces of china!
[or: How I know myself how to accompany my dance!]
Sit down there, Don José, and I'll begin!

(Elle fait asseoir Don José dans un coin du théâtre. Petite danse. Carmen, du bout des lèvres fredonne un air qu'elle accompagne avec ses castagnettes. Don José la dévore des yeux.)

La la la la la la la la [22]
La la la la la la la etc.

(On entend au loin, très loin, des clairons qui sonnent la retraite. Don José prête l'oreille. Il croit entendre les clairons, mais les castagnettes de Carmen claquent très bruyamment.)

La la la la la la la la
La la la la la la la etc.

(Don José s'approche de Carmen, lui prend le bras, et l'oblige à s'arrêter.)

DON JOSÉ
Attends un peu, Carmen, rien qu'un moment, arrête !

CARMEN *(étonnée)*
Et pourquoi, s'il te plait ?

DON JOSÉ
Il me semble… là-bas…
Oui, ce sont nos clairons qui sonnent la retraite.

(Les clairons se rapprochent.)

Ne les entends-tu pas ?

CARMEN *(avec entrain)*
Bravo ! bravo ! j'avais beau faire ; il est mélancolique de danser sans orchestre… Et vive la musique qui nous tombe du ciel !

(Elle reprend sa chanson qui se rythme sur la retraite sonnée au dehors par les clairons. Carmen se remet à danser et Don José se remet à regarder Carmen. La retraite approche… approche… approche… passe sous les fenêtres de l'auberge… puis s'éloigne…)

ACT TWO SCENE 5

(She makes Don José sit down in a corner of the stage. Short dance. Carmen sings a tune that she accompanies with her castanets. Don José feasts on her with his eyes.)

La la la la la la la la [22]
la la la la la la la etc.

(In the distance, far away, the bugles sound the retreat. Don José tries to listen and he thinks he can hear them, but Carmen's castanets are clicking away too noisily.)

La la la la la la la la
la la la la la la la etc.

(Don José approaches Carmen, takes her arm and makes her stop.)

DON JOSÉ
Wait a moment, Carmen, just for a moment, stop!

CARMEN *(astonished)*
Why, if you please?

DON JOSÉ
I think... out there...
Yes, I can hear the bugles beating the retreat.

(The bugles get nearer.)

Can't you hear them?

CARMEN *(excitedly)*
Bravo! bravo! I've tried, but in vain, it's really sad dancing without a band... Long live this music which the heavens have sent!

(She continues her song, timing it to the rhythm of the music of the retreat sounding from afar on the bugles. She begins her dance again, and Don José watches her again. The retreat approaches and gets nearer and nearer, passing right under the windows of the tavern, then it fades away.)

CARMEN
La la la la la la la la
La la la la la la la etc.

(Le son des clairons va s'affaiblissant. Nouvel effort de Don José pour s'arracher à cette contemplation de Carmen... Il lui prend le bras et l'oblige encore à s'arrêter.)

DON JOSÉ
Tu ne m'a pas compris. Carmen... c'est la retraite !
Il faut que moi, je rentre au quartier pour l'appel !

(Le bruit de la retraite cesse tout à coup.)

CARMEN *(stupéfaite et regardant Don José qui remet sa giberne et rattache le ceinturon de son sabre)*
Au quartier !... pour l'appel !...

(éclatant)

Ah ! j'étais vraiment trop bête !
Je me mettais en quatre et je faisais des frais,
Oui, je faisais des frais
Pour amuser monsieur !
Je chantais ! je dansais !
Je crois, Dieu me pardonne,
Qu'un peu plus, je l'aimais !
Ta ra ta ta...
C'est le clairon qui sonne !
Ta ra ta ta...
Il part... il est parti !
Va-t'en donc, canari !

(avec fureur, lui envoyant son shako à la volée)

Tiens ! prends ton shako, ton sabre, ta giberne,
Et va-t'en, mon garçon, va-t'en !
Retourne à ta caserne !

ACT TWO SCENE 5

CARMEN
>La la la la la la la la
>la la la la la la la etc.

(The sound of the bugles gradually fades away into the distance. Don José tries once again to tear himself away from his fixation with Carmen... He takes her arm and once more forces her to stop.)

DON JOSÉ
>You haven't understood me, Carmen... they're beating the retreat!
>It means that I must return to quarters for the roll-call.

(The sound of the bugles stops suddenly.)

CARMEN *(surprised to see Don José putting back on his bullet belt and the scabbard for his sword)*
>Back to quarters! For roll-call!

(exploding)

>Ah! How stupid I've been!
>I cut myself in four and spent my every penny,
>yes, spent my every penny
>to amuse the gentleman!
>I sang! I danced!
>And God forgive me, I think,
>a little longer and I would have loved him!
>Ta ra ta ta...
>It's the bugle sounding!
>Ta ra ta ta...
>He's leaving... he's gone!
>Off you go then, canary!

(furiously throwing his shako at him)

>Here! Take your shako, your sword and your belt,
>and go away, boy. Go away!
>Back to your barracks!

DON JOSÉ *(avec tristesse)*
C'est mal à toi, Carmen, de te moquer de moi !
Je souffre de partir,
Car jamais, jamais femme, jamais femme avant toi,
Aussi profondément n'avait troublé mon âme !

CARMEN
Ta ra ta ta…
Ô mon Dieu ! c'est la retraite !
Ta ra ta ta…
Je vais être en retard !
Il perd la tête ! il court !
Et voilà son amour !

DON JOSÉ
Ainsi tu ne crois pas à mon amour ?

CARMEN
Mais non !

DON JOSÉ
Eh bien ! tu m'entendras !

CARMEN
Je ne veux rien entendre !

DON JOSÉ
Tu m'entendras !

CARMEN
Tu vas te faire attendre !

DON JOSÉ
Tu m'entendras !

CARMEN
Tu vas te faire attendre !

DON JOSÉ
Oui, tu m'entendras !

ACT TWO SCENE 5

DON JOSÉ *(sadly)*
>It's bad of you, Carmen, to mock me!
>It pains me to leave you,
>for never, never a woman before you
>has stirred up my heart like you!

CARMEN
>Ta ra ta ta...
>Heavens! It's the retreat!
>Ta ra ta ta...
>I'm going to be late!
>He goes into a panic! He's running!
>So much for his love!

DON JOSÉ
>So you don't believe in my love for you?

CARMEN
>Not at all!

DON JOSÉ
>Well, then you must listen to me!

CARMEN
>I don't want to hear a word!

DON JOSÉ
>You must listen to me!

CARMEN
>You're keeping them waiting!

DON JOSÉ
>You must listen to me!

CARMEN
>You're keeping them waiting!

DON JOSÉ
>Yes, you must listen to me!

(violemment)

Je le veux ! Carmen, tu m'entendras !

(De la main gauche, il a saisi brusquement le bras de Carmen ; de la main droite, il va chercher sous sa veste d'uniforme la fleur de cassie que Carmen lui a jetée au premier acte. Il montre cette fleur à Carmen.)

La fleur que tu m'avais jetée [23]
Dans ma prison m'était restée ;
Flétrie et sèche, cette fleur
Gardait toujours sa douce odeur ;
Et pendant des heures entières,
Sur mes yeux, fermant mes paupières,
De cette odeur je m'enivrais
Et dans la nuit je te voyais !
Je me prenais à te maudire,
À te détester, à me dire :
Pourquoi faut-il que le destin
L'ait mise là sur mon chemin !
Puis je m'accusais de blasphème,
Et je ne sentais en moi-même,
Je ne sentais qu'un seul désir,
Un seul désir, un seul espoir :
C'était, ô ma Carmen, oui,
Te revoir, ô Carmen, oui, te revoir !
Car tu n'avais eu qu'à paraître,
Qu'à jeter un regard sur moi,
Pour t'emparer de tout mon être,
Ô ma Carmen !
Et j'étais une chose à toi !
Carmen, je t'aime !

CARMEN
Non ! tu ne m'aimes pas !

DON JOSÉ
Que dis-tu ?

ACT TWO SCENE 5

(violently)

I demand it! Carmen, you must listen to me!

(With his left hand, he has roughly seized Carmen by the arm; with his right he feels under the vest of his uniform for the cassia flower that Carmen threw him in the first act. He shows the flower to Carmen.)

The flower that you threw me [23]
I kept in my prison cell;
wilted and dry, that flower
still kept its sweet scent;
and for hours and hours
under my eyes, my eyelids shut,
I was drunk on its scent
and in the night I saw you!
I took to cursing you,
to hating you, and to asking
why it was that fate
had put you in my way!
Then I accused myself of blasphemy,
feeling in myself only one desire,
one desire and one hope:
to see you again,
yes, to see you again, Carmen,
to see you again, Carmen!
For you only had to appear before me,
to glance at me just once, to make me
possessed with you with all my being,
oh my Carmen!
And I was your possession!
Carmen, I love you!

CARMEN
No, you don't love me at all!

DON JOSÉ
What did you say?

CARMEN
　Non ! tu ne m'aimes pas ! Non !
　Car si tu m'aimais,
　Là-bas, là-bas tu me suivrais !

DON JOSÉ
　Carmen !

CARMEN
　Oui ! Là-bas, là-bas dans la montagne ! [24]

DON JOSÉ
　Carmen !

CARMEN
　Là-bas, là-bas tu me suivrais !
　Sur ton cheval tu me prendrais,
　Et comme un brave à travers la campagne,
　En croupe, tu m'emporterais !
　Là-bas, là-bas dans la montagne !

DON JOSÉ *(troublé)*
　Carmen !

CARMEN
　Là-bas, là-bas tu me suivrais !
　Si tu m'aimais !
　Tu n'y dépendrais de personne ;
　Point d'officier à qui tu doives obéir,
　Et point de retraite qui sonne
　Pour dire à l'amoureux qu'il est temps de partir !
　Le ciel ouvert, la vie errante,
　Pour pays tout l'univers,
　Et pour loi ta volonté !
　Et surtout la chose enivrante :
　La liberté ! la liberté !

DON JOSÉ
　Mon Dieu !

ACT TWO SCENE 5

CARMEN
>No! You don't love me at all.
>Because if you did,
>you'd come there with me!

DON JOSÉ
>Carmen!

CARMEN
>Yes, you'd come there to the mountains! [24]

DON JOSÉ
>Carmen!

CARMEN
>Yes, you'd come there!
>You'd take me on your horse,
>like a real brave man, you'd take me
>riding behind you through the fields,
>there across the mountains!

DON JOSÉ *(worried)*
>Carmen!

CARMEN
>You'd follow me there
>if you loved me!
>You'd have no one to answer to –
>no officer whom you'd have to obey –
>and there'd be no retreat sounded
>to warn my lover that it was time to leave!
>The open sky, the wandering life,
>the whole world at your disposal,
>and your own will as the law!
>And the most intoxicating thing:
>freedom! Freedom!

DON JOSÉ
>Heavens!

CARMEN
  Là-bas, là-bas dans la montagne !

DON JOSÉ *(très ébranlé, presque vaincu)*
  Carmen !

CARMEN
  Là-bas, là-bas si tu m'aimais…

DON JOSÉ
  Tais-toi !

CARMEN
  Là-bas, là-bas tu me suivrais !
  Sur ton cheval tu me prendrais…

DON JOSÉ
  Ah ! Carmen, hélas ! tais-toi !
  Tais-toi ! mon Dieu !

CARMEN
  Sur ton cheval tu me prendrais
  Et comme un brave, à travers la campagne,
  Oui, tu m'emporterais, si tu m'aimais !

DON JOSÉ
  Hélas ! hélas !

CARMEN
  Oui, n'est-ce pas ?

DON JOSÉ
  Pitié ! Carmen, pitié !

CARMEN
  Là-bas, là-bas tu me suivras !
  Tu me suivras !

DON JOSÉ
  Ô mon Dieu ! Hélas !

ACT TWO SCENE 5

CARMEN
>There in the mountains!

DON JOSÉ *(very shaken and almost persuaded)*
>Carmen!

CARMEN
>Come with me, come with me, if you love me...

DON JOSÉ
>Shut up!

CARMEN
>Come with me, come with me!
>Take me on your horse...

DON JOSÉ
>Ah! Carmen, alas, don't say that!
>Don't, for heaven's sake!

CARMEN
>You'd take me across the country
>on your horse, like a brave man,
>yes, you'd take me away, if you loved me!

DON JOSÉ
>Alas! Alas!

CARMEN
>Isn't that so?

DON JOSÉ
>Have mercy, Carmen, mercy!

CARMEN
>Come with me, come with me!
>Come along with me!

DON JOSÉ
>Heavens, alas!

CARMEN
  Là-bas, là-bas tu me suivras, tu m'aimes et tu me suivras !
  Là-bas, là-bas emporte-moi !

DON JOSÉ
  Ah ! tais-toi ! tais-toi !

DON JOSÉ *(s'arrachant brusquement des bras de Carmen)*
  Non ! je ne veux plus t'écouter !
  Quitter mon drapeau... déserter...
  C'est la honte... c'est l'infamie !...
  Je n'en veux pas !

CARMEN *(durement)*
  Eh bien ! pars !

DON JOSÉ *(suppliant)*
  Carmen, je t'en prie !

CARMEN
  Non ! je ne t'aime plus !

DON JOSÉ
  Écoute !

CARMEN
  Va ! je te hais !

DON JOSÉ
  Carmen !

CARMEN
  Adieu ! mais adieu pour jamais !

DON JOSÉ *(avec douleur)*
  Eh bien ! soit ! adieu ! adieu pour jamais !

CARMEN
  Va-t'en !

DON JOSÉ
  Carmen ! adieu ! adieu pour jamais !

ACT TWO SCENE 5

CARMEN
> Come with me, come with me, you love me and you'll come with me!
> Take me there! Take me there!

DON JOSÉ
> Be quiet! Be quiet!

DON JOSÉ *(breaking free from Carmen's arms)*
> No! I don't want to listen to you any more!
> Betray my flag... desert?
> That would be dishonour... infamy!
> I don't want that!

CARMEN *(harshly)*
> Then go!

DON JOSÉ *(suppliant)*
> Carmen, I implore you!

CARMEN
> No, I don't love you any more!

DON JOSÉ
> Listen!

CARMEN
> Go away! I hate you!

DON JOSÉ
> Carmen!

CARMEN
> Goodbye! Goodbye for ever!

DON JOSÉ *(painfully)*
> All right! So be it! Goodbye! Goodbye for ever!

CARMEN
> Get out!

DON JOSÉ
> Carmen! Goodbye! Goodbye for ever!

CARMEN
   Adieu !

(Il va en courant vers la porte… Au moment où il y arrive, on frappe… Don José s'arrête, silence. On frappe encore.)

Scène VI

Les mêmes, le lieutenant Zuniga

N° 18 Final

ZUNIGA *(au dehors)*
   Holà ! Carmen ! Holà ! Holà !

DON JOSÉ
   Qui frappe ? qui vient là ?

CARMEN
   Tais-toi !… tais-toi !

ZUNIGA *(faisant sauter la porte)*
   J'ouvre moi-même… et j'entre…

(Il voit Don José. À Carmen, légèrement)

   Ah ! fi ! ah ! fi ! la belle !
   Le choix n'est pas heureux ! c'est se mésallier
   De prendre le soldat quand on a l'officier.

(à Don José)

   Allons, décampe !

DON JOSÉ *(calme, mais résolu)*
   Non !

ZUNIGA
   Si fait ! tu partiras.

DON JOSÉ
   Je ne partirai pas.

ACT TWO SCENE 6

CARMEN
Goodbye!

(He runs towards the door... At the very moment he gets there, someone knocks at the door... Don José stops, in silence. There's another knock.)

Scene 6

The same, Lieutenant Zuniga

No. 18 Finale

ZUNIGA *(outside)*
Hey there! Carmen! Hey! Hey!

DON JOSÉ
Who's knocking? Who is it?

CARMEN
Be quiet! Be quiet!

ZUNIGA *(pushing the door open)*
I can open it myself... and I'm in...

(He sees Don José. To Carmen, humorously)

Ah! Yes! Ah! Yes! My pretty one!
Not a very good choice! It's stooping a little low
to choose a mere soldier when there's an officer on offer.

(to Don José)

Now then, clear off!

DON JOSÉ *(calmly but resolutely)*
No!

ZUNIGA
Come on! Off you go!

DON JOSÉ
I am not leaving.

ZUNIGA *(le frappant)*
   Drôle !

DON JOSÉ *(sautant sur son sabre)*
   Tonnerre !… il va pleuvoir des coups !

(Zuniga dégaine à moitié.)

CARMEN *(se jetant entre Don José et Zuniga)*
   Au diable le jaloux !

(appelant)

   À moi ! à moi !

(Le Dancaïre, Le Remendado, Mercédès, Frasquita, les bohémiens et les bohémiennes paraissent de tous les côtés. Carmen d'un geste montre Zuniga aux bohémiens ; Le Dancaïre et Le Remendado se jettent sur lui, le désarment.)

CARMEN *(à Zuniga, d'un ton moqueur)*
   Bel officier, bel officier, l'amour
   Vous joue en ce moment un assez vilain tour !
   Vous arrivez fort mal !
   Vous arrivez fort mal hélas !
   Et nous sommes forcés,
   Ne voulant être dénoncés,
   De vous garder au moins… pendant une heure.

LE REMENDADO *(à Zuniga, le pistolet à la main, gracieusement)*
   Mon cher monsieur !

LE DANCAÏRE *(à Zuniga, le pistolet à la main, gracieusement)*
   Mon cher monsieur !

LE REMENDADO
   Mon cher monsieur !

LE DANCAÏRE
   Mon cher monsieur !

ZUNIGA *(hitting him)*
   Very amusing!

DON JOSÉ *(drawing his sword)*
   To hell with you! We'll fight!

(Zuniga half-draws his sword.)

CARMEN *(throwing herself between Don José and Zuniga)*
   To hell with jealousy!

(calling)

   Come here! Come here!

(Dancaïre, Remendado, Mercédès, Frasquita and the other gypsies appear from all around. Carmen points to Zuniga, and Dancaïre and Remendado throw themselves on him and disarm him.)

CARMEN *(to Zuniga, mockingly)*
   Handsome officer, love has dealt you
   a poor hand at the moment!
   You've arrived at a bad time!
   You've arrived at a bad time, alas!
   And I'm afraid that we need
   to keep you under arrest for an hour at least,
   so that you don't give the game away!

REMENDADO *(to Zuniga, his pistol in his hand, politely)*
   Dear Sir!

DANCAÏRE *(to Zuniga, his pistol in his hand, politely)*
   Dear Sir!

REMENDADO
   Dear Sir!

DANCAÏRE
   Dear Sir!

LE DANCAÏRE, LE REMENDADO
Nous allons, s'il vous plaît, quitter cette demeure. Vous viendrez avec nous ?

CARMEN *(riant)*
C'est une promenade !

LE REMENDADO, LE DANCAÏRE
Consentez-vous ?

LE DANCAÏRE, LE REMENDADO *(le pistolet à la main)*, **CHŒUR DES BOHÉMIENS**
Répondez, camarade !

ZUNIGA
Certainement.

(avec ironie)

> D'autant plus que votre argument
> Est un de ceux auxquels
> On ne résiste guère !

(changeant de ton)

> Mais gare à vous !

(court)

> Gare à vous plus tard !

LE DANCAÏRE *(avec philosophie)*
La guerre, c'est la guerre !
En attendant, mon officier,
Passez devant sans vous faire prier !

LE REMENDADO, BOHÉMIENS
Passez devant sans vous faire prier !

(L'officier sort, emmené par quatre bohémiens, le pistolet à la main.)

ACT TWO SCENE 6

DANCAÏRE, REMENDADO
>If you don't mind, we're going to leave this place. Will you come with us?

CARMEN *(laughing)*
>Just for a little walk!

REMENDADO, DANCAÏRE
>Is that all right?

DANCAÏRE, REMENDADO *(hands on their pistols),* **CHORUS OF GYPSIES**
>Reply, my friend!

ZUNIGA
>Certainly.

(ironically)

>And the more so because your proposal
>is one of those
>one can hardly resist!

(changing his tone)

>But be careful!

(curtly)

>You'll have to watch it in the future!

DANCAÏRE *(philosophically)*
>I'm afraid it's war!
>Meanwhile, officer,
>lead the way without having to be asked!

REMENDADO, GYPSIES
>Lead the way without having to be asked!

(The officer leaves, led by four gypsies with their pistols drawn.)

CARMEN *(à Don José)*
   Es-tu des nôtres maintenant ?

DON JOSÉ
   Il le faut bien !

CARMEN
   Ah ! le mot n'est pas galant !
   Mais, qu'importe ! va... tu t'y feras
   quand tu verras comme c'est beau, la vie errante !
   Pour pays tout l'univers,
   Et pour loi ta volonté !
   Et surtout, la chose enivrante :
   La liberté ! la liberté !

FRASQUITA, MERCÉDÈS, CARMEN, BOHÉMIENNES
   Suis-nous à travers la campagne,
   Viens avec nous dans la montagne,
   Suis-nous et tu t'y feras, tu t'y feras
   Quand tu verras, là-bas,

LE REMENDADO, LE DANCAÏRE, BOHÉMIENS
   Ami, suis-nous dans la campagne,
   Viens avec nous dans la montagne,
   Tu t'y feras, tu t'y feras
   Quand tu verras, là-bas, là-bas,

FRASQUITA, MERCÉDÈS, CARMEN, LE REMENDADO, LE DANCAÏRE, CHŒUR
   Comme c'est beau, la vie errante,
   Pour pays tout l'univers,
   Et pour loi ta volonté !
   Et surtout, la chose enivrante :
   La liberté !

ACT TWO SCENE 6

CARMEN *(to Don José)*
>Are you now one of us?

DON JOSÉ
>I have to be!

CARMEN
>Well, that wasn't very nicely put!
>But no matter! You'll get used to it
>when you see how lovely the wandering life is!
>The whole world at your disposal,
>and your own will as the law!
>And the most intoxicating thing:
>freedom, freedom!

FRASQUITA, MERCÉDÈS, CARMEN, GYPSIES
>Follow us across the countryside,
>come with us up into the mountains,
>follow us and you'll soon get used to it
>when you see what it's like up there.

REMENDADO, DANCAÏRE, GYPSIES
>Friend, follow us across the countryside,
>come with us up into the mountains,
>you'll soon get used to it, you'll soon get used to it
>when you see it up there, up there.

FRASQUITA, MERCÉDÈS, CARMEN, REMENDADO, DANCAÏRE, CHORUS
>How lovely the wandering life is!
>The whole world at your disposal,
>and your own will as the law!
>And the most intoxicating thing :
>freedom!

TROISIÈME ACTE

Entr'acte [25]

Scène 1

Carmen, Don José, Le Dancaïre, Le Remendado, Frasquita, Mercédès, contrebandiers.

N° 18 Introduction [26]

Le rideau se lève sur des rochers... site pittoresque et sauvage... Solitude complète et nuit noire. Prélude musical. Au bout de quelques instants, un contrebandier paraît au haut des rochers et sonne de la trompe, puis un autre, puis deux autres, puis vingt autres çà et là, descendant et escaladant des rochers. Des hommes portent de gros ballots sur les épaules.

CHŒUR *(La moitié seulement)*
    Écoute, écoute, compagnon, écoute !
    La fortune est là-bas, là-bas !
    Mais prends garde, pendant la route,
    Prends garde de faire un faux pas !
    Écoute, compagnon, écoute, écoute !
    La fortune est là-bas, là-bas !
    Prends garde, prends garde, pendant la route,
    Prends garde de faire un faux pas !

FRASQUITA, MERCÉDÈS, CARMEN, DON JOSÉ, LE REMENDADO, LE DANCAÏRE
    Notre métier est bon, mais pour le faire il faut
    Avoir, avoir une âme forte !
    Et le péril, le péril est en haut,
    Il est en bas, il est en haut,
    Il est partout, qu'importe !
    Nous allons en avant

ACT THREE

Entr'acte [25]

Scene 1

Carmen, Don José, Dancaïre, Remendado, Frasquita, Mercédès, smugglers.

No. 18 Introduction [26]

The curtain opens on a rocky landscape... a picturesque and wild place... The scene is totally empty and the night pitch-black. Musical prelude. After a few moments, a smuggler appears on top of the rocks and sounds a horn, another follows suit, and then two others, then follow twenty more here and there, coming down and scaling the rocks. The men carry heavy packages on their shoulders.

CHORUS *(only half of them)*
    Listen, listen, friend, listen!
    Down there lies our fortune!
    But take care as you go,
    take care not to make a false step!
    Listen, listen, friend, listen!
    Our fortune awaits us down there!
    But take care, take care, as you go,
    take care not to make a false step!

FRASQUITA, MERCÉDÈS, CARMEN, DON JOSÉ, REMENDADO, DANCAÏRE
    Our job is a good one, but to do it
    you need to have a strong heart!
    And danger lurks above
    and below: above and below,
    it's everywhere, but never mind!
    We go forward

Sans souci du torrent,
Sans souci de l'orage,
Sans souci du soldat qui là-bas nous attend,
Qui là-bas nous attend
Et nous guette au passage !
Sans souci nous allons en avant !

CHŒUR
Ami, là-bas est la fortune,
Écoute, écoute, compagnon,
Prends garde, pendant la route,
Prends garde de faire un faux pas !
Oui, la fortune est là-bas !
Écoute, écoute, écoute !
Oui, la fortune est là-bas !
Prends garde de faire un faux pas !

FRASQUITA, MERCÉDÈS, CARMEN, DON JOSÉ, LE REMENDADO, LE DANCAÏRE, CHŒUR
Écoute, compagnon, écoute, écoute !
La fortune est là-bas, là-bas !
Prends garde, prends garde, pendant la route
Prends garde de faire un faux pas !

TOUS
Prends garde ! prends garde !

Dialogue [ou Récitatif 17, p. 356, suivi de douze mesures pour orchestre seul, puis Récitatif 18]

LE DANCAÏRE
Halte ! nous allons nous arrêter ici… ceux qui ont sommeil pourront dormir pendant une demi-heure…

LE REMENDADO *(s'étendant avec volupté)*
Ah !

despite the torrent,
despite the storm,
despite the soldiers who lie in wait for us,
in wait for us down there
and who watch out for us to pass!
Without a care we go on forward!

CHORUS
Friend, down there lies our fortune,
listen, listen, my friend,
but take care as you go,
take care not to make a false step!
Yes, our fortune lies down there!
Listen, listen, listen!
Yes, our fortune lies down there!
Take care not to make a false step!

FRASQUITA, MERCÉDÈS, CARMEN, DON JOSÉ, REMENDADO, DANCAÏRE, CHORUS
Listen, friend, listen, listen!
Down there, down there lies our fortune!
But take care as you go,
take care not to make a false step!

ALL
Take care! Take care!

Dialogue [or Recitative 17, p. 357, followed by twelve bars of orchestral music, then Recitative 18]

DANCAÏRE
Halt! We're going to stop here... those who are sleepy can have half an hour's sleep...

REMENDADO *(stretching out languidly)*
Ah!

LE DANCAÏRE
Je vais, moi, voir s'il y a moyen de faire entrer les marchandises dans la ville… une brèche s'est faite dans le mur d'enceinte et nous pourrions passer par là ; malheureusement on a mis un factionnaire pour garder cette brèche.

DON JOSÉ
Lillas Pastia nous a fait savoir que, cette nuit, ce factionnaire serait un homme à nous…

LE DANCAÏRE
Oui, mais Lillas Pastia a pu se tromper… le factionnaire qu'il veut dire a pu être changé. Avant d'aller plus loin je ne trouve pas mauvais de m'assurer par moi-même.

(appelant)

Remendado !

LE REMENDADO *(se réveillant)*
Hé ?

LE DANCAÏRE
Debout, tu vas venir avec moi…

LE REMENDADO
Mais, patron…

LE DANCAÏRE
Qu'est-ce que c'est ?

LE REMENDADO *(se levant)*
Voilà, patron, voilà !…

LE DANCAÏRE
Allons, passe devant.

LE REMENDADO
Et moi, qui rêvais que j'allais pouvoir dormir… C'était un rêve, hélas, c'était un rêve !…

(Il sort suivi du Dancaïre.)

ACT THREE SCENE I

DANCAÏRE
As for me, I'm going to see if I can find a way of getting the goods into the town... there's a breach in the surrounding wall, and we can get in through that: unfortunately they've put a sentry to guard it.

DON JOSÉ
Lillas Pastia has let us know that it's a sentry who's on our side...

DANCAÏRE
Yes, but Lillas Pastia could be wrong... the sentry of whom he was talking may have been changed. Before we go any further it wouldn't be a bad idea for me to make sure.

(calling)

Remendado!

REMENDADO *(waking up)*
Eh?

DANCAÏRE
Up you get, you're coming with me...

REMENDADO
But, boss...

DANCAÏRE
What is it?

REMENDADO *(getting up)*
There we are, boss!...

DANCAÏRE
Come on then, you come first.

REMENDADO
And I thought I was going to get some sleep... It was just a dream, alas, just a dream!

(He exits, followed by Dancaïre.)

Scène II

Les mêmes, moins Le Dancaïre et Le Remendado

Pendant la scène entre Carmen et Don José, quelques bohémiens allument un feu près duquel Mercédès et Frasquita viennent s'asseoir, les autres se roulent dans leurs manteaux, se couchent et s'endorment.

DON JOSÉ
Voyons, Carmen… si je t'ai parlé trop durement, je t'en demande pardon, faisons la paix.

CARMEN
Non.

DON JOSÉ
Tu ne m'aimes plus alors ?

CARMEN
Ce qui est sûr c'est que je t'aime beaucoup moins qu'autrefois… et que si tu continues à t'y prendre de cette façon-là, je finirai par ne plus t'aimer du tout… Je ne veux pas être tourmentée ni surtout commandée. Ce que je veux c'est être libre et faire ce qui me plaît.

DON JOSÉ
Tu es le diable, Carmen ?

CARMEN
Oui. Qu'est-ce que tu regardes là, à quoi penses-tu ?…

DON JOSÉ
Je me dis que là-bas… à sept ou huit lieues d'ici tout au plus, il y a un village, et dans ce village une bonne vieille femme qui croit que je suis encore un honnête homme.

CARMEN
Une bonne vieille femme ?

DON JOSÉ
Oui ; ma mère.

ACT THREE SCENE 2

Scene 2

The same but without Dancaïre and Remendado

During this scene between Carmen and Don José, some gypsies light a fire beside which Mercédès and Frasquita come and sit; the others wrap themselves in their overcoats, lie down and go to sleep.

DON JOSÉ
> You see, Carmen... if I've spoken too harshly, I ask you to forgive me, let's make peace.

CARMEN
> No.

DON JOSÉ
> Then you don't love me any more?

CARMEN
> What's for sure is that I love you a lot less than before... and if you continue to behave in that way, I'll end up by not loving you at all... I don't want to be tormented nor bossed around. What I want is to be free and to do as I please.

DON JOSÉ
> Are you the devil, Carmen?

CARMEN
> Yes. What are you looking at, and what are you thinking?

DON JOSÉ
> I was thinking that over there... seven or eight leagues away at the most, there's a village where a fine old lady still thinks I'm a respectable young man.

CARMEN
> A fine old lady?

DON JOSÉ
> Yes, my mother.

CARMEN
Ta mère… Eh bien là, vrai, tu ne ferais pas mal d'aller la retrouver, car décidément tu n'es pas fait pour vivre avec nous… chien et loup ne font pas longtemps bon ménage…

DON JOSÉ
Carmen…

CARMEN
Sans compter que le métier n'est pas sans péril pour ceux qui, comme toi, refusent de se cacher quand ils entendent des coups de fusil… plusieurs des nôtres y ont laissé leur peau, ton tour viendra.

DON JOSÉ
Et le tien aussi… si tu me parles encore de nous séparer et si tu ne te conduis pas avec moi comme je veux que tu conduises…

CARMEN
Tu me tuerais, peut-être ?…

(Don José ne répond pas.)

À la bonne heure… j'ai vu plusieurs fois dans les cartes que nous devions finir ensemble.

(faisant claquer ses castagnettes)

Bah ! arrive qui plante…

DON JOSÉ
Tu es le diable, Carmen ?…

CARMEN
Mais oui, je te l'ai déjà dit…

(Elle tourne le dos à Don José et va s'asseoir près de Mercédès et de Frasquita. Après un instant d'indécision, Don José s'éloigne à son tour et va s'étendre sur les rochers. Pendant les dernières répliques de la scène, Mercédès et Frasquita ont étalé des cartes devant elles.)

ACT THREE SCENE 2

CARMEN

Your mother... Ah well, you could do worse than to go over there and see her again, for you're certainly not suited to living with us... the dog and the wolf don't make a good household...

DON JOSÉ

Carmen...

CARMEN

And that's not to mention how the job isn't without its dangers for those, like you, who refuse to hide when they hear shots fired... several of us have lost their lives: your turn will come.

DON JOSÉ

Yours too... and if you mention our separation again, and if you don't behave like I want you to behave...

CARMEN

You'll kill me perhaps?

(Don José doesn't reply.)

And so be it... I've seen it several times in the cards that we're bound to die together.

(clicking her castanets)

Well, what will be will be!

DON JOSÉ

Are you the devil, Carmen?

CARMEN

Why yes, I've already told you that...

(She turns her back on Don José and sits down near Mercédès and Frasquita. After a moment of hesitation, Don José also goes away and stretches out on the rocks. During the final exchanges of the scene Mercédès and Frasquita have laid out a pack of cards in front of themselves.)

N° 19 Trio

FRASQUITA, MERCÉDÈS
    Mêlons !
    Coupons !

FRASQUITA, MERCÉDÈS
    Bien ! c'est cela !

    Trois cartes ici, quatre là !

    Et maintenant, parlez, mes belles,   [27]
    De l'avenir, donnez-nous des nouvelles.

    Dites-nous qui nous trahira !
    Dites-nous qui nous aimera !
    Parlez, parlez !

MERCÉDÈS
    Moi, je vois un jeune amoureux
    Qui m'aime on ne peut davantage ;

FRASQUITA
    Le mien est très riche et très vieux ;
    Mais il parle de mariage !

MERCÉDÈS *(fièrement)*
    Je me campe sur son cheval
    Et dans la montagne il m'entraîne !

FRASQUITA
    Dans un château presque royal,
    Le mien m'installe en souveraine !

MERCÉDÈS
    De l'amour à n'en plus finir,
    Tous les jours, nouvelles folies !

FRASQUITA *(avec joie)*
    De l'or tant que j'en puis tenir,
    Des diamants, des pierreries !

ACT THREE SCENE 2

No. 19 Trio

FRASQUITA, MERCÉDÈS
　Shuffle!
　Cut!

FRASQUITA, MERCÉDÈS
　Yes, that's fine!

　Three cards here, four there!

　And now tell us, my beauties,   [27]
　of the future, give us some news.

　Tell us who's going to betray us!
　Tell us who's going to love us!
　Speak, speak!

MERCÉDÈS
　I can see a young lover
　who couldn't love me more;

FRASQUITA
　Mine's very rich and very old,
　but he's talking of marriage!

MERCÉDÈS *(proudly)*
　I'm mounted on his horse
　and he takes me off to the mountains.

FRASQUITA
　In an almost regal castle
　mine installs me as queen!

MERCÉDÈS
　Making love all the time,
　every day something new!

FRASQUITA *(joyfully)*
　As much gold as I can hold in my hands,
　and diamonds and precious stones!

MERCÉDÈS
  Le mien devient un chef fameux,
  Cent hommes marchent à sa suite !

FRASQUITA
  Le mien… le mien… en croirai-je mes yeux ?…
  Oui… Il meurt !

(avec ivresse)

  Ah ! je suis veuve et j'hérite !

FRASQUITA, MERCÉDÈS
  Ah ! Parlez encor, parlez, mes belles,
  De l'avenir, donnez-nous des nouvelles.
  Dites-nous qui nous trahira !
  Dites-nous qui nous aimera !

(Elles recommencent à consulter les cartes.)

FRASQUITA
  Fortune !

MERCÉDÈS
  Amour !

(Carmen depuis le commencement de la scène suivait du regard le jeu de Mercédès et de Frasquita.)

CARMEN
  Donnez, que j'essaie à mon tour.

(Elle se met à tourner les cartes.)

Musique de scène.

  Carreau ! Pique !

(tournant encore les cartes)

MERCÉDÈS
>Mine becomes a famous chief
>with a hundred men behind him!

FRASQUITA
>Mine... mine... can I believe my eyes?
>Yes, he dies!

(deliriously)

>Ah! I'm a widow and an heiress!

FRASQUITA, MERCÉDÈS
>And now tell us again, my beauties,
>of the future, give us some news.
>Tell us who's going to betray us!
>Tell us who's going to love us!

(Once again they consult the cards.)

FRASQUITA
>Fortune!

MERCÉDÈS
>Love!

(Carmen since the beginning of the scene has been following the game between Mercédès and Frasquita.)

CARMEN
>Give me the cards, it's my turn.

(She begins to shuffle the cards.)

Stage music.

>Diamonds! Spades!

(shuffling the cards again)

La mort !
J'ai bien lu !...
Moi d'abord
Ensuite lui...

(montrant Don José endormi)

Pour tous les deux, la mort.

(très également et simplement)

En vain, pour éviter les réponses amères, [28]
En vain tu mêleras !
Cela ne sert à rien, les cartes sont sincères
Et ne mentiront pas !
Dans le livre d'en haut si ta page est heureuse,
Mêle et coupe sans peur,
La carte sous tes doigts se tournera joyeuse,
T'annonçant le bonheur.
Mais si tu dois mourir,
Si le mot redoutable
Est écrit par le sort,
Recommence vingt fois, la carte impitoyable
Répétera : la mort !

(tournant les cartes)

Encore !... encore!... toujours la mort !

FRASQUITA, MERCÉDÈS
Ah ! Parlez encor, parlez, mes belles,
De l'avenir, donnez-nous des nouvelles.
Dites-nous qui nous trahira !
Dites-nous qui nous aimera !

CARMEN
Le désespoir !
La mort ! la mort !
Encor la mort !

Death!
I read it clearly!...
Me first.
Then him...

(pointing at Don José, asleep)

Death for the two of us.

(in an even tone and simply)

In vain, to avoid such a painful reply, [28]
in vain you cut the cards again!
There is no point, the cards tell the truth
and do not lie.
If in heaven's book your page reads happily,
shuffle and cut without fear,
the cards you feel with your fingers will spell
good fortune and happiness.
But if you have to die,
if that terrible word
is spelt in the way they fall,
you can begin twenty times and the pitiless cards
will repeat the word 'death'!

(turning over the cards)

Again! again! always death!

FRASQUITA, MERCÉDÈS
And now tell us again, my beauties,
of the future, give us some news.
Tell us who's going to betray us!
Tell us who's going to love us!

CARMEN
Despair!
Death! Death!
Again, death!

FRASQUITA
Fortune !

MERCÉDÈS
Amour !

CARMEN
Toujours la mort !

FRASQUITA, MERCÉDÈS, CARMEN
Encor ! encor !

(Rentrent Le Dancaïre et Le Remendado.)

Scène III

Carmen, Don José, Frasquita, Mercédès, Le Dancaïre, Le Remendado

Dialogue [ou Récitatif 19, p. 358]

CARMEN
Eh bien ?...

LE DANCAÏRE
Eh bien, j'avais raison de ne pas me fier aux renseignements de Lillas Pastia ; nous n'avons pas trouvé son factionnaire, mais en revanche nous avons aperçu trois douaniers qui gardaient la brèche et qui la gardaient bien, je vous assure...

CARMEN
Savez-vous leurs noms à ces douaniers ?...

LE REMENDADO
Certainement nous savons leurs noms ; qui est-ce qui connaîtrait les douaniers si nous ne les connaissions pas ? Il y avait Eusebio, Perez et Bartolomé...

FRASQUITA
Eusebio...

MERCÉDÈS
Perez...

FRASQUITA
Fortune!

MERCÉDÈS
Love!

CARMEN
Always death!

FRASQUITA, MERCÉDÈS, CARMEN
Again! Again!

(Dancaïre and Remendado re-enter.)

Scene 3

Carmen, Don José, Frasquita, Mercédès, Dancaïre, Remendado

Dialogue [or Recitative 19, p. 359]

CARMEN
Well?...

DANCAÏRE
Well, I was right not to trust what Lillas Pastia told us; we didn't find his sentry, but rather we saw three customs men guarding the breach, and guarding it very carefully, I can tell you...

CARMEN
Do you know the names of these customs men?

REMENDADO
Of course we know their names: if we didn't know them, who on earth would? They're called Eusebio, Perez and Bartolomé...

FRASQUITA
Eusebio...

MERCÉDÈS
Perez...

CARMEN
Et Bartolomé...

(en riant)

N'ayez pas peur, Dancaïre, nous vous en répondons de vos trois douaniers...

DON JOSÉ *(furieux)*
Carmen !

LE DANCAÏRE
Ah ! toi, tu vas nous laisser tranquilles avec ta jalousie... le jour vient et nous n'avons pas de temps à perdre... En route, les enfants...

(On commence à prendre les ballots.)

Quant à toi...

(s'adressant à Don José)

je te confie la garde des marchandises que nous n'emporterons pas... Tu vas te placer là, sur cette hauteur tu y seras à merveille pour voir si nous sommes suivis ; dans le cas où tu apercevrais quelqu'un, je t'autorise à passer ta colère sur l'indiscret. Nous y sommes ?

LE REMENDADO
Oui, patron.

LE DANCAÏRE
En route alors...

(aux femmes)

Mais vous ne vous flattez pas, vous me répondez vraiment de ces trois douaniers ?

CARMEN
N'ayez pas peur, Dancaïre.

CARMEN
And Bartolomé...

(laughing)

Don't worry, Dancaïre, we can look after your three customs men...

DON JOSÉ *(furious)*
Carmen!

DANCAÏRE
Oh, you and your jealousy! Just don't bother us with it... It's nearly light and we have no time to lose... Come on, fellows...

(They start picking up the goods.)

As for you...

(addressing Don José)

I'm giving you the task of guarding the stuff we're not taking... You're going to take up position up there, on that ledge: it'll be an excellent place from where you can see if we're being followed... If you do see someone, you have my permission to vent your anger on the cheeky fellow. Are we ready?

REMENDADO
Yes, boss.

DANCAÏRE
Off we go then...

(to the women)

You're not kidding yourselves, you will look after the three customs men?

CARMEN
Don't worry, Dancaïre.

N° 20 *Morceau d'Ensemble*

FRASQUITA, MERCÉDÈS, CARMEN, CHŒUR DES
BOHÉMIENNES [29]
    Quant au douanier, c'est notre affaire !
    Tout comme un autre, il aime à plaire,
    Il aime à faire le galant ;
    Ah ! Laissez-nous passer en avant !

FRASQUITA
    Le douanier sera clément !

TOUS
    Il est galant !

CARMEN
    Le douanier sera charmant !

TOUS
    Il aime à plaire !

MERCÉDÈS
    Le douanier sera galant !

FRASQUITA
    Oui, le douanier sera même entreprenant !

FRASQUITA, MERCÉDÈS, CARMEN, CHŒUR DES
BOHÉMIENNES
    Quant au douanier, c'est notre affaire !
    Tout comme un autre, il aime à plaire,
    Il aime à faire le galant ;
    Ah ! Laissez-nous passer en avant !
    Il ne s'agit pas de bataille ;
    Non, il s'agit tout simplement
    De se laisser prendre la taille
    Et d'écouter un compliment.
    S'il faut aller jusqu'au sourire,
    Que voulez-vous ! on sourira !
    Et d'avance, je puis le dire,
    La contrebande passera !

ACT THREE SCENE 3

No. 20 Ensemble

FRASQUITA, MERCÉDÈS, CARMEN, CHORUS OF GYPSIES [29]
As for the customs officer, we'll look after him!
Like all the rest, he'll want to please us,
and to flirt with us.
Ah! Let's go in front!

FRASQUITA
The customs officer will be kind!

ALL
And gallant!

CARMEN
The customs officer will be charming!

ALL
He'll want to please us!

MERCÉDÈS
The customs officer will be gallant!

FRASQUITA
Yes, he might even be enterprising!

FRASQUITA, MERCÉDÈS, CARMEN, CHORUS OF GYPSIES
As for the customs officer, we'll look after him!
Like all the rest, he'll want to please us,
and to flirt with us.
Ah! Let us go in front.
There won't be any battle ;
no, it'll be simply a matter of letting them
put their arms round our waists
and listening to their compliments.
If they want us to smile, we'll smile!
Why not? We'll smile!
And I can tell you in advance,
the contraband will get through!

FRASQUITA, MERCÉDÈS, CARMEN
En avant ! marchons ! allons ! en avant !

FRASQUITA, MERCÉDÈS, CARMEN, LE REMENDADO, LE DANCAÏRE, CHŒUR
Le douanier, c'est notre affaire !
Tout comme un autre, il aime à plaire,
Il aime à faire le galant !
Oui, passez en avant !
Marchons en avant.

(Tout le monde sort. Don José ferme la marche et sort en examinent l'amorce de sa carabine ; un peu avant qu'il soit sorti, on voit un homme passer sa tête au-dessus du rocher. C'est un guide.)

Scène IV

Le Guide, puis Micaëla

Dialogue [ou Récitatif 20, p. 360]

LE GUIDE *(s'avance avec précaution, puis fait un signe à Micaëla que l'on ne voit pas encore)*
Nous y sommes.

MICAËLA *(entrant)*
C'est ici.

LE GUIDE
Oui, vilain endroit, n'est-ce pas, et pas rassurant du tout ?

MICAËLA
Je ne vois personne.

LE GUIDE
Ils viennent de partir, mais ils reviendront bientôt car ils n'ont pas emporté toutes leurs marchandises... je connais leurs habitudes... prenez garde... l'un de leurs doit être en sentinelle quelque part et si l'on nous apercevait...

FRASQUITA, MERCÉDÈS, CARMEN
On we go! Quick march, let's go!

FRASQUITA, MERCÉDÈS, CARMEN, REMENDADO, DANCAÏRE, CHORUS
As for the customs man, we'll look after him!
Like all the rest, they'll want to please us,
and to flirt with us.
Ah! Let us go first.
We'll go in front.

(Everyone leaves. Don José brings up the rear and exits looking at the priming pin of his gun; just before he leaves, a man is seen, raising his head above the rocks. It's a guide.)

Scene 4

The Guide, then Micaëla

Dialogue [or Recitative 20, p. 361]

GUIDE *(advancing carefully, signalling to Micaëla, who cannot yet be seen)*
Here we are.

MICAËLA *(entering)*
It's here.

GUIDE
Yes, an evil place, isn't it, not at all safe?

MICAËLA
I can't see anyone.

GUIDE
They've just left, but they'll come back soon, because they haven't taken all their goods with them... I know how they operate... be careful... one of them must be on guard somewhere, and if he sees us...

MICAËLA
> Je l'espère bien qu'on m'apercevra... puisque je suis venue ici tout justement pour parler à... pour parler à un de ces contrebandiers...

LE GUIDE
> Eh bien là, vrai, vous pouvez vous vanter d'avoir du courage... tout à l'heure quand nous nous sommes trouvés au milieu de ce troupeau de taureaux sauvages que conduisait le célèbre Escamillo, vous n'avez pas tremblé... Et maintenant venir ainsi affronter ces bohémiens...

MICAËLA
> Je ne suis pas facile à effrayer.

LE GUIDE
> Vous dites cela parce que je suis près de vous, mais si vous étiez toute seule...

MICAËLA
> Je n'aurais pas peur, je vous assure.

LE GUIDE
> Bien vrai ?...

MICAËLA
> Bien vrai...

LE GUIDE *(naïvement)*
> Alors je vous demanderai la permission de m'en aller. J'ai consenti à vous servir de guide parce que vous m'avez bien payé ; mais maintenant que vous êtes arrivée... si ça ne vous fait rien, j'irai vous attendre là où vous m'avez pris... à l'auberge qui est au bas de la montagne.

MICAËLA
> C'est cela, allez m'attendre !

LE GUIDE
> Vous restez décidément ?

MICAËLA

I rather hope someone does see me... since I've come especially to speak to... to speak to one of the smugglers...

GUIDE

In that case, it's true, you can certainly be proud of yourself for being courageous... just now, when we were in the middle of a herd of wild bulls that the celebrated Escamillo was leading, you didn't so much as tremble... And now you've come here to confront the gypsies...

MICAËLA

I'm not easy to scare.

GUIDE

You say that because I'm near you, but if you were all alone...

MICAËLA

I wouldn't be afraid, I can assure you.

GUIDE

Is that true?

MICAËLA

Yes, quite true.

GUIDE *(naively)*

Well then, I'd like to ask your permission to leave you now. I agreed to be your guide because you paid me handsomely; but now you're here... if you don't mind, I'll go back and wait for you where I met you... at the inn at the foot of the mountain.

MICAËLA

That's fine, go and wait for me!

GUIDE

Are you sure you're staying?

MICAËLA
   Oui, je reste !

LE GUIDE
   Que tous les saints du paradis vous soient en aide alors, mais c'est une drôle d'idée que vous avez là…

(Il sort.)

Scène V

Micaëla

MICAËLA *(regardant autour d'elle)*
   Mon guide avait raison… l'endroit n'a rien de bien rassurant…

N° 21 Air

MICAËLA
   Je dis que rien ne m'épouvante, [30]
   Je dis, hélas ! que je réponds de moi ;
   Mais j'ai beau faire la vaillante,
   Au fond du cœur, je meurs d'effroi !
   Seule en ce lieu sauvage,
   Toute seule j'ai peur,
   Mais j'ai tort d'avoir peur ;
   Vous me donnerez du courage,
   Vous me protégerez, Seigneur !
   Je vais voir de près cette femme
   Dont les artifices maudits
   Ont fini par faire un infâme
   De celui que j'aimais jadis !
   Elle est dangereuse… elle est belle !…
   Mais je ne veux pas avoir peur !
   Non, non, je ne veux pas avoir peur !…
   Je parlerai haut devant elle,
   Ah ! Seigneur, vous me protégerez !
   Seigneur, vous me protégerez !

MICAËLA
Yes, I'm staying!

GUIDE
Well, let all the saints in heaven come to your aid, it's a mad idea you have in mind...

(He leaves.)

Scene 5

Micaëla

MICAËLA *(looking around)*
My guide was right... this place doesn't make you feel very comfortable...

No. 21 Air

MICAËLA
I said that nothing terrifies me, [30]
I say, alas, that I can take care of myself;
I've tried in vain to be valiant,
but deep down I'm dying of fright!
Alone in this wild place,
all alone I'm quite afraid,
but I'm wrong to feel afraid,
for you, dear Lord, will give me courage,
you, dear Lord, will protect me!
I'm going to see close up this woman
whose wicked cunning
has caused the man who meant the world to me
to ruin himself!
She is dangerous... she is beautiful!
But I don't want to be afraid!
No, no, I won't be afraid!
I'll speak up before her!
Ah! Lord, protect me!
You'll protect me, Lord!

Ah ! Je dis que rien ne m'épouvante,
Je dis, hélas ! que je réponds de moi ;
Mais j'ai beau faire la vaillante,
Au fond du cœur je meurs d'effroi !
Seule en ce lieu sauvage,
Toute seule j'ai peur,
Mais j'ai tort d'avoir peur ;
Vous me donnerez du courage,
Vous me protégerez, Seigneur !
Protégez-moi ! O Seigneur !
Donnez moi du courage !

Dialogue [ou Récitatif 21, p. 360]

MICAËLA

Mais... je ne me trompe pas... à cent pas d'ici... sur ce rocher, c'est José.

(appelant)

José ! José !

(avec terreur)

Mais que fait-il ?... il ne regarde pas de mon coté... il arme sa carabine, il ajuste... il fait feu...

(On entend un coup de feu.)

Ah ! mon Dieu, j'ai trop présumé de mon courage... j'ai peur... j'ai peur...

(Elle disparait derrière les rochers. Au même moment, entre Escamillo tenant son chapeau à la main.)

Scène VI

Escamillo, puis Don José

ESCAMILLO *(regardant son chapeau)*

Quelques lignes plus bas et ce n'est pas moi qui, à la course prochaine, aurais eu le plaisir de combattre les taureaux que je suis en train de conduire...

I said that nothing terrifies me,
I say, alas, that I can take care of myself;
I've tried in vain to be valiant
but deep down I'm dying of fright!
Alone in this wild place,
all alone I'm quite afraid,
but I'm wrong to feel afraid,
because you, dear Lord, will give me courage
and protect me!
Protect me! O Lord!
Give me courage!

Dialogue [or Recitative 21, p. 361]

MICAËLA
> But... I'm sure I'm not mistaken... just a hundred paces away... on that rock, it's José.

(calling)

> José! José!

(afraid)

> But what's he doing? He's not looking in my direction... he's loading his gun, he's taking aim... he's firing...

(A shot is heard.)

> Ah! My God, I've trusted my courage too much... I'm really frightened...

(She disappears behind the rocks. As she does, Escamillo enters, holding his hat in his hand.)

Scene 6

Escamillo, then Don José

ESCAMILLO *(examining his hat)*
> Had the bullet been a little lower, it wouldn't have been me who at the next fight would have had the pleasure of fighting the bulls I've been leading...

(Entre Don José.)

DON JOSÉ *(son couteau à la main)*
   Qui êtes-vous ? répondez.

ESCAMILLO *(très calme)*
   Eh là doucement !

N° 22 Duo

ESCAMILLO
   Je suis Escamillo, torero de Grenade.

DON JOSÉ
   Escamillo !

ESCAMILLO
   C'est moi !

DON JOSÉ *(remettant son couteau à sa ceinture)*
   Je connais votre nom.
   Soyez le bienvenu ; mais vraiment, camarade,
   Vous pouviez y rester.

ESCAMILLO
   Je ne vous dis pas non.
   Mais je suis amoureux, mon cher, à la folie !
   Et celui-là serait un pauvre compagnon
   Qui pour voir ses amours ne risquerait sa vie !

DON JOSÉ
   Celle que vous aimez est ici ?

ESCAMILLO
   Justement.
   C'est une zingara, mon cher...

DON JOSÉ
   Elle s'appelle ?

ESCAMILLO
   Carmen.

ACT THREE SCENE 6

(Enter Don José.)

DON JOSÉ *(his knife drawn)*
   Who are you? Reply.

ESCAMILLO *(calmly)*
   Well then! Gently please!

No. 22 Duo

ESCAMILLO
   I am Escamillo, the bullfighter from Granada.

DON JOSÉ
   Escamillo!

ESCAMILLO
   It's me!

DON JOSÉ *(putting his knife back into his belt)*
   I know your name.
   Welcome! But really, friend,
   you could have been killed there.

ESCAMILLO
   I won't refuse.
   But I'm in love, my dear fellow, madly so!
   And whoever wouldn't risk their life for love
   would be a poor companion!

DON JOSÉ
   And she whom you love is here?

ESCAMILLO
   Absolutely.
   It's a gypsy, dear friend…

DON JOSÉ
   What's her name?

ESCAMILLO
   Carmen.

DON JOSÉ
    Carmen !

ESCAMILLO
    Carmen ! oui, mon cher.
    Elle avait pour amant,
    Un soldat qui jadis a déserté pour elle.

DON JOSÉ *(à part)*
    Carmen !

ESCAMILLO
    Ils s'adoraient ! mais c'est fini, je crois,
    Les amours de Carmen ne durent pas six mois.

DON JOSÉ
    Vous l'aimez cependant !

ESCAMILLO
    Je l'aime !

DON JOSÉ
    Vous l'aimez cependant !…

ESCAMILLO
    Je l'aime,
    Oui, mon cher, je l'aime,
    Je l'aime à la folie !

DON JOSÉ
    Mais pour nous enlever nos filles de Bohème
    Savez-vous bien qu'il faut payer ?…

ESCAMILLO *(gaiment)*
    Soit ! on paiera, soit ! on paiera.

DON JOSÉ *(menaçant)*
    Et que le prix se paie à coups de navaja !

ESCAMILLO *(surpris)*
    À coups de navaja !

ACT THREE SCENE 6

DON JOSÉ
Carmen!

ESCAMILLO
Carmen! Yes, dear friend,
she used to have a soldier,
a soldier who deserted for her.

DON JOSÉ *(aside)*
Carmen!

ESCAMILLO
They were madly in love, but it's finished, I think:
Carmen's lovers never last beyond six months.

DON JOSÉ
But despite that you love her!

ESCAMILLO
I love her!

DON JOSÉ
Despite that you love her!

ESCAMILLO
I love her,
Yes, my friend, I love her,
I love her madly!

DON JOSÉ
But for taking away our gypsy girls
do you know you have to pay?

ESCAMILLO *(happily)*
Well, if I have to pay I'll pay.

DON JOSÉ *(threateningly)*
And the price is to be paid in knife blows!

ESCAMILLO *(surprised)*
In knife blows!

DON JOSÉ
　Comprenez-vous ?

ESCAMILLO
　Le discours est très net.

(avec une légère teinte d'ironie)

　　Ce déserteur, ce beau soldat qu'elle aime,
　　Ou du moins qu'elle aimait, c'est donc vous ?

DON JOSÉ
　Oui, c'est moi-même !

ESCAMILLO
　J'en suis ravi, mon cher !
　Et le tour est complet !

(Tous les deux, la navaja à la main, se drapent dans leurs manteaux.)

DON JOSÉ
　Enfin ma colère
　Trouve à qui parler,
　Le sang, oui, le sang, je l'espère,
　Va bientôt couler !

ESCAMILLO
　Quelle maladresse,
　J'en rirais, vraiment !
　Chercher la maîtresse
　Et trouver, trouver l'amant !

DON JOSÉ, ESCAMILLO
　Mettez-vous en garde
　Et veillez sur vous !
　Tant pis pour qui tarde
　À parer les coups !

(Ils se mettent en garde à une certaine distance.)

ACT THREE SCENE 6

DON JOSÉ
Do you understand?

ESCAMILLO
The meaning seems pretty clear.

(with a hint of irony)

This deserter, the handsome soldier she loves,
or rather used to love, is you?

DON JOSÉ
Yes it's me!

ESCAMILLO
Delighted to hear it, dear friend!
But now it's my turn!

(Knives in hand, both wrap themselves in their cloaks.)

DON JOSÉ
At last my anger
finds the rival I need to speak to,
and blood, yes blood, I hope,
will soon be flowing!

ESCAMILLO
What a blunder –
you have to laugh!
Searching for your mistress
and finding, finding her lover!

DON JOSÉ, ESCAMILLO
Be on your guard
and watch out for yourself!
So much the worse for the one who's tardy
in rebuffing the blows.

(They stand on guard at a certain distance from each other.)

ESCAMILLO
>Je la connais, ta garde navarraise,
>Et je te préviens en ami
>Qu'elle ne vaut rien.

(Sans répondre Don José marche sur le torero.)

>À ton aise !
>Je t'aurai du moins averti.

(Combat ; musique de scène.) [31]

(Escamillo très calme cherche seulement à se défendre.)

DON JOSÉ
>Tu m'épargnes, maudit !

ESCAMILLO
>À ce jeu de couteau
>Je suis trop fort pour toi !

DON JOSÉ
>Voyons cela !

(Rapide et très vif engagement corps à corps. Don José se trouve à la merci d'Escamillo qui ne le frappe pas.)

ESCAMILLO
>Tout beau !
>Ta vie est à moi, mais en somme,
>J'ai pour métier de frapper le taureau,
>Non de trouer le cœur de l'homme !

DON JOSÉ
>Frappe ou bien meurs ! Ceci n'est pas un jeu !

ESCAMILLO *(se dégageant)*
>Soit ! mais au moins, respire un peu !

DON JOSÉ
>En garde !

ACT THREE SCENE 6

ESCAMILLO
>I know that, your Navarrese defence,
>and I tell you as a friend
>that it's of no use at all.

(Don José advances towards the torero without replying.)

>At ease!
>At least I warned you.

(Fighting; stage music.) [31]

(Escamillo fights calmly, merely defending himself.)

DON JOSÉ
>You're sparing me, a curse on you!

ESCAMILLO
>At this knife game
>I'm too good for you!

DON JOSÉ
>We'll see about that!

(Quick, lively close engagement. Don José finds himself at the mercy of Escamillo, who doesn't attack.)

ESCAMILLO
>There you are!
>You're at my mercy, but in the end
>my job is killing bulls,
>not piercing men's hearts!

DON JOSÉ
>Strike or die, this is no game!

ESCAMILLO *(drawing away)*
>So be it! But at least let's take breath!

DON JOSÉ
>On guard!

ESCAMILLO
  En garde !

DON JOSÉ, ESCAMILLO
  Mettez-vous en garde
  Et veillez sur vous !
  Tant pis pour qui tarde
  À parer les coups !

ESCAMILLO, DON JOSÉ
  En garde ! Allons ! En garde !
  Veillez sur vous !

(Après le dernier ensemble, reprise du combat. Escamillo glisse et tombe sur le gazon. Don José va le frapper. Entrent Carmen et Le Dancaïre; Carmen arrête le bras de Don José. Escamillo se relève ; Le Remendado, Mercédès, Frasquita et les contrebandiers rentrent pendant ce temps.)

N° 23 Final

CARMEN *(arrêtant le bras de Don José)*
  Holà ! holà ! José !

ESCAMILLO *(se relevant, galant)*
  Vrai ! j'ai l'âme ravie
  Que ce soit vous, Carmen, qui me sauviez la vie !

CARMEN
  Escamillo !

ESCAMILLO *(à Don José)*
  Quant à toi, beau soldat :
  Nous sommes manche à manche, et nous jouerons la belle,
  Oui nous jouerons la belle
  Le jour où tu voudras reprendre le combat.

LE DANCAÏRE *(s'interposant)*
  C'est bon, c'est bon ! plus de querelle !
  Nous, nous allons partir.

ACT THREE SCENE 6

ESCAMILLO
On guard!

DON JOSÉ, ESCAMILLO
Be on your guard
and watch out for yourself!
So much the worse for the one who's tardy
in rebuffing the blows.

ESCAMILLO, DON JOSÉ
On guard! Come on!
Watch out!

(After the last exchange, the fight resumes. Escamillo slips and falls on the ground. Don José goes to strike him. Enter Carmen and Dancaïre; Carmen seizes Don José's arm. Escamillo gets up again and Remendado, Mercédès, Frasquita and the smugglers enter as this is happening.)

No. 23 Finale

CARMEN *(seizing Don José's arm)*
Hey! Hey! José!

ESCAMILLO *(getting up, gallantly)*
Really! How heart-warming
that it was you, Carmen, who saved my life!

CARMEN
Escamillo!

ESCAMILLO *(to Don José)*
As for you, soldier boy:
we're equal now, and we'll play the last round,
yes, we'll play the last round
any day when you want to continue our fight.

DANCAÏRE *(standing between them)*
All right, all right! No more quarrelling!
We've got to leave.

(à Escamillo)

    Et toi l'ami, bonsoir !

ESCAMILLO
    Souffrez au moins qu'avant de vous dire au revoir
    Je vous invite tous aux courses de Séville,
    Je compte pour ma part y briller de mon mieux...

(avec intention)

    Et qui m'aime y viendra !

(Froidement, à Don José qui fait un geste de menace)

    L'ami, tiens-toi tranquille !

(regardant Carmen)

    J'ai tout dit...
    Oui, j'ai tout dit... et je n'ai plus ici qu'à faire mes adieux !...

(Jeu de scène. Don José veut s'élancer sur Escamillo. Le Dancaïre et Le Remendado le retiennent. Escamillo sort très lentement.)

DON JOSÉ *(à Carmen, menaçant, mais contenu)*
    Prends garde à toi Carmen, je suis las de souffrir !

(Carmen lui répond par un léger mouvement d'épaules et s'éloigne de lui.)

LE DANCAÏRE, CHŒUR
    En route, en route, il faut partir !

LE REMENDADO
    Halte ! quelqu'un est là qui cherche à se cacher.

(Il amène Micaëla.)

CARMEN
    Une femme !

(to Escamillo)

    And as for you, my friend, goodnight!

ESCAMILLO
    Just let me say one more thing before I say goodbye:
    I invite you all to the bullfight in Seville;
    I am hoping to be at my brilliant best...

(meaningfully)

    And all those who love me will be there!

(Coldly, to Don José, who makes a threatening gesture)

    Calm down, friend!

(looking at Carmen)

    That's all I have to say...
    Yes, that's all... All that remains is to say adieu.

(Action. Don José tries to throw himself on Escamillo. Dancaïre and Remendado hold him back. Escamillo exits very slowly.)

DON JOSÉ *(to Carmen, threateningly but controlled)*
    Be careful Carmen, I can't take much more!

(Carmen replies with a shrug of the shoulders and moves away from him.)

DANCAÏRE, CHORUS
    Let's go, let's go, we must go!

REMENDADO
    Halt! There's someone here trying to hide.

(He brings in Micaëla.)

CARMEN
    A woman!

LE DANCAÏRE
   Pardieu ! la surprise est heureuse !

DON JOSÉ *(reconnaissant Micaëla)*
   Micaëla !

MICAËLA
   Don José !

DON JOSÉ
   Malheureuse !
   Que viens-tu faire ici ?

MICAËLA
   Moi ! je viens te chercher !
   Là-bas est la chaumière
   Où sans cesse priant,
   Une mère, ta mère,
   Pleure, hélas ! sur son enfant !
   Elle pleure et t'appelle,
   Elle pleure et te tend les bras !
   Tu prendras pitié d'elle,
   José, ah ! José, tu me suivras !

CARMEN *(à Don José, martelé)*
   Va-t'en, va-t'en, tu feras bien,
   Notre métier ne te vaut rien !

DON JOSÉ *(à Carmen)*
   Tu me dis de la suivre !

CARMEN
   Oui, tu devrais partir !

DON JOSÉ
   Tu me dis de la suivre…
   Pour que toi tu puisses courir

DANCAÏRE
Good Lord! Well, here's a nice surprise!

DON JOSÉ *(recognizing Micaëla)*
Micaëla!

MICAËLA
Don José!

DON JOSÉ
Unluckily for you!
What brings you here?

MICAËLA
Me? I've come to find you!
There is the cottage
where, endlessly praying,
a mother, your mother,
weeps, alas, for her child!
She weeps and calls for you,
she weeps and holds out her arms!
Take pity on her,
José, ah! José, come with me!

CARMEN *(to Don José, insistently)*
Go! Go! It's best for you:
you're no good at this job!

DON JOSÉ *(to Carmen)*
You're telling me to go with her!

CARMEN
Yes, you should go!

DON JOSÉ
You're telling me to go with her
so that you can chase

Après ton nouvel amant !
Non ! non vraiment !

(résolument)

Dût-il m'en coûter la vie,
Non, Carmen, je ne partirai pas !
Et la chaîne qui nous lie
Nous liera jusqu'au trépas !...
Dût-il m'en coûter la vie,
Non, non, non, je ne partirai pas !

MICAËLA
Écoute-moi, je t'en prie,
Ta mère te tend les bras !
Cette chaîne qui te lie,
José, tu la briseras !

FRASQUITA, MERCÉDÈS, LE REMENDADO, LE DANCAÏRE, CHŒUR
Il t'en coûtera la vie,
José, si tu ne pars pas,
Et la chaîne qui vous lie
Se rompra par ton trépas !

DON JOSÉ *(à Micaëla)*
Laisse-moi !

MICAËLA
Hélas ! José !

DON JOSÉ
Car je suis condamné !

FRASQUITA, MERCÉDÈS, LE REMENDADO, LE DANCAÏRE, CHŒUR
José ! prends garde !

after your new lover!
No! No, I won't!

(resolutely)

Even if it costs me my life,
no, Carmen, I'm not leaving!
And the bond that links us
will link us unto death!
Even if it costs me my life,
no, Carmen, I'm not leaving!

MICAËLA
Listen to me, I beseech you,
your mother holds out her arms!
This bond which links you,
José, you'll break it!

FRASQUITA, MERCÉDÈS, REMENDADO, DANCAÏRE, CHORUS
It will cost you your life,
José, if you don't leave,
and the bond which binds you
will be broken by your death!

DON JOSÉ *(to Micaëla)*
Leave me!

MICAËLA
Alas! José!

DON JOSÉ
For I know I am damned!

FRASQUITA, MERCÉDÈS, REMENDADO, DANCAÏRE, CHORUS
José! Take care!

DON JOSÉ (*à Carmen, avec emportement*)
 Ah ! je te tiens, fille damnée !
 Je te tiens, et je te forcerai bien
 À subir la destinée
 Qui rive ton sort au mien !
 Dût-il m'en coûter la vie,
 Non, non, non, je ne partirai pas !

FRASQUITA, MERCÉDÈS, LE REMENDADO, LE DANCAÏRE, CHŒUR
 Ah ! prends garde, prends garde, Don José !

MICAËLA (*avec autorité*)
 Une parole encor ;

(*tristement*)

 Ce sera la dernière !
 Ta mère, hélas !
 Ta mère se meurt et ta mère
 Ne voudrait pas mourir sans t'avoir pardonné !

DON JOSÉ
 Ma mère ! elle se meurt !

MICAËLA
 Oui, Don José !

DON JOSÉ
 Partons ! ah ! partons !

(*à Carmen*)

 Sois contente… je pars… mais… nous nous reverrons !

(*Il entraine Micaëla. On entend Escamillo.*)

ESCAMILLO (*au loin*)
 Toréador, en garde !
 Toréador ! Toréador !
 Et songe bien, oui, songe en combattant

ACT THREE SCENE 6

DON JOSÉ *(to Carmen, heatedly)*
  Ah! I still have you, accursed woman!
  I have a hold on you, and I'll force you
  to submit to the destiny
  which welds your death to mine!
  Even if it costs me my life,
  no, no, no, I won't leave!

FRASQUITA, MERCÉDÈS, REMENDADO, DANCAÏRE, CHORUS
  Ah! take care, take care, Don José!

MICAËLA *(with authority)*
  One more thing:

(sadly)

  this will be the last!
  Your mother, alas!
  Your mother is dying,
  and she doesn't want to die without having forgiven you!

DON JOSÉ
  My mother! She's dying?

MICAËLA
  Yes, Don José!

DON JOSÉ
  Let's go, ah, let's go!

(to Carmen)

  Rest assured... I'm going... but... we'll see each other again!

(He drags Micaëla out. Escamillo is heard.)

ESCAMILLO *(in the distance)*
  Toreador, on guard!
  Toreador! Toreador!
  And bear in mind, yes bear in mind, while fighting,

Qu'un œil noir te regarde
Et que l'amour t'attend,
Toréador, l'amour, l'amour t'attend !

(Don José s'arrête au fond, dans les rochers, regardant Carmen qui écoute. Il hésite, puis après un instant, résolument :)

DON JOSÉ
　Micaëla, partons !

ESCAMILLO
　…l'amour t'attend !

(Carmen écoute et se penche sur les rochers. Les bohémiens ont pris leurs ballots et se mettent en marche.)

that dark eyes are fixed on you
and that love awaits you,
Toreador, love, yes, love awaits you!

(Don José stops at the back, among the rocks, watching Carmen, who is listening. He hesitates, then, after a moment, resolutely:)

DON JOSÉ
Micaëla, let's go!

ESCAMILLO
… love awaits you!

(Carmen listens and leans against the rocks. The gypsies have taken their goods and have set off walking.)

QUATRIÈME ACTE

Scène I [32]

Le lieutenant Zuniga, Frasquita, Mercédès, etc., puis Carmen et Escamillo

N° 24 *Chœur* [33]

MARCHANDS DE CIGARETTES, DE VIN, DE PROGRAMMES, D'EAU. MARCHANDES D'ÉVENTAILS ET D'ORANGES
    À deux cuartos ! À deux cuartos !

MARCHANDES D'ÉVENTAILS
    Des éventails pour s'éventer !

(Pendant le chœur paraissent Zuniga et l'officier avec Mercédès et Frasquita.)

MARCHANDES D'ORANGES
    Des oranges pour grignoter !

MARCHANDS DE PROGRAMMES
    Le programme avec les détails !

MARCHANDS DE VIN
    Du vin !

MARCHANDS D'EAU
    De l'eau !

MARCHANDS DE CIGARETTES
    Des cigarettes !

MARCHANDES D'ÉVENTAILS
    Des éventails pour s'éventer !

ACT FOUR

Scene 1 [32]

Lieutenant Zuniga, Frasquita, Mercédès, etc., then Carmen and Escamillo

No. 24 Chorus [33]

SELLERS OF CIGARETTES, WINE, PROGRAMMES, WATER, FANS AND ORANGES
    Two cuartos apiece! Two cuartos apiece!

FAN-SELLERS
    Fans to cool yourselves!

(During this chorus Zuniga and the officer appear with Mercédès and Frasquita.)

ORANGE-SELLERS
    Oranges to munch on!

PROGRAMME-SELLERS
    The programme with details!

WINE-SELLERS
    Wine!

WATER-SELLERS
    Water!

CIGARETTE-SELLERS
    Cigarettes!

FAN-SELLERS
    Fans to cool yourselves!

MARCHANDS DE CIGARETTES
　Des cigarettes !

TOUS LES MARCHANDS
　À deux cuartos !
　Voyez ! à deux cuartos !
　Séñoras et Caballeros !

(Pendant ce premier chœur sont entrés les deux officiers du deuxième acte ayant au bras les deux bohémiennes Mercédès et Frasquita.)

ZUNIGA *(aux marchandes)*
　Des oranges... vite.

PLUSIEURS MARCHANDES D'ORANGES *(se précipitant)*
　En voici...
　Prenez, prenez, mesdemoiselles.

UNE MARCHANDE *(à l'officier qui paie)*
　Merci, mon officier, merci !

MARCHANDES D'ORANGES *(à Zuniga)*
　Celles-ci, señor, sont plus belles !

MARCHANDES D'ÉVENTAILS
　Des éventails pour s'éventer !

MARCHANDES D'ORANGES
　Des oranges pour grignoter !

MARCHANDS DE PROGRAMMES
　Le programme avec les détails !

MARCHANDS DE VINS
　Du vin !

MARCHANDS D'EAU
　De l'eau !

MARCHANDS DE CIGARETTES
　Des cigarettes !

ACT FOUR SCENE 1

CIGARETTE-SELLERS
Cigarettes!

ALL THE MERCHANTS
Two cuartos apiece!
All at two cuartos apiece!
Ladies and gentlemen!

(During this first chorus the two officers from Act Two enter with the two gypsies Mercédès and Frasquita on their arms.)

ZUNIGA *(to the merchants)*
Oranges... quick.

SEVERAL ORANGE-SELLERS *(rushing towards them)*
Here you are...
Help yourselves, young ladies.

A MERCHANT *(to the officer who's paying)*
Thank you officer, thank you!

ORANGE-SELLERS *(à Zuniga)*
These, señor, are the best!

FAN-SELLERS
Fans to cool yourselves!

ORANGE-SELLERS
Oranges to munch on!

PROGRAMME-SELLERS
The programme with details!

WINE-SELLERS
Wine!

WATER-SELLERS
Water!

CIGARETTE-SELLERS
Cigarettes!

UN OFFICIER
    Holà ! des éventails !

UN BOHÉMIEN *(se précipitant)*
    Voulez-vous aussi des lorgnettes ?

TOUS LES MARCHANDS
    À deux cuartos !
    Voyez ! à deux cuartos !
    Séñoras et Caballeros !
    À deux cuartos ! Voyez ! voyez !

Dialogue [supprimé dans la version avec récitatifs, suivi directement par le N° 25, p. 318]

ZUNIGA
    Qu'avez-vous donc fait de la Carmencita ? je ne la vois pas.

FRASQUITA
    Nous la verrons tout à l'heure… Escamillo est ici, la Carmencita ne doit pas être loin.

UN OFFICIER
    Ah ! c'est Escamillo, maintenant ?…

MERCÉDÈS
    Elle en est folle…

FRASQUITA
    Et son ancien amoureux José, sait-on ce qu'il est devenu ?

ZUNIGA
    Il a reparu dans le village où sa mère habitait… l'ordre avait même été donné de l'arrêter, mais quand les soldats sont arrivés, José n'était plus là…

MERCÉDÈS
    En sorte qu'il est libre ?

ZUNIGA
    Oui, pour le moment.

ACT FOUR SCENE 1

AN OFFICER
  Hey! Fans!

A GYPSY *(rushing forward)*
  Would you like a pair of eye-glasses?

ALL THE MERCHANTS
  Two cuartos apiece!
  All at two cuartos apiece!
  Ladies and gentlemen!
  Everything at two cuartos, look!

Dialogue [recitative version omits this, cut to No. 25, p. 319]

ZUNIGA
  What have you done with Carmencita? I can't see her.

FRASQUITA
  We'll soon be seeing her... Escamillo's here, so Carmencita can't be far away.

AN OFFICER
  Ah! It's Escamillo now, is it?

MERCÉDÈS
  She's mad about him...

FRASQUITA
  And her former lover José, do we know what's become of him?

ZUNIGA
  He turned up in the village where his mother lived... a warrant for his arrest was issued, but when the soldiers arrived he was no longer there...

MERCÉDÈS
  So he's free then?

ZUNIGA
  Yes, for the moment.

FRASQUITA
> Hum ! je ne serais pas tranquille à la place de Carmen, je ne serais pas tranquille du tout.

N° 25 *Chœur et Scène*

On entend de grands cris au dehors... des fanfares, etc., etc. C'est l'arrivée de la quadrille.

ENFANTS *(au dehors)*
> Les voici, les voici,
> Voici la quadrille !

(Entrée des enfants.)

ENFANTS, CHŒUR
> Les voici ! voici la quadrille,
> La quadrille des toreros.
> Sur les lances, le soleil brille !
> En l'air toques et sombreros !
> Les voici, voici la quadrille,
> La quadrille des toreros !

(Défilé de la quadrille. Pendant ce défilé, le chœur chante le morceau suivant. Entrée des alguazils.)

ENFANTS
> Voici, débouchant sur la place,
> Voici d'abord, marchant au pas,
> L'alguazil à vilaine face.
> À bas ! à bas ! à bas ! à bas !

CHŒUR, ENFANTS
> À bas l'alguazil ! à bas !

(Entrée des chulos et des banderilleros.)

CHŒUR
> Et puis saluons au passage,
> Saluons les hardis chulos !
> Bravo ! viva ! gloire au courage !

ACT FOUR SCENE 1

FRASQUITA
Hmm! I wouldn't feel comfortable about that if I was Carmen, not at all comfortable.

No. 25 Chorus and Scene

Shouting is heard from outside… fanfares, etc., etc. The cuadrilla arrives.

CHILDREN *(from outside)*
Here they are, here they are,
here's the cuadrilla!

(Enter the children.)

CHILDREN, CHORUS
Here they are! Here's the cuadrilla,
the procession of the bullfighters.
Look how the sun shines on their lances!
In the air their caps and sombreros!
Here they are, here's the cuadrilla,
the procession of the bullfighters!

(The procession passes by. During this, the chorus sings the following number. Enter the alguazils.)

CHILDREN
Here they are, spilling into the square,
and in the lead, marching slowly,
is the alguazil with the evil face.
Down with him! Down with him!

CHORUS AND CHILDREN
Down with the alguazil! Down with him!

(Enter the chulos and banderilleros.)

CHORUS
And let's salute, as they pass,
the brave and hardy chulos!
Bravo, bravo, all hail their courage!

Voici les hardis chulos !
Voyez les banderilleros,
Voyez quel air de crânerie !

CHŒUR, ENFANTS
Voyez !

CHŒUR
Voyez quels regards, et de quel éclat
Étincelle la broderie
De leur costume de combat !

(Entrée des picadors.)

ENFANTS, CHŒUR
Une autre quadrille s'avance !
Voyez les picadors ! Comme ils sont beaux !
Comme ils vont du fer de leur lance
Harceler le flanc des taureaux !

CHŒUR
L'Espada !

ENFANTS, CHŒUR
Escamillo !

(Paraît enfin Escamillo ayant près de lui Carmen radieuse et dans un costume éclatant.)

C'est l'Espada, la fine lame,
Celui qui vient terminer tout,
Qui paraît à la fin du drame
Et qui frappe le dernier coup !
Vive Escamillo ! Vive Escamillo ! ah ! bravo !

ENFANTS, CHŒUR,
Les voici ! voici la quadrille,
La quadrille des toreros.
Sur les lances, le soleil brille !
En l'air toques et sombreros !

> There are the hardy chulos!
> Look at the banderilleros,
> see how they swagger!

CHORUS, CHILDREN
> Look!

CHORUS
> See the look in their eye,
> and the way their embroidery shines
> on their fighting costumes!

(Enter the picadors.)

CHILDREN, CHORUS
> Another cuadrilla is coming!
> Look at the picadors! How fine they are!
> How they are going to wound
> the bull's flanks with their lances!

CHORUS
> The swordsman!

CHILDREN, CHORUS
> Escamillo!

(At last Escamillo appears accompanied by Carmen, looking radiant and wearing a striking costume.)

> It's the swordsman with the fine blade,
> he who comes to end it all,
> who appears at the end of the drama
> and who strikes the final blow!
> Long live Escamillo! Long live Escamillo! Ah, bravo!

CHILDREN, CHORUS
> Here they are! Here's the cuadrilla,
> the procession of the bullfighters.
> Look how the sun shines on their lances!
> In the air their caps and sombreros!

Les voici, voici la quadrille,
La quadrille des toreros !
Vive Escamillo !
Ah ! Vive Escamillo ! Bravo ! Viva !

ESCAMILLO *(à Carmen)*
Si tu m'aimes, Carmen, [34]
Tu pourras, tout à l'heure,
Être fière de moi !
Si tu m'aimes, si tu m'aimes !

CARMEN
Ah ! je t'aime, Escamillo, je t'aime, et que je meure
Si j'ai jamais aimé quelqu'un autant que toi !

CARMEN, ESCAMILLO
Ah ! je t'aime !
Oui, je t'aime !

PLUSIEURS VOIX
Place ! place ! place au seigneur Alcade !

(L'Alcade paraît au fond, accompagné d'alguazils, il entre dans le cirque suivi de la quadrille, de la foule, etc.)

FRASQUITA *(sotto voce)*
Carmen, un bon conseil… ne reste pas ici.

CARMEN
Et pourquoi, s'il te plaît ?

MERCÉDÈS
Il est là…

CARMEN
Qui donc ?

MERCÉDÈS
Lui !
Don José ! dans la foule il se cache, regarde…

ACT FOUR SCENE 1

Here they are! Here's the cuadrilla,
the procession of the bullfighters.
Long live Escamillo!
Ah! Long live Escamillo! Bravo! Viva!

ESCAMILLO *(to Carmen)*
    If you love me, Carmen,   [34]
    you'll soon
    be proud of me!
    If you love me! If you love me!

CARMEN
    Ah! I love you Escamillo, I love you, and let me die,
    if I've ever loved anyone as much as I love you!

CARMEN, ESCAMILLO
    Ah! I love you!
    Yes, I love you!

SEVERAL VOICES
    Make way, make way for the Mayor!

(The Mayor appears at the back accompanied by alguazils; he enters the bullring followed by the cuadrilla, the crowd, etc.)

FRASQUITA *(sotto voce)*
    Carmen, some advice for you… don't stay here.

CARMEN
    And why, if you please?

MERCÉDÈS
    He's here…

CARMEN
    Who do you mean?

MERCÉDÈS
    Him!
    Don José! hiding over there in the crowd, look…

CARMEN
   Oui, je le vois.

FRASQUITA
   Prends garde !

CARMEN
   Je ne suis pas femme à trembler devant lui… Je l'attends et je vais lui parler.

MERCÉDÈS
   Carmen, crois-moi, prends garde !

CARMEN
   Je ne crains rien !

FRASQUITA
   Prends garde !

(L'Alcade est entré dans le cirque. Derrière l'Alcade, le cortège de la quadrille reprend sa marche et entre dans le cirque. Le populaire suit… L'orchestre joue le motif « Les voici, voici la quadrille » et la foule en se retirant a dégagé Don José… Carmen reste seule au premier plan. Tous deux se regardent pendant que la foule se dissipe et que le motif de la marche va diminuant et mourant à l'orchestre. Sur les dernières notes, Carmen et Don José restent seuls, en présence l'un de l'autre.)

Scène II

Carmen, Don José

N° 26 Duo final

CARMEN *(bref)*
   C'est toi !

DON JOSÉ
   C'est moi !

CARMEN
   L'on m'avait avertie
   Que tu n'étais pas loin, que tu devais venir ;

CARMEN
Yes, I can see him.

FRASQUITA
Be careful!

CARMEN
I am not the kind of woman who would be frightened of him...
I'll wait for him and talk to him.

MERCÉDÈS
Carmen, believe me, you need to be careful!

CARMEN
I am afraid of nothing!

FRASQUITA
Be careful!

(The Mayor has entered the bullring. Behind him the procession of the cuadrilla starts up again and enters the bullring. Everyone follows... The orchestra plays the motif 'Here they are, here's the cuadrilla' and, as the crowd leaves Don José has detached himself... Carmen is alone at the front of the stage. They look at each other as the crowd melts away and the motif in the orchestra fades out. On its last notes, Carmen and Don José find themselves alone together.)

Scene 2

Carmen, Don José

No. 26 Final duet

CARMEN *(curtly)*
It's you!

DON JOSÉ
Yes, it's me!

CARMEN
I was warned you weren't far away,
and that you'd be coming;

L'on m'avait même dit de craindre pour ma vie.
Mais je suis brave ! et n'ai pas voulu fuir !

DON JOSÉ
Je ne menace pas ! j'implore... je supplie !
Notre passé, Carmen, notre passé, je l'oublie !...
Oui, nous allons tous deux
Commencer une autre vie,
Loin d'ici, sous d'autres cieux !

CARMEN
Tu demandes l'impossible !
Carmen jamais n'a menti !
Son âme reste inflexible ;
Entre elle et toi... c'est fini !
Jamais je n'ai menti !
Entre nous tout est fini !

DON JOSÉ
Carmen, il est temps encore, [35]
Oui, il est temps encore...
Ô ma Carmen, laisse-moi
Te sauver, toi que j'adore,
Ah ! laisse-moi te sauver
Et me sauver avec toi !

CARMEN
Non ! je sais bien que c'est l'heure,
Je sais bien que tu me tueras ;
Mais que je vive ou que je meure,
Non, non, non, je ne te céderai pas !

DON JOSÉ
Carmen ! il est temps encore
Oui, il est temps encore...
Ô ma Carmen, laisse-moi
Te sauver, toi que j'adore !
Ah ! laisse-moi te sauver
Et me sauver avec toi...

I was even warned to fear for my life;
but I'm brave and didn't want to run away!

DON JOSÉ

I'm not threatening you! I implore you... I beg you!
Our past, Carmen, I have forgotten!
Yes, the two of us could
begin another life together,
far from here, in another place.

CARMEN

You are asking the impossible!
Carmen has never lied!
Her heart remains unmoved;
between her and you... it's over!
Never have I lied!
Between us it is finished!

DON JOSÉ

Carmen, there's still time... [35]
Yes there's still time...
O my Carmen, let me
save you, you whom I adore,
Ah! Let me save you
and save myself with you.

CARMEN

No! I know the time has come
I know you are going to kill me;
but whether I live or whether I die,
no, no, no, I won't give in to you!

DON JOSÉ

Carmen! There's still time...
Yes there's still time...
O my Carmen, let me
save you, you whom I adore!
Ah! Let me save you
and save myself with you...

CARMEN
    Pourquoi t'occuper encore
    D'un cœur qui n'est plus à toi !
    Non, ce cœur n'est plus à toi !
    En vain tu dis : « je t'adore ! »
    Tu n'obtiendras rien, non, rien de moi,
    Ah ! c'est en vain…
    Tu n'obtiendras rien, rien de moi !

DON JOSÉ *(avec anxiété)*
    Tu ne m'aimes donc plus ?

(Silence de Carmen et Don José répète, avec désespoir.)

    Tu ne m'aimes donc plus ?

CARMEN *(simplement)*
    Non ! je ne t'aime plus.

DON JOSÉ *(avec passion)*
    Mais moi, Carmen, je t'aime encore,
    Carmen, hélas ! moi, je t'adore !

CARMEN
    À quoi bon tout cela ? que de mots superflus !

DON JOSÉ
    Carmen, je t'aime, je t'adore !
    Eh bien ! S'il le faut, pour te plaire,
    Je resterai bandit… tout ce que tu voudras…
    Tout ! tu m'entends tout, tu m'entends tout !
    Mais ne me quitte pas,
    Ô ma Carmen ! ah ! souviens-toi,
    Souviens-toi du passé !
    Nous nous aimions, naguère !

(désespéré)

    Ah ! ne me quitte pas, Carmen,
    Ah ! ne me quitte pas !

CARMEN
> Why bother any more
> with a heart that is no longer yours!
> No, my heart is no longer for you!
> It's in vain that you say: 'I adore you'!
> You'll have nothing more from me, nothing.
> Ah! It's all in vain…
> You'll have nothing, nothing more from me!

DON JOSÉ *(anxiously)*
> So you don't love me any more?

(Carmen doesn't answer, and Don José repeats his question, desperately)

> So you don't love me any more?

CARMEN *(simply)*
> No! I don't love you any more.

DON JOSÉ *(passionately)*
> But as for me, Carmen, I still love you,
> Carmen, alas, I still adore you!

CARMEN
> What's the use of that? They are nothing but worthless words!

DON JOSÉ
> Carmen, I love you, I adore you!
> Ah well! If it pleases you,
> I'll stay a bandit… whatever you want…
> Anything! Do you hear me? Anything you want!
> But don't leave me,
> O my Carmen! Remember the past!
> Don't you remember the past?
> How we loved each other only a while ago!

(desperately)

> Ah! Don't leave me, Carmen,
> Ah! don't leave me!

CARMEN
>   Jamais Carmen ne cédera !
>   Libre elle est née et libre elle mourra !

CHŒUR ET FANFARES *(dans le cirque)*
>   Viva ! Viva ! la course est belle !
>   Sur le sable sanglant
>   Le taureau qu'on harcèle
>   S'élance en bondissant...
>   Frappé juste en plein cœur !

CHŒUR
>   Voyez ! Victoire !
>   La course est belle !

(Pendant ce chœur, silence de Carmen et de Don José... Tous deux écoutent... En entendant les cris de: « Victoire, victoire ! » Carmen a laissé échapper un « Ah ! » d'orgueil et de joie... Don José ne perd pas Carmen de vue... Le chœur terminé, Carmen fait un pas du côté du cirque.)

DON JOSÉ *(se plaçant devant elle)*
>   Où vas-tu ?

CARMEN
>   Laisse-moi.

DON JOSÉ
>   Cet homme qu'on acclame,
>   C'est ton nouvel amant !

CARMEN *(voulant passer)*
>   Laisse-moi... laisse-moi...

DON JOSÉ
>   Sur mon âme,
>   Tu ne passeras pas,
>   Carmen, c'est moi que tu suivras !

CARMEN
>Carmen will never give in!
>Free she was born and free she will die!

CHORUS AND FANFARES *(in the bullring)*
>Viva! Viva! The fight's going well!
>On the bloodstained sand
>the wounded bull
>attacks leaping...
>Struck right in the heart!

CHORUS
>Look! He's won!
>What a good fight!

(During this chorus, Carmen and Don José remain silent... Both listen... Hearing the cries of 'He's won, he's won!' Carmen utters an 'Ah!' of pride and joy... Don José doesn't let her out of his sight... The chorus ends, Carmen takes a step towards the side of the bullring.)

DON JOSÉ *(barring her way)*
>Where are you going?

CARMEN
>Leave me alone.

DON JOSÉ
>That man they're applauding,
>he's your new lover!

CARMEN *(wanting to get past him)*
>Leave me alone... leave me alone...

DON JOSÉ
>I swear on my soul
>You won't get away,
>Carmen, you're going to come with me!

CARMEN
　　Laisse-moi, Don José, je ne te suivrai pas.

DON JOSÉ
　　Tu vas le retrouver, dis…

(avec rage)

　　Tu l'aimes donc ?

CARMEN
　　Je l'aime !
　　Je l'aime et devant la mort même,
　　Je répèterais que je l'aime !

CHŒUR ET FANFARES *(dans le cirque)*
　　Viva ! viva ! la course est belle !
　　Viva ! sur le sable sanglant,
　　Le taureau s'élance.
　　Voyez ! voyez !
　　Le taureau qu'on harcèle
　　En bondissant s'élance.
　　Voyez !

DON JOSÉ *(avec violence)*
　　Ainsi, le salut de mon âme [36]
　　Je l'aurai perdu pour que toi,
　　Pour que tu t'en ailles, infâme,
　　Entre ses bras rire de moi !
　　Non, par le sang, tu n'iras pas !
　　Carmen, c'est moi que tu suivras !

CARMEN
　　Non, non ! jamais !

DON JOSÉ
　　Je suis las de te menacer !

CARMEN *(avec colère)*
　　Eh bien ! frappe-moi donc, ou laisse-moi passer.

ACT FOUR SCENE 2

CARMEN
Leave me, Don José, I am not coming with you.

DON JOSÉ
You're going to find him, aren't you...

(in a rage)

So you love him?

CARMEN
I love him!
Even under the threat of death
I would repeat that I love him!

CHORUS AND FANFARES *(in the bullring)*
Viva! Viva! What a good fight!
Viva! On the bloodstained sand
the bull leaps forward.
Look! Look!
The wounded bull
leaps forward.
Look!

DON JOSÉ *(violently)*
So I have lost my soul's salvation [36]
just so that you
can go into his arms
laughing at me, you monster.
No, by my blood, you will not go!
Carmen, you're going to come with me!

CARMEN
No, no! Never!

DON JOSÉ
I'm tired of threatening you!

CARMEN *(angrily)*
Go on then! Strike me, or else let me by.

CHŒUR *(dans le cirque)*
   Victoire !

DON JOSÉ *(éperdu)*
   Pour la dernière fois, démon,
   Veux-tu me suivre ?

CARMEN
   Non ! non !

(à demi voix, avec rage)

   Cette bague, autrefois, tu me l'avais donnée… Tiens !

(Elle la jette à la volée.)

DON JOSÉ *(le poignard à la main, s'avançant sur Carmen)*
   Eh bien ! damnée !

(Carmen recule… Don José la poursuit… Pendant ce temps fanfares et chœur dans le cirque.)

CHŒUR *(dans le cirque)*
   Victoire ! Bravo !
   Toréador, en garde !
   Toréador ! Toréador !
   Et songe bien, oui, songe en combattant
   Qu'un œil noir te regarde
   Et que l'amour t'attend,
   Toréador, l'amour t'attend !

(Don José a frappé Carmen… Elle tombe morte… Le vélum s'ouvre. La foule sort du cirque.)

DON JOSÉ *(se levant)*
   Vous pouvez m'arrêter… c'est moi qui l'ai tuée !

(Escamillo paraît sur les marches du cirque entouré de la foule qui l'acclame, entre elle Mercédès, Frasquita and Zuniga. Escamillo aperçoit Carmen étendue morte par terre.)

   Ah ! Carmen ! ma Carmen adorée !

ACT FOUR SCENE 2

CHORUS *(in the bullring)*
   He's won!

DON JOSÉ *(madly)*
   For the last time, you demon,
   are you going to come with me?

CARMEN
   No! no!

(in a low voice, in a rage)

   This ring you once gave me... Here!

(She throws it into the air.)

DON JOSÉ *(his dagger in his hand, approaching Carmen)*
   Damn you!

(Carmen recoils... Don José follows her... During all this, fanfares and the chorus in the bullring.)

CHORUS *(in the bullring)*
   Victory! Bravo!
   Toreador, on guard!
   Toreador! Toreador!
   And bear in mind, yes bear in mind, while fighting,
   that dark eyes are fixed on you
   and that love awaits you,
   Toreador, love, yes love awaits you!

(Don José has stabbed Carmen... She falls dead... The arena curtain opens. The crowd comes out of the bullring.)

DON JOSÉ *(getting up)*
   You can arrest me... it is I who have killed her!

(Escamillo appears on the steps of the bullring surrounded by the crowd who applaud him, among them Mercédès, Frasquita and Zuniga. Escamillo sees Carmen lying dead on the ground.)

   Ah! Carmen! My adored Carmen!

Recitatives

Récitatif 1 (p. 116)

MORALÈS
    Une jeune fille charmante
    Vient de nous demander si tu n'étais pas là !
    Jupe bleue et natte tombante …

DON JOSÉ
    Ce doit être Micaëla !

[suivi du N° 2bis, p. 116]

Récitatif 2 (p. 118)

ZUNIGA
    C'est bien là, n'est-ce pas, dans ce grand bâtiment
    Que travaillent les cigarières ?

DON JOSÉ
    C'est là, mon officier, et bien certainement
    On ne vit nulle part filles aussi légères.

ZUNIGA
    Mais, au moins, sont-elles jolies ?

DON JOSÉ
    Mon officier, je n'en sais rien.
    Et m'occupe assez peu de ces galanteries.

ZUNIGA
    Ce qui t'occupe, ami, je le sais bien ;
    Une jeune fille charmante
    Qu'on appelle Micaëla.
    Jupe bleue et natte tombante ;
    Tu ne réponds rien à cela ?

DON JOSÉ
    Je réponds que c'est vrai,
    Je réponds que je l'aime.

RECITATIVES

Recitative 1 (p. 117)

MORALÈS
A charming young girl
was asking whether you were here.
Blue skirt and plaits ...

DON JOSÉ
That sounds like Micaëla!

[segue No. 2b, p. 117]

Recitative 2 (p. 119)

ZUNIGA
It's there, isn't it, in that big building
that the cigar girls work?

DON JOSÉ
Yes, sir, it's in there and one thing's for sure,
you'll never find such loose girls.

ZUNIGA
But at least they're pretty, aren't they?

DON JOSÉ
Sir, I know nothing about it:
I'm not interested in their affairs.

ZUNIGA
What interests you, my friend, I know well!
A charming young girl
called Micaëla.
Blue skirts and plaits!
What do you say to that?

DON JOSÉ
I say it's true
and I reply that I love her.

Quant aux ouvrières d'ici,
Quant à leur beauté, les voici !
Et vous pouvez juger vous-même.

[suivi du N° 3, p. 124]

Récitatif 3 (p. 138)

DON JOSÉ
    Quels regards ! Quelle effronterie !
    Cette fleur-là m'a fait l'effet
    D'une balle qui m'arrivait !
    Le parfum en est fort et la fleur est jolie !
    Et la femme …
    S'il est vraiment des sorcières,
    C'en est une, certainement.

(Entre Micaëla)

MICAËLA
    Don José !

DON JOSÉ
    Micaëla !

MICAËLA
    Me voici !

DON JOSÉ
    Quelle joie !

MICAËLA
    C'est votre mère qui m'envoie.

[suivi du N° 7, p. 140]

Récitatif 4 (p. 148)

DON JOSÉ
    Reste là maintenant,
    Pendant que je lirai.

RECITATIVES

But regarding the working girls round here,
as for their beauty, well there they are!
And you'll have to judge for yourself.

[segue No. 3, p. 125]

Recitative 3 (p. 139)

DON JOSÉ
What looks! What effrontery!
That flower was like
a bullet hitting me!
Its scent is so strong and the flower so pretty!
And as for the woman...
If there are really such things as witches,
she's surely one of them.

(Enter Micaëla)

MICAËLA
Don José!

DON JOSÉ
Micaëla!

MICAËLA
Here I am!

DON JOSÉ
What a pleasure!

MICAËLA
It's your mother who sent me.

[segue No. 7, p. 141]

Recitative 4 (p. 149)

DON JOSÉ
Stay there now,
while I read it.

MICAËLA
  Non pas, lisez d'abord,
  Et puis je reviendrai.

DON JOSÉ
  Pourquoi t'en aller ?

MICAËLA
  C'est plus sage.
  Cela me convient davantage.
  Lisez ! puis je reviendrai.

DON JOSÉ
  Tu reviendras ?

MICAËLA
  Je reviendrai !

DON JOSÉ
  Ne crains rien ma mère, ton fils t'obéira,
  Fera ce que tu lui dis ; j'aime Micaëla.
  Je la prendrai pour femme.
  Quant à tes fleurs, sorcière infâme !

[suivi du N° 8, p. 152]

Récitatif 5 (p. 164)

DON JOSÉ
  Mon officier, c'ètait une querelle ;
  Des injures d'abord, puis à la fin, des coups.
  Une femme blessée.

ZUNIGA
  Et par qui ?

DON JOSÉ
  Mais par elle !

MICAËLA
   No, you read it first,
   and then I'll come back.

DON JOSÉ
   Why go away?

MICAËLA
   It's more sensible.
   And it suits me better.
   Read it and then I'll come back.

DON JOSÉ
   You'll come back?

MICAËLA
   Yes I'll come back!

DON JOSÉ
   Don't worry, mother, your son will obey;
   he'll do what you say: I love Micaëla.
   I'll take her for a wife.
   As for those flowers, wicked witch!

[segue No. 8, p. 153]

Recitative 5 (p. 165)

DON JOSÉ
   Sir, it was a quarrel,
   insults at first, then it finally came to blows.
   A woman was hurt.

ZUNIGA
   By whom?

DON JOSÉ
   By her!

ZUNIGA (*à Carmen*)
    Vous entendez ? que nous répondrez-vous ?

[suivi du N° 9, p. 168, «Tra la, la»]

Récitatif 6 (p. 168)

ZUNIGA
    Fais-nous grâce de tes chansons.
    Et puisque l'on t'a dit de répondre, réponds !

[suivi directement de «Tra la, la», p. 168]

Récitatif 7 (p. 170)

ZUNIGA
    Puisque tu le prends sur ce ton
    Tu chanteras ton air aux murs de la prison.

[suivi directement de «Tra la, la», p. 170]

Récitatif 8 (p. 170)

ZUNIGA
    La peste !
    Décidément vous avez la main leste.

Récitatif 9 (p. 170)

ZUNIGA
    C'est dommage,
    C'est grand dommage.
    Car elle est gentille, vraiment.
    Mais il faut bien la rendre sage.
    Attachez ces deux jolis bras !

RECITATIVES

ZUNIGA (*to Carmen*)
Do you understand? We want an answer.

[segue No. 9, p. 169 'Tra la, la']

Recitative 6 (p. 169)

ZUNIGA
Spare us your songs.
And since we've asked you to reply, please reply!

[segue 'Tra la, la' immediately following p. 169]

Recitative 7 (p. 171)

ZUNIGA
Since you're taking that attitude,
you can sing your songs to the prison walls.

[segue 'Tra la, la' immediately following p. 171]

Recitative 8 (p. 171)

ZUNIGA
Damn!
You're certainly nimble-fingered.

Recitative 9 (p. 171)

ZUNIGA
What a pity,
what a great pity.
Because she's really lovely,
but she needs teaching a lesson:
tie her lovely arms together!

CARMEN
   Où me conduirez-vous ?

DON JOSÉ
   À la prison et je n'y puis rien faire.

CARMEN
   Vraiment tu n'y peux rien faire ?

DON JOSÉ
   Non, rien, j'obéis à mes chefs.

CARMEN
   Eh bien moi, je sais bien
   Qu'en dépit de tes chefs eux-mêmes
   Tu feras tout ce que je veux,
   Et cela parce que tu m'aimes !

DON JOSÉ
   Moi t'aimer ?

CARMEN
   Oui, Don José ! la fleur, dont je t'ai fait présent,
   Tu sais, la fleur de la sorcière,
   Tu peux la jeter maintenant,
   Le charme opère !

DON JOSÉ
   Ne me parle plus, tu m'entends,
   Ne parle plus, je le défends !

[suivi du Nº 10, p. 176]

Récitatif 10 (p. 186)

FRASQUITA
   Messieurs, Pastia me dit …

ZUNIGA
   Que nous veut-il encore maître Pastia ?

CARMEN
>Where are you taking me?

DON JOSÉ
>To prison, and I can't do anything about it.

CARMEN
>Can't you really do anything about it?

DON JOSÉ
>No, nothing at all, I obey my superiors.

CARMEN
>Ah, but I know that
>in spite of your superiors
>you'll do exactly what I ask,
>because you're in love with me!

DON JOSÉ
>Me in love with you?

CARMEN
>Yes, Don José! The flower I gave you as a present,
>you know, the witch's flower,
>you can throw it away now:
>the spell is working!

DON JOSÉ
>Don't speak to me again, do you hear me?
>Don't speak at all, I forbid it!

[segue No. 10, p. 177]

Recitative 10 (p. 187)

FRASQUITA
>Messieurs, Pastia tells me …

ZUNIGA
>What more does he want from us, Master Pastia?

FRASQUITA
   Il dit que le corrégidor
   Veut que l'on ferme l'auberge.

ZUNIGA
   Eh bien, nous partirons ;
   Vous viendrez avec nous.

FRASQUITA
   Non pas, nous, nous restons.

ZUNIGA
   Et toi, Carmen, tu ne viens pas ?
   Écoute ! Deux mots dits tout bas ;
   Tu m'en veux.

CARMEN
   Vous en vouloir ! Pourquoi ?

ZUNIGA
   Ce soldat, l'autre jour,
   Emprisonné pour toi …

CARMEN
   Qu'a-t-on fait de ce malheureux ?

ZUNIGA
   Maintenant il est libre !

CARMEN
   Il est libre ! tant mieux.
   Bonsoir, messieurs nos amoureux !

FRASQUITA, MERCÉDÈS, CARMEN
   Bonsoir, messieurs nos amoureux !

[suivi du N° 12, p. 194]

Récitatif 11 (p. 194)

ZUNIGA
   Une promenade aux flambeaux !
   C'est le vainqueur des courses de Grenade.

FRASQUITA
   He says the corregidor
   wants the inn to close.

ZUNIGA
   All right, we'll go;
   you'll come with us.

FRASQUITA
   No, not us, we're staying.

ZUNIGA
   And you, Carmen? Aren't you coming?
   Listen! Just whisper two words;
   are you angry with me?

CARMEN
   Angry with you? Why should I be?

ZUNIGA
   That soldier the other day,
   he was put in prison because of you…

CARMEN
   What happened to the poor man?

ZUNIGA
   Now he's free!

CARMEN
   He's free! So much the better.
   Goodnight, lovers!

FRASQUITA, MERCÉDÈS, CARMEN
   Goodnight, lovers!

[segue No. 12, p. 195]

Recitative 11 (p. 195)

ZUNIGA
   A torchlight procession!
   It's the winner of the Granada tournament.

Voulez-vous avec nous boire, mon camarade,
À vos succès anciens, à vos succès nouveaux ?

[suivi de «Vivat ! vivat ! vivat !», p. 194]

Récitatif 12 *(p. 202)*

ESCAMILLO
La belle, un mot :
Comment t'appelle-t-on ?
Dans mon premier danger
Je veux dire ton nom.

CARMEN
Carmen ! Carmencita !
Cela revient au même.

ESCAMILLO
Et si l'on disait que l'on t'aime …

CARMEN
Je répondrais qu'il ne faut pas m'aimer.

ESCAMILLO
Cette réponse n'est pas tendre,
Je me contenterai d'espérer et d'attendre.

CARMEN
Il est permis d'attendre, il est doux d'espérer.

ZUNIGA
Puisque tu ne viens pas, Carmen, je reviendrai.

CARMEN
Et vous aurez grand tort

ZUNIGA
Bah ! je me risquerai.

[suivi de «Tout le monde sort» avant la Scène III, p. 208]

RECITATIVES

Won't you have a drink with us, my friend,
To your former triumphs, and to your success in the future?

[segue 'Vivat! Vivat! Vivat!', p. 195]

Recitative 12 (p. 203)

ESCAMILLO
   A little question, my beauty:
   what's your name?
   The first time I'm in danger
   I want to say your name.

CARMEN
   Carmen! Carmencita!
   It's all the same to me.

ESCAMILLO
   And if someone said they were in love with you...

CARMEN
   I'd say that they mustn't be in love with me.

ESCAMILLO
   That's not a very nice reply,
   so I'll have to make do with hoping and waiting!

CARMEN
   Well, waiting is allowed, and it's nice to hope ...

ZUNIGA
   Since you won't come, Carmen, I'll have to come back.

CARMEN
   That would be a serious mistake.

ZUNIGA
   Bah! Well, I'll risk it.

[segue 'Exit all' before Scene 3, p. 209]

Récitatif 13 (p. 208)

FRASQUITA
  Eh bien, vite, quelles nouvelles ?

LE DANCAÏRE
  Pas trop mauvaises, les nouvelles
  Et nous pouvons encor faire quelques beaux coups,
  Mais nous avons besoin de vous ...

FRASQUITA, MERCÉDÈS, CARMEN
  Besoin de nous ?

LE DANCAÏRE
  Oui, nous avons besoin de vous.

[suivi du Nº 14, p. 210]

Récitatif 14 (p. 224)

LE DANCAÏRE
  Mais qui donc attends-tu ?

CARMEN
  Presque rien, un soldat, qui l'autre jour pour me rendre service,
  S'est fait mettre en prison.

LE REMONDADO
  Le fait est délicat.

LE DANCAÏRE
  Il se peut qu'après tout ton soldat réfléchisse.
  Es-tu bien sûre qu'il viendra ?

[suivi du Nº 15, p. 228]

Récitatif 15 (p. 228)

FRASQUITA
  C'est un beau dragon.

RECITATIVES

Recitative 13 (p. 209)

FRASQUITA
Quickly, what's the news?

DANCAÏRE
Not such bad news.
We can still make a few nice raids,
but we need your help...

FRASQUITA, MERCÉDÈS, CARMEN
Our help?

DANCAÏRE
Yes, we need your help!

[segue No. 14, p. 211]

Recitative 14 (p. 225)

DANCAÏRE
But who are you waiting for?

CARMEN
Oh, nothing, a soldier who did me a favour the other day
and got himself put in prison.

REMONDADO
That's a little awkward.

DANCAÏRE
Your soldier could change his mind.
Are you sure he's going to come?

[segue No. 15, p. 229]

Recitative 15 (p. 229)

FRASQUITA
He's a fine dragoon.

MERCÉDÈS
   Un très beau dragon.

LE DANCAÏRE
   Qui serait pour nous un fier compagnon.

LE REMONDADO
   Dis-lui de nous suivre.

CARMEN
   Il refusera.

LE REMONDADO
   Mais, essaye, au moins.

CARMEN
   Soit ! on essayera.

[suivi du 2ᵉ couplet de la chanson de José «Halte-là !», p. 230]

Récitatif 16 (p. 232)

CARMEN
   Enfin c'est toi !

DON JOSÉ
   Carmen !

CARMEN
   Et tu sors de prison ?

DON JOSÉ
   J'y suis resté deux mois.

CARMEN
   Tu t'en plains ?

DON JOSÉ
   Ma foi non !
   Et, si c'était pour toi, j'y voudrais être encore.

MERCÉDÈS
A very fine dragoon.

DANCAÏRE
Who would be a faithful companion.

REMONDADO
Tell him to come with us.

CARMEN
He'd refuse.

REMONDADO
Well, at least try.

CARMEN
So be it! I'll try.

[segue 2nd verse of José's song 'Halt there!', p. 231]

Recitative 16 (p. 233)

CARMEN
It's you at last!

DON JOSÉ
Carmen!

CARMEN
So you're out of prison?

DON JOSÉ
I was there for two months.

CARMEN
Do you regret it?

DON JOSÉ
My word, no!
If it was for you I wouldn't have minded still being there!

CARMEN
  Tu m'aimes donc ?

DON JOSÉ
  Moi je t'adore !

CARMEN
  Vos officiers sont venus tout à l'heure ;
  Ils nous ont fait danser.

DON JOSÉ
  Comment, toi !

CARMEN
  Que je meure si tu n'es pas jaloux !

DON JOSÉ
  Eh oui !… je suis jaloux.

CARMEN
  Tout doux, monsieur, tout doux.

[suivi du Nº 16, p. 238]

Récitatif 17 (p. 264)

LE DANCAÏRE
  Reposons-nous une heure ici, mes camarades.
  Nous, nous allons nous assurer
  Que le chemin est libre
  Et que sans algarades,
  La contrebande peut passer.

[suivi d'une reprise orchestrale, absente de la version avec dialogue, puis du Récitatif 18]

Récitatif 18 (p. 264)

CARMEN (*à Don José*)
  Que regardes-tu donc ?

CARMEN
    You're in love with me, then?

DON JOSÉ
    I adore you!

CARMEN
    Your officers were here just now.
    They made us dance for them.

DON JOSÉ
    What, you?

CARMEN
    Strike me dead if you're not jealous!

DON JOSÉ
    Ah yes, I'm jealous.

CARMEN
    Quiet, sir, quiet.

[segue No. 16, p. 239]

Recitative 17 (p. 265)

DANCAÏRE
    Let's rest here for an hour, my friends.
    We need to make sure
    the way is clear
    and that we can get the contraband through
    without being raided.

[segue orchestral reprise not in dialogue version, then Recitative 18]

Recitative 18 (p. 265)

CARMEN (*to Don José*)
    What are you looking at?

DON JOSÉ
>   Je me dis que, là-bas,
>   Il existe une bonne et brave vieille femme
>   Qui me croit honnête homme.
>   Elle se trompe, hélas.

CARMEN
>   Qui donc est cette femme ?

DON JOSÉ
>   Ah ! Carmen, sur mon âme, ne raille pas,
>   Car c'est ma mère …

CARMEN
>   Eh bien ! va la retrouver tout de suite ;
>   Notre métier, vois-tu, ne te vaut rien
>   Et tu ferais fort bien de partir au plus vite.

DON JOSÉ
>   Partir, nous séparer !

CARMEN
>   Sans doute !

DON JOSÉ
>   Nous séparer, Carmen ?
>   Écoute, si tu redis ce mot !…

CARMEN
>   Tu me tuerais peut-être ?
>   Quel regard ! tu ne réponds rien.
>   Que m'importe après tout, le destin est le maître.

[suivi du N° 19, p. 272]

Récitatif 19 (p. 278)

CARMEN
>   Eh bien !

DON JOSÉ
I was saying to myself that over there
there is a good, brave old lady
who thinks I'm a good man.
Alas, she's making a mistake.

CARMEN
Who is this woman?

DON JOSÉ
Ah! Carmen, upon my soul, don't mock:
it's my mother...

CARMEN
Ah well! Go and find her at once!
Our profession isn't for you, can't you see that?
The best thing for you would be to go as soon as possible.

DON JOSÉ
To leave and split up from you?

CARMEN
Absolutely!

DON JOSÉ
Split up, Carmen?
Listen, if you say that again...

CARMEN
You'd kill me, perhaps?
What a look! And you're saying nothing.
But what does it matter to me, we're all in the hands of fate.

[segue No. 19, p. 273]

Recitative 19 (p. 279)

CARMEN
Well then!

LE DANCAÏRE
   Eh bien, nous essaierons de passer
   Et nous passerons !
   Reste là-haut, Don José, garde les marchandises.

FRASQUITA
   La route est-elle libre ?

LE DANCAÏRE
   Oui ! mais gare aux surprises.
   J'ai, sur la brèche où nous devons passer,
   Vu trois douaniers ;
   Il faut nous en débarrasser.

CARMEN (*mesuré*)
   Prenez les ballots et partons !
   Il faut passer, nous passerons.

[suivi du N° 20, p. 282]

Récitatif 20 (p. 284)

MICAËLA
   C'est des contrebandiers le refuge ordinaire ;
   Il est ici, je le verrai !
   Et le devoir que m'imposa sa mère,
   Sans trembler je l'accomplirai.

[suivi du N° 21, p. 288]

Récitatif 21 (p. 290)

MICAËLA
   Je ne me trompe pas ... c'est lui sur le rocher !
   À moi, José ... José ! Je ne puis approcher.
   Mais que fait-il ? il ajuste ! il fait feu !

(On entend un coup de feu.)

RECITATIVES

DANCAÏRE
Well then, we'll try to get through,
and we'll do it!
You stay up there, Don José, and guard the goods.

FRASQUITA
Is the road clear?

DANCAÏRE
Yes, but beware of surprises.
Through the gap where we enter I've seen
three customs men;
we'll have to get rid of them.

CARMEN (*measured*)
Take the bundles and leave!
We need to get through, we'll do it.

[segue No. 20, p. 283]

Recitative 20 (p. 285)

MICAËLA
This is the normal hiding place of the smugglers.
He is here, I'll find him.
And the task his mother has set me,
I'll accomplish without any fear.

[segue No. 21, p. 289]

Recitative 21 (p. 291)

MICAËLA
I'm not mistaken, that's him on the rock!
Look over here, José... José! I can't come any nearer.
What's he doing? He's taking aim! He's firing!

(A shot is heard.)

Ah ! J'ai trop présumé de mes forces, mon Dieu !

(Elle disparaît derrière les rochers.)

ESCAMILLO
Quelques lignes plus bas, et tout était fini …

DON JOSÉ
Votre nom, répondez !

ESCAMILLO
Eh ! doucement l'ami.

[suivi du N° 22, p. 292]

RECITATIVES

Ah, my God, I overestimated my courage.

(She disappears behind the rocks.)

ESCAMILLO
A few inches lower and all would have been over…

DON JOSÉ
Your name! Reply!

ESCAMILLO
Hey, gently my friend!

[segue No. 22, p. 293]

Select Discography

To date there have been more than 225 audio recordings of the complete opera or substantial sections of it. Some forty of these were issued in the days of 78s or come from early radio broadcasts. Of special interest are: the first-ever recording of the opera made in Berlin in 1908 (in German) with Emmy Destinn as Carmen; the first recording (1911) made at the Opéra-Comique in Paris with Marguerite Mérentié as Carmen, which includes alterations to the score and offers much insight into the way the dialogue was delivered there at the time; and two live Metropolitan Opera performances with Rosa Ponselle as Carmen and Gennaro Papi conducting (1937) and with Lily Djanel as Carmen and Thomas Beecham conducting (1943). For full details of these and other historic recordings, visit operadis-opera-discography.org.uk/CLBICARM.HTM#207.

The more modern recordings (from 1950 on) have been chosen for their ease of current availability and the interest of their performers. There is no up-to-date survey in English of *Carmen* on CD. For discussions of selected recordings up to 1979, see Alan Blyth, '*Carmen*', *Opera on Record*, ed. Alan Blyth (London: Hutchinson, 1979), pp. 461–80, and, up to 1993, Mark Swed, '*Carmen*', *The Metropolitan Opera Guide to Recorded Opera*, ed. Paul Gruber (London and New York: Thames and Hudson, 1993), pp. 48–59.

CARMEN

YEAR	CAST	CONDUCTOR / ORCHESTRA	MOST RECENT LABEL (2020)
	CARMEN DON JOSÉ MICAËLA ESCAMILLO FRASQUITA MERCÉDÈS LE DANCAÏRE LE REMENDADO		
1950	Solange Michel Raoul Jobin Martha Angelici Michel Dens Germaine Chellet Raymonde Notti-Pagès Jean Vieuille Frédéric Leprin	André Cluytens Théâtre National de l'Opéra-Comique	Naxos (dialogue)
1951	Risë Stevens Jan Peerce Licia Albanese Robert Merrill Paula Lenchner Margaret Roggero George Cehanovsky Alessio de Paolis	Fritz Reiner RCA Victor Orchestra	Sony (recitatives)
1959	Victoria de los Angeles Nicolai Gedda Janine Micheau Ernest Blanc Denise Monteil Monique Linval/ Marcelle Croisier Jean-Christophe Benoît Michel Hamel	Thomas Beecham Orchestre National de la Radiodiffusion Française	Warner (recitatives)
1961	Christa Ludwig Rudolf Schock Melitta Muszely Hermann Prey Ursula Schirrmacher Ursula Gust Leopold Clam Karl-Ernst Mercker	Horst Stein Berlin Symphony	EMI (recitatives) (in German)

SELECT DISCOGRAPHY

1963	Regina Resnik Mario del Monaco Joan Sutherland Tom Krause Georgette Spanellys Yvonne Minton Alfred Hallet Jean Prudent	Thomas Schippers Orchestre de la Suisse Romande	Decca (recitatives)
1963	Leontyne Price Franco Corelli Mirella Freni Robert Merrill Monique Linval Geneviève Macaux Jean-Christophe Benoît Maurice Besançon	Herbert von Karajan Vienna Philharmonic	Sony (recitatives)
1964	Maria Callas Nicolai Gedda Andrea Guiot Robert Massard Nadine Sautereau Jane Berbié Jean-Paul Vauquelin Jacques Pruvost/ Maurice Maïevski	Georges Prêtre Orchestre du Théâtre National de l'Opéra de Paris	Warner (recitatives)
1967	Grace Bumbry Jon Vickers Mirella Freni Justino Díaz Olivera Miljaković Julia Hamari John van Kesteren Milen Paunov	Herbert von Karajan Vienna Philharmonic	Orfeo (recitatives)
1970	Grace Bumbry Jon Vickers Mirella Freni Kostas Paskalis Éliane Lublin Viorica Cortez Michel Trempont Albert Voli	Rafael Frühbeck de Burgos Orchestre de l'Opéra Paris	Warner (dialogue spoken by actors)

CARMEN

1972	Marilyn Horne James McCracken Adriana Maliponte Tom Krause Colette Boky Marcia Baldwin Russell Christopher Andrea Velis	Leonard Bernstein Metropolitan Opera	DG (dialogue)
1974	Régine Crespin Gilbert Py Jeannette Pilou José van Dam Mariarosa Carminati Nadine Denize Jacques Trigeau Rémy Corazza	Alain Lombard Strasbourg Philharmonic	Erato (recitatives)
1975	Tatiana Troyanos Plácido Domingo Kiri Te Kanawa José van Dam Norma Burrowes Jane Berbié Michel Roux Michel Sénéchal	Georg Solti London Philharmonic	Decca (dialogue)
1978	Teresa Berganza Plácido Domingo Ileana Cotrubas Sherrill Milnes Yvonne Kenny Alicia Nafé Gordon Sandison Geoffrey Pogson	Claudio Abbado London Symphony Orchestra	DG (dialogue)
1982	Julia Migenes-Johnson Plácido Domingo Faith Esham Ruggero Raimondi Lilian Watson Susan Daniel Jean-Philippe Lafont Gérard Garino	Lorin Maazel Orchestre National de France	Erato (dialogue; soundtrack of Francesco Rosi film)

SELECT DISCOGRAPHY

1982	Agnes Baltsa José Carreras Katia Ricciarelli José van Dam Christine Barbaux Jane Berbié Gino Quilico Heinz Zednik	Herbert von Karajan Berlin Philharmonic	DG (dialogue)
1988	Jessye Norman Neil Shicoff Mirella Freni Simon Estes Ghyslaine Raphanel Jean Rigby François Le Roux Gérard Garino	Seiji Ozawa Orchestre National de France	Decca (dialogue)
2003	Angela Gheorghiu Roberto Alagna Inva Mula Thomas Hampson Elisabeth Vidal Isabelle Cals Nicolas Rivenq Yann Beuron	Michel Plasson Orchestre National du Capitole de Toulouse	Warner (recitatives) (includes original version of Carmen's entrance aria)
2012	Magdalena Kožená Jonas Kaufmann Genia Kühmeier Kostas Smoriginas Christina Landshamer Rachel Frenkel Simone del Savio Jean-Paul Fouchécourt	Simon Rattle Berlin Philharmonic	Warner (dialogue; Oeser reconstruction)
2012 (recorded 2002)	Anne Sofie von Otter Marcus Haddock Lisa Milne Laurent Naouri Mary Hegarty Christine Rice Quentin Hayes Colin Judson	Philippe Jordan London Philharmonic	Glyndebourne (dialogue)

Carmen on DVD: a Selection

For a fuller listing to 2003, including non-commercial and television films, see Ken Wlaschin, *Encyclopedia of Opera on Screen* (New Haven: Yale University Press, 2004), pp. 110–20.

YEAR	CAST	CONDUCTOR / ORCHESTRA	DIRECTOR / COMPANY / LABEL
	CARMEN DON JOSÉ MICAËLA ESCAMILLO FRASQUITA MERCÉDÈS LE DANCAÏRE LE REMENDADO		
1967	Grace Bumbry Jon Vickers Mirella Freni Justino Díaz Nadine Sautereau Jane Berbié Gérard Dunan Milen Paunov	Herbert von Karajan Vienna Philharmonic	Herbert von Karajan Salzburg Festival Philips/DG (recitatives)
1978	Elena Obraztsova Plácido Domingo Isobel Buchanan Yuri Mazurok Cheryl Kanfoush Axelle Gall Paul Wolfrum Heinz Zednik	Carlos Kleiber Vienna State Opera	Franco Zeffirelli Vienna State Opera TDK/Arthaus Musik (recitatives)

CARMEN ON DVD: A SELECTION

1984	Julia Migenes-Johnson Plácido Domingo Faith Esham Ruggero Raimondi Lilian Watson Susan Daniel Jean-Philippe Lafont Gérard Garino	Lorin Maazel Orchestre National de France	Francesco Rosi Feature film Columbia TriStar (dialogue)
1985	Maria Ewing Barry McCauley Marie McLaughlin David Holloway Elizabeth Collier Jean Rigby Gordon Sandison Petros Evangelides	Bernard Haitink London Philharmonic	Peter Hall Glyndebourne Festival Pioneer/Warner (dialogue)
1987	Agnes Baltsa José Carreras Leona Mitchell Samuel Ramey Myra Merritt Diane Kesling Bruce Hubbard Anthony Laciura	James Levine Metropolitan Opera	Peter Hall Metropolitan Opera DG (recitatives)
1989	Maria Ewing Jacque Trussel Miriam Gauci Alain Fondary Rosemary Ashe Ludmilla Andrew David Hamilton Emile Belcourt	Jacques Delacôte National Philharmonic	Steven Pimlott Earl's Court Arena, London Stax Entertainment (dialogue)
2002	Anne-Sofie von Otter Marcus Haddock Lisa Milne Laurent Naouri Mary Hegarty Christine Rice Quentin Hayes Colin Judson	Philippe Jordan London Philharmonic	David McVicar Glyndebourne Festival Opus Arte (dialogue)

2007	Anna C. Antonacci Jonas Kaufmann Norah Amsellem Ildebrando D'Arcangelo Elena Xanthoudakis Viktoria Vizin Jean-Sébastien Bou Jean-Paul Fouchécourt	Antonio Pappano Royal Opera House	Francesca Zambello Royal Opera House Decca/Opus Arte (dialogue)
2010	Elīna Garanča Roberto Alagna Barbara Frittoli Teddy Tahu Rhodes Elizabeth Cabellero Sandra Piques Eddy Earle Patriarco Keith Jameson	Yannick Nézet-Séguin Metropolitan Opera	Richard Eyre Metropolitan Opera Decca (recitatives)
2010	Anna C. Antonacci Andrew Richards Anne-C. Gillet Nicolas Cavallier Virginie Pochon Annie Gill Francis Dudziak Vincent Ordoneau	John Eliot Gardiner Orchestre Révolutionnaire et Romantique	Adrian Noble Théâtre National de l'Opéra-Comique (includes the Act One *Scène de l'Anglais*) (dialogue)
2011	Christine Rice Bryan Hymel Maija Kovalevska Aris Argiris Elena Xanthoudakis Paula Murrihy Adrian Clarke Harry Nicoll	Constantinos Carydis Royal Opera House	Francesca Zambello Royal Opera House Opus Arte (Blu-Ray, also on 3D) (dialogue)
2011	Béatrice Uria-Monzon Roberto Alagna Marina Poplavskaya Erwin Schrott Eliana Bayón Itxaro Mentxaka Marc Canturri Francisco Vas	Marc Piollet Gran Teatre del Liceu	Calixto Bieito Gran Teatre del Liceu Unitel Classica (dialogue)

Select Bibliography

Baker, Evan, 'The Scene Designs for the First Performances of Bizet's *Carmen*', *19th-Century Music* 13, no. 3 (1990)

Bizet, Georges, *Lettres de Georges Bizet: Impressions de Rome (1857–60), La Commune (1871)*, ed. Louis Ganderax (Paris: Calmann-Lévy, 1905)

Clément, Catherine, *Opera or the Undoing of Women*, trans. Betsy Wing (London: Virago Press, 1989)

Christoforidis, Michael and Elizabeth Kertesz, *Carmen and the Staging of Spain* (New York: Oxford University Press, 2019)

Dibbern, Mary, *'Carmen': A Performance Guide* (New York: Pendragon Press, 2000)

Doré, Gustave, *Doré's Spain: All 236 Illustrations from Spain* (Mineola: Dover Publications, 2004)

Fauser, Annegret and Everist, Mark (eds.), *Music, Theater and Cultural Transfer, Paris 1830–1914* (Chicago: University of Chicago Press, 2009)

Furman, Nelly, *George Bizet's 'Carmen'* (New York: Oxford University Press, 2020)

Hansen, Eric C., *Ludovic Halévy: A Study of Frivolity and Fatalism in Nineteenth-Century France* (Lanham, MD: University Press of America, 1987)

Lacombe, Hervé, *Georges Bizet* (Paris: Fayard, 2000)

Lacombe, Hervé, *The Keys to French Opera in the Nineteenth Century*, trans. Edward Schneider (Berkeley: University of California Press, 2001)

Lacombe, Hervé and Rodriguez, Christine, *La Habanera de Carmen: naissance d'un tube.* (Paris: Fayard, 2014)

Langham Smith, Richard and Rowden, Clair (eds.), *Carmen Abroad: Bizet's Opera on the Global Stage* (Cambridge: Cambridge University Press, 2020)

Langham Smith, Richard, *Bizet's Carmen Uncovered.* (Woodbridge: Boydell & Brewer, 2020)

Macdonald, Hugh, *Bizet* (Oxford: Oxford University Press, 2014)

McClary, Susan, *Georges Bizet: 'Carmen'* (Cambridge: Cambridge University Press, 1992)

Mérimée, Prosper, *Carmen*, trans. Lady Mary Loyd (London: The Folio Society, 1949)

Mérimée, Prosper, *Carmen* and *Vénus de l'Ille*, trans. Andrew Brown (London: Hesperus Classics, 2004)

Nietzsche, Friedrich, *The Birth of Tragedy and The Case of Wagner*, trans. Walter Kaufmann (New York: Random House, 1967)

Raitt, A.W., *Prosper Mérimée* (London: Eyre & Spottiswoode, 1970)

Stricker, Rémy, *Georges Bizet* (Paris: Gallimard, 1999)

Villamil, Victoria Etnier, *'O ma Carmen': Bizet's Fateful Gypsy in Portrayals from 1875 to the Present* (New York: McFarland, 2017)

Wright, Lesley A. (ed.), *Georges Bizet: Letters in the Nydahl Collection* (Stockholm: Royal Swedish Academy of Music, 1988)

Bizet Websites*

List of stage works — opera.stanford.edu/Bizet/

Complete *Carmen* Discography
    operadis-opera-discography.org.uk/CLBICARM.HTM#207

Bibliothèque Nationale de France (French only)
    data.bnf.fr/13891543/georges_bizet/

Les Amis de Bizet (French only) — lesamisdebizet.com

Maison Georges Bizet (French only) — maisongeorgesbizet.com

The Bizet Catalogue — digital.wustl.edu/bizet
(compiled by Hugh Macdonald)

Carmen Abroad — carmenabroad.org
(curated by Clair Rowden and Richard Langham Smith)

---

* Links valid at the time of publication in 2020.

Note on the Contributors

George Hall writes widely about classical music in general and opera in particular for various publications, including *The Stage*, *Opera*, *Opera News* and *BBC Music Magazine*. He has also contributed to many books, including such reference works as *The Oxford Companion to Music* and the *New Penguin Opera Guide*.

Gary Kahn has been series editor of the Overture/ENO opera guides since 2010. He has previously worked for BBC Television and English National Opera. He is currently a freelance dramaturg. His book *The Power of the Ring* was published by the Royal Opera House in 2007 and reissued in a revised edition in 2012.

Richard Langham Smith is Research Professor at the Royal College of Music. He is co-editor of the Cambridge Opera Handbook on *Pelléas et Mélisande* and editor of *Debussy Studies*. His performance urtext of *Carmen* is published by Peters Edition. He was made Chevalier de l'Ordre des Arts et des Lettres in 1995 for services to French music.

Lesley A. Wright is Professor Emerita of Music at the University of Hawaii. She has published extensively on Bizet, Massenet and their generation, concentrating on musical institutions and the press in Paris during the Second Empire and Third Republic. She has contributed to the *New Penguin Opera Guide* and is the editor of *Georges Bizet: Letters in the Nydahl Collection*.

Acknowledgements

We would like to thank John Allison of *Opera*, John Pennino of the Metropolitan Opera, Charles Johnston and Mike Ashman for their assistance and advice in the preparation of this guide.